T0301487

Achieving Proof of Concept in Drug Discovery and Development

Achieving Proof of Concept in Drug Discovery and Development

The Role of Competition Law in Collaborations between Public Research Organizations and Industry

Helen Yu

University of Copenhagen, Denmark

Cheltenham, UK • Northampton, MA, USA

Published by
Edward Elgar Publishing Limited
The Lypiatts
15 Lansdown Road
Cheltenham
Glos GL50 2JA
UK

Edward Elgar Publishing, Inc.
William Pratt House
9 Dewey Court
Northampton
Massachusetts 01060
USA

A catalogue record for this book
is available from the British Library

Library of Congress Control Number: 2016942190

This book is available electronically in the **Elgar**online
Law subject collection
DOI 10.4337/9781785369377

ISBN 978 1 78536 938 4 (cased)
ISBN 978 1 78536 937 7 (eBook)

Typeset by Columns Design XML Ltd, Reading
Printed and bound by CPI Group (UK) Ltd, Croydon, CR0 4YY

Contents

PART IV   CONCLUSION

Acknowledgements

First and foremost, I would like to thank my supervisor Jens Schovsbo for his advice, support, and patience while I embarked on this journey of finding my academic voice. His persistence, insights, and critique have been invaluable to my academic development.

I would also like to express my gratitude to the following people at the integrated drug discovery organizations who gave up their time and provided me with the data necessary to complete my research: Karimah Es Sabar, Dave Rogers, and Michel Roberge at the Centre for Drug Research and Development; Patrick Chaltin and Bruno Lambrecht at the Centre for Drug Design and Discovery; Bert Klebl and Thomas Hegen-dorfer at the Lead Discovery Centre; and Mike Johnson and Dave Pardoe at MRCT.

Finally, I would like to thank my family, especially my partner Søren Harbel for his love, patience, and encouragement. Thank you for giving me the courage to leave private practice to follow my heart and pursue my passion in teaching and research.

Table of cases

COMMISSION DECISIONS

Table of legislation

PART I

Landscape of drug discovery and development

1. Introduction

A. WHAT IS THE PROBLEM WITH THE CURRENT DRUG DEVELOPMENT PROCESS?

To the benefit of individuals and society, medical innovations and technologies have the ability to lead to better healthcare, improve quality of life, and increase longevity. As stated in the 2009 Pharmaceutical Sector Inquiry, a comprehensive study of the European pharmaceutical sector put together by the European Commission (EC), '[i]nnovation in human medicines has enabled patients to benefit from treatments that were unimaginable a few decades ago'.[1] In addition to providing a better quality of life, research relied upon by the United States National Institute of Health (NIH) on the economic impact and potential of improved health claims that the decline in mortality rate from 1970 to 2000 translated to approximately an added $3 trillion a year in economic activity.[2] However, the cost of healthcare and research and development (R&D) to bring new drugs to market is reportedly ever increasing. The average cost of bringing a new drug to market is US$2.6 billion and the average time to develop a new drug is more than ten years.[3] In another

---

[1] European Commission Pharmaceutical Sector Inquiry, Final Report, July 8, 2009, page 11.
[2] Kevin M. Murphy and Robert H. Topel, *The Value of Health and Longevity.* JOURNAL OF POLITICAL ECONOMY, 114(5), 871 (2006). See also National Institute of Health 2012, Economic Impact Factsheet (accessible at http://www.researchamerica.org/sites/default/files/uploads/EconomicFactSheet.pdf), which further claims that the ability to decrease cancer deaths by 1% has a present value to the current and future generations of Americans of nearly US$500 billion.
[3] Asher Mullard, *New Drugs Cost US$2.6 Billion to Develop.* NATURE REVIEWS DRUG DISCOVERY, 13, 877 (2014). See also Pharmaceutical Research and Manufacturers of America, *2015 Biopharmaceutical Research Industry Profile*, Washington, DC: PhRMA (2015); Jorge Mestre-Ferrandiz, Jon Sussex and Adrian Towse, *The R&D Cost of a New Medicine*, London, UK: Office of Health Economics (2012); Steven M. Paul, Daniel S. Mytelka, Christopher T. Dunwiddie, Charles C. Persinger, Bernard H. Munos, Stacy R.

study, it was reported that the economic burden to society associated with the treatment of chronic diseases such as heart disease, diabetes, and cancer is estimated at US$1.3 trillion or €700 billion a year.[4] Worldwide,

---

Lindborg, and Aaron L. Schacht, *How to Improve R&D Productivity: The Pharmaceutical Industry's Grand Challenge*. NATURE REVIEWS DRUG DIS-COVERY, 9(3), 203–214 (2010); Michael Dickson and Jean P. Gagnon, *Key Factors in the Rising Cost of New Drug Discovery and Development*. NATURE REVIEWS DRUG DISCOVERY, 3(5), 417–429 (2004); Joseph A. DiMasi, Ronald W. Hansen, and Henry G. Grabowski, *The Price of Innovation: New Estimates of Drug Development Costs*. JOURNAL OF HEALTH ECONOMICS, 22(2), 151–185 (2003). However, there is some debate and conflicting reports over the actual cost of drug development. In Donald W. Light and Rebecca Warburton, *Demythologizing the High Costs of Pharmaceutical Research.* BIOSOCIETIES, 6(1), 34–50 (2011) it was reported that an unrepresentative sample of drug companies provided unverifiable and exaggerated R&D costs data to the Tufts Center for the Study of Drug Development (Tufts CSDD), which formed the basis of the finding of the excessively high average cost to bring a new drug to market. See also Donald W. Light and Joel R. Lexchin, *Pharmaceutical Research and Development: What Do We Get for All That Money?* BRITISH MEDICAL JOURNAL, 345 (2012), which argued that the often quoted cost data have been used by industry and academics alike when discussing the various views on the drug development process and explaining industry behavior, such as the need for high profit margins associated with new drugs as a means to recuperate sunk R&D costs and to fund further R&D. Kenneth Kaitin, Professor and Director of the Tufts CSDD, asserts that there is no conflict of interest in the articles he publishes that rely upon the DiMasi and Grabowski data. He asserts Tufts CSDD is a nonprofit academic research center at Tufts University, Boston, Massachusetts, which is funded in part by unre-stricted grants from pharmaceutical and biotechnology firms, as well as com-panies that provide related services (e.g., contract research, consulting, and technology firms).

    [4] European Commission, Health and Consumers Directorate-General (2014) The 2014 EU Summit on Chronic Diseases Conference Conclusions, Brussels; Giuseppe Garcea and Ashley Dennison, *The Economic Burden of Chronic Ill Health*. EUROPEAN JOURNAL FOR PERSON CENTERED HEALTHCARE, 3(2), 238–244 (2015). See also The Council for American Medical Innovation (CAMI), *Gone Tomorrow: A Call to Promote Medical Innovation, Create Jobs, and Find Cures in America*, prepared by the Battelle Technology Partnership Practice, June 10, 2010. The Centre for Disease Control and Prevention also published similar statistics on its website in May 2014 in association with its Chronic Disease and Health Promotion awareness campaign (see http://www.cdc.gov/chronicdisease/overview/).

global spending on pharmaceuticals in 2013 approached US$1 trillion.[5] Although in 2014, the United States Food and Drug Administration approved 41 new drugs (17 of which had fast track status and a further eight drugs were approved under the 'accelerated approval' program),[6] in the immediate ten years prior, the number of new drugs approved was approximately the same number of drugs approved in the 1950s.[7] Given the available statistics and metrics on the drug development process (illustrated in Figure 1.1), researchers and the pharmaceutical sector alike have commented that the current drug development model may be too cumbersome and therefore stalling the translation of basic science into pharmaceutical products.[8]

---

[5] The Global Use of Medicines: Outlook Through 2018, IMS Institute for Healthcare Informatics, November 2014 (accessible at http://apps.who.int/medicinedocs/documents/s20306en/s20306en.pdf).

[6] U.S. Food and Drug Administration Center for Drug Evaluation and Research (2015) New Molecular Entity Approvals for 2014 Summary Report. However, it should be noted that fast track status is a designation that accelerates the approval of new drugs which show promise in treating life-threatening medical conditions for which no drug or treatment exists or works well. As such, the increased pace of new drug launches may be reflective of greater efficiency in the approval process as opposed to increased drug discovery and development productivity. Perhaps the encouraging signs of pick-up in new drug approvals, which is anticipated to continue, should be viewed with some cautious optimism.

[7] Micheal Hay, David W. Thomas, John L. Craighead, Celia Economides, and Jesse Rosenthal, *Clinical Development Success Rates for Investigational Drugs.* NATURE BIOTECHNOLOGY, 32(1) 40–51 (2014); Joseph A. DiMasi, L. Feldman, A. Seckler, and A. Wilson, *Trends in Risks Associated with New Drug Development: Success Rates for Investigational Drugs.* CLINICAL PHARMACOLOGY AND THERAPEUTICS, 87(3), 272–277 (2010). While there are over 7,000 diseases that affect the human population, only 600 of these diseases have treatments and there are even fewer FDA-approved treatments for rare diseases which affect one in ten Americans.

[8] Fabio Pammolli, Laura Magazzini, and Massimo Riccaboni, *The Productivity Crisis in Pharmaceutical R&D.* NATURE REVIEWS DRUG DISCOVERY, 10(6), 428–438 (2011). See also Ian M. Cockburn, *The Changing Structure of the Pharmaceutical Industry.* HEALTH AFFAIRS, 23(1), 10–22 (2004); Fredric J. Cohen, *Macro Trends in Pharmaceutical Innovation.* NATURE REVIEWS DRUG DISCOVERY, 4(1), 78–84 (2005); Arti K. Rai, Jerome H. Reichman, Paul F. Uhlir, and Colin R. Crossman, *Pathways Across the Valley of Death: Novel Intellectual Property Strategies for Accelerated Drug Discovery.* YALE JOURNAL OF HEALTH POLICY, LAW AND ETHICS, 8(1), 53–89 (2008); Robert F. Service, *Surviving the Blockbuster Syndrome.* SCIENCE (New York, NY), 303(5665), 1796 (2004).

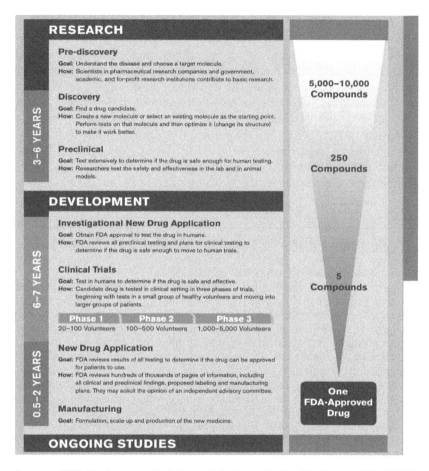

RESEARCH

Pre-discovery
Goal: Understand the disease and choose a target molecule.
How: Scientists in pharmaceutical research companies and government,
      academic, and for-profit research institutions contribute to basic research.

Discovery
Goal: Find a drug candidate.
How: Create a new molecule or select an existing molecule as the starting point.
      Perform tests on that molecule and then optimize it (change its structure)
      to make it work better.

Preclinical
Goal: Test extensively to determine if the drug is safe enough for human testing.
How: Researchers test the safety and effectiveness in the lab and in animal
      models.

3–6 YEARS

5,000–10,000
Compounds

250
Compounds

DEVELOPMENT

Investigational New Drug Application
Goal: Obtain FDA approval to test the drug in humans.
How: FDA reviews all preclinical testing and plans for clinical testing to
      determine if the drug is safe enough to move to human trials.

Clinical Trials
Goal: Test in humans to determine if the drug is safe and effective.
How: Candidate drug is tested in clinical setting in three phases of trials,
      beginning with tests in a small group of healthy volunteers and moving into
      larger groups of patients.

| Phase 1 | Phase 2 | Phase 3 |
| 20–100 Volunteers | 100–500 Volunteers | 1,000–5,000 Volunteers |

New Drug Application
Goal: FDA reviews results of all testing to determine if the drug can be approved
      for patients to use.
How: FDA reviews hundreds of thousands of pages of information, including
      all clinical and preclinical findings, proposed labeling and manufacturing
      plans. They may solicit the opinion of an independent advisory committee.

Manufacturing
Goal: Formulation, scale-up and production of the new medicine.

6–7 YEARS

0.5–2 YEARS

5
Compounds

One
FDA-Approved
Drug

ONGOING STUDIES

Source: 2013 Biopharmaceutical Research Industry Profile, Washington, DC: PhRMA 2013. Reproduced by permission of Pharmaceutical Research and Manufacturers of America (PhRMA).

Figure 1.1   Drug discovery and development process

Those involved in the drug discovery and development process have expressed a serious concern regarding the rising R&D expenditures in the pharmaceutical sector, which can create productivity challenges,[9] cost

---

[9]   Kenneth I. Kaitin, *Deconstructing the Drug Development Process: The New Face of Innovation.* CLINICAL PHARMACOLOGY AND THERA-PEUTICS, 87(3), 356–361 (2010), which asserts that the pharmaceutical sector, as currently structured, is unable to deliver enough new products to market to

containment pressures from government[10] and investors[11] and an increased demand in industry for a competitive edge in the market to maintain shareholder value, thereby unwittingly promoting an over-protective (as opposed to collaborative) environment within the pharmaceutical sector. Much of the cost associated with drug discovery and development is related to the high risk of failure in translating discoveries into safe and effective products, demonstrating how challenging it is to move a molecule from discovery to commercialization.[12] Furthermore, it has been reported that on average, only three in ten new products generate revenues equal to or greater than average industry R&D costs.[13] Given that industry is the only player in the drug discovery and development process that manufactures and makes products derived from basic research available to the public, it is understandable why industry and investors tend to shy away from investing in early stage research and

---

generate revenues sufficient to sustain its own growth and that major drug developers are critically examining their R&D practices and considering different R&D models. To understand why 'business as usual' is no longer an option for the pharmaceutical industry, the author cites three main challenges: loss of revenue due to patent expirations, increased demand for proof of concept, and stringent regulatory compliance requirements. Similarly, Clint Gartin, the head of healthcare banking at Morgan Stanley, states: 'R&D in pharma and biotech is a very risky exercise. Most projects that are started end in failure', see Andrew Jack, 'Pharma Tries to Avoid Falling Off "Patent Cliff"'. *Financial Times* (London, 6 May 2012) (accessible at http://www.ft.com/cms/s/0/572ea510-9452-11e1-bb47-00144feab49a.html#axzz4EmCT0HIL).

[10] For example, see the initial decision of the National Institute for Health and Clinical Excellence in April 2012 where the UK's drug rationing body decided not to cover the cost of GSK's Benlysta, claiming the drug was not cost effective despite there being no alternative treatments for lupus. See article entitled *Benlysta in the UK – Not Covered by the NHS* at http://www.lupus.org.uk/news-events/general/267-benlysta-lupus-drug-not-covered-by-nhs-2

[11] Andrew Jones and Les Clifford, *Drug Discovery Alliances*. NATURE REVIEWS DRUG DISCOVERY, 4(10), 807–808 (2005).

[12] DiMasi, et al., *supra* note 7 and Hay et al., *supra* note 7.

[13] Henry G. Grabowski, John M. Vernon, and Joseph A. DiMasi, *Returns on Research and Development for 1990s New Drug Introductions*. PHARMACO-ECONOMICS, 20(3), 11–29 (2002); and Joseph A. DiMasi and Henry G. Grabowski, 'R&D Costs and Returns to New Drug Development: A Review of the Evidence'. *The Oxford Handbook of the Economics of the Biopharmaceutical Industry*, Oxford University Press, Oxford, 21–46 (2012).

discoveries in favor of innovations with established indications of viability, such as proof of concept.[14]

One of the most problematic areas in the drug discovery and development process that has been the subject of much discussion in the
literature is the lack of competencies to advance innovations beyond
early stage development,[15] despite large government investments in
university R&D, education, equipment, and apparatus in the fields of
medicine and pharmaceutical sciences.[16] University technology transfer
offices (TTOs) have generally been criticized for their slow rate of
commercialization,[17] particularly in the field of pharmaceutical sciences
because TTOs have limited resources and skills to advance early stage
research through to proof of concept. Specifically, the pre-clinical and
target validation processes associated with drug discovery and the
defining of leads and candidates are complex, lengthy, and unpredictable.[18] As previously mentioned, the nature of pharmaceutical research is
such that very few early stage discoveries actually deliver promising

---

[14]   European Commission, Enterprise and Industry. The financing of biopharmaceutical product development in Europe: The Framework Contract of
Sector Competitiveness Studies – ENTR/06/054 Final Report 2009; Jones and
Clifford, supra note 11; Bruce L. Booth, *From the Analyst's Couch: Valuation
with Cash Multiples.* NATURE REVIEWS DRUG DISCOVERY, 4(7), 533–534
(2005). Without better validation tools to allow researchers and industry to
identify which candidates have the greatest likelihood of successful development,
investors will continue to be risk adverse.

[15]   See for example, Rai et al., *supra* note 8; Constance E. Bagley and
Christina D. Tvarnø, *Pharmaceutical Public-Private Partnerships: Moving from
the Bench to the Bedside.* HARVARD BUSINESS LAW REVIEW, 4, 373
(2014); Nuala Moran, *Public Sector Seeks to Bridge 'Valley of Death'.* NATURE
BIOTECHNOLOGY, 25, 266 (2007); Barry S. Coller and Robert M. Califf,
*Traversing the Valley of Death: A Guide to Assessing Prospects for Translational
Success.* SCIENCE TRANSLATIONAL MEDICINE, 1(10), 109 (2009).

[16]   Cancer Center, University of Kansas, Cancer Research, Friends of, Authority, Kansas Bioscience, American Medical Innovation, Council for and Foundation, Ewing Marion Kauffman, *The New Role of Academia in Drug Discovery
and Development: New Thinking, New Competencies, New Results* (December 1,
2010). Ewing Marion Kauffman Foundation Research Paper. Available at SSRN:
http://ssrn.com/abstract=1718465.

[17]   See for example Paul M. Swamidass, and Vulasa Venubabu, *Why University Inventions Rarely Produce Income? Bottlenecks in University Technology
Transfer.* THE JOURNAL OF TECHNOLOGY TRANSFER, 34(4), 343–363
(2009).

[18]   See for example Declan Butler, *Translational Research: Crossing the
Valley of Death.* NATURE NEWS, 453(7197), 840–842 (2008); Cohen, *supra*
note 8; Service, *supra* note 8.

results due to a high risk of failure compared to other industry sectors. Without the funding or expertise to decide which discoveries have potential, TTOs have a difficult time assessing and marketing early stage research to investors for translation into therapies that may ultimately improve human health. If TTOs fail to attract licensing revenue from investors, basic research projects fail to receive further funding to establish proof of concept to demonstrate commercial and clinical viability.

The European Commission, Directorate General Enterprise and Industry, has reported that venture capitalists (VCs), which have largely driven success in funding medical innovation in the recent past,[19] have effectively stopped making early-stage investments since 2001/2002, citing too many failures and too high a risk/return ratio.[20] The available data and statistics therefore point to a hesitance by VCs to invest in early stage pharmaceutical research, presumably because of their growing intolerance of the unpredictability and risk associated with unproven technologies and discoveries.[21] In other words, the gap between academic research and the evidence of viability demanded by VCs to justify investment has widened. A consequence of industry preference to invest in later-stage technologies is that researchers potentially face increasing difficulty finding funding to translate and develop their early-stage discoveries to provide proof of concept, thereby creating a vicious cycle: investors need proof of concept to invest in the further development of basic research but researchers need investors to invest in early-stage discoveries in order to have the funding to achieve proof of concept.

---

[19]   European Commission *supra*, note 14. As stated in the report, venture capital is the most important source of capital for European pharmaceutical companies and drug development, particularly at early stages of development. By participating in early validation of technology, any resulting success may be used to attract other investors.

[20]   Jones and Clifford., *supra* note 11, stating that venture capital investors have altered their investment behavior by favoring companies with critical mass or opportunities with existing or near-term products and revenue. See also Arthur Klausner, *Mind the (Biomedical Funding) Gap*. NATURE BIOTECHNOLOGY, 23(10), 1217–1218 (2005) and Booth, *supra* note 14, where industry analysts have also reported on the 'funding gap' resulting from the increasing reluctance of venture capitalists to invest in early stage discoveries.

[21]   The European Federation of Pharmaceutical Industries and Associations, *The Pharmaceutical Industry in Figures*, Edition 2012 (accessible at http://www.efpia.eu/uploads/Modules/Documents/efpia_figures_2012_final-20120622-003-en-v1.pdf).

From the perspective of those critical of the traditional university technology transfer model, there appears to be a general consensus that this model is an inefficient means to facilitate the translation and commercialization of pharmaceutical discoveries and technologies.[22] Specifically, the traditional technology transfer model fails to provide a mechanism to bridge the gap between early stage academic research and pre-clinical research. Technology transfer consists of the transfer of technological information or knowledge wherein one party gains access to another party's information for a fee in order to utilize such information. At the risk of stating the obvious, successful technology transfer therefore presupposes the technology is developed to the point where third parties deem it a worthwhile investment (or can reasonably assess the technology's value) to license the associated intellectual property for commercialization or further R&D purposes. In order to attract investors to license university research, TTOs assert intellectual property rights in university research results in order to have something proprietary to license to interested parties. Without proof of concept, industry partners are unable to assess the risk and rewards to make an informed decision as to whether to make a substantial financial investment in early-stage discoveries. Known as the 'Valley of Death', innovations that may be the next 'blockbuster success' could potentially fall through the gap and be left undeveloped at the early stages of research because of lack of funding and expertise to bring discoveries to a clinically and commercially investible point to attract industry involvement in translation and commercialization.[23]

[22]   Joshua B. Powers, *Between Lab Bench and Marketplace: The Pitfalls of Technology Transfer.* THE CHRONICLE OF HIGHER EDUCATION, 53, 5, B18 (2006); Gary P. Pisano, *Can Science be a Business? Lessons from Biotech.* HARVARD BUSINESS REVIEW, 114–125 (2006); Robert E. Litan and Lesa Mitchell, *A Faster Path from Lab to Market.* HARVARD BUSINESS REVIEW, 88(1–2), 52 (2010).

[23]   Michelle G. Habets, Johannes J. van Delden, and Annelien L. Bredenoord, *The Social Value of Clinical Research.* BMC MEDICAL ETHICS, 15(1), 66 (2014); Maureen Kelley, Kelly Edwards, Helene Starks, Stephanie M. Fullerton, Rosalina James, Sara Goering, Suzanne Holland, Mary L. Disis, and Wylie Burke, *Values in Translation: How Asking the Right Questions Can Move Translational Science towards Greater Health Impact.* CLINICAL AND TRANSLATIONAL SCIENCE, 5(6), 445–451 (2012); Karl E. Friedl, *Overcoming the 'Valley of Death': Mouse Models to Accelerate Translational Research.* DIABETES TECHNOLOGY & THERAPEUTICS, 8(3), 413–414 (2006); Coller and Califf, *supra* note 15.

B. COLLABORATIVE DRUG DISCOVERY AND DEVELOPMENT

Due to the increasing cost of R&D and budgetary and funding challenges in the public research sector, collaborative partnerships between industry and public research organizations, such as universities, hospitals, and other publically funded research institutions may be a pragmatic solution as a means to pool resources and reduce duplication efforts.[24] If collaborative partnerships are to be supported as a means to facilitate the drug discovery and development process, the question then becomes how public research organizations and industry can forge closer ties through partnerships and research collaborations while preserving academic core values and providing industry with the incentive required to justify investment in basic research.[25] It is conceivable to anticipate polarization within academic institutions between those who want to partner with industry as a means to secure research funds required to translate publically funded basic research into pharmaceutical products for the benefit of the public and those who view collaboration with industry as a betrayal of academic objectives and principles.[26] As stated by Louis Berneman, Past President of the Association of University Technology

---

[24] See Moran, *supra* note 15, on bridging the funding gap between the finishing point of research that is funded by academic grants and development of clinical and therapeutic applications funded by the private sector. For example, in June 2011, Pfizer entered into a USD$100 million five-year partnership with eight research institutions in the Boston area to discover and develop new candidate drugs. This came after Pfizer unveiled its plans to cut its research and development spending, including closing its research facility in Sandwich, UK and letting go almost all of the 2,400 employees there. Pfizer also announced it will cut its R&D expenditure by $1–2 billion for the next fiscal year.

[25] See John P. Walsh, Wesley M. Cohen, and Charlene Cho, *Where Excludability Matters: Material Versus Intellectual Property in Academic Biomedical Research*. RESEARCH POLICY, 36(8), 1184–1203 (2007), which cited empirical data that indicates 70% of agreements between academia and industry for academic researchers to gain access to industry proprietary materials for the purposes of R&D included reach-through rights on improvements and some restrictions on publication, which may impede future collaborations.

[26] University–industry collaborations can restrict or delay academic publication in favor of preserving a company's proprietary rights. As stated by Eric Campbell, a sociologist at Harvard Medical School in Boston, 'You should not in any way accept the notion that these giant institutional agreements are without tremendous danger', see Heidi Ledford, *Drug Buddies*. NATURE, 474(7352), 433–434 (2011) at 434.

Managers, the tension between conflicting priorities of the parties must be recognized and respected in order for the collaboration to be successful:

> The two worlds – university and industry – can be bridged. In fact, their widely divergent missions and institutional obligations (public vs. private interests) can be complementary, synergistic, and beneficial to all.[27]

Public–private collaboration in product development is not a new idea and appears to be an obvious model to explore in the pharmaceutical sector since none of the individual players in the drug discovery and development process have all the necessary skills and resources to research and develop pharmaceutical products alone. Academia is a rich source of basic research and discovery but lacks the funding and translational expertise of how new therapies reach the market. Industry has core competencies in clinical translational activities and procedures required to convert early-stage research into new therapies, but they generally outsource the discovery of new molecules to external partners.[28] There are many different models that attempt to foster the translation of ideas from academia to industry as a means to bridge the translation gap. These range from strategic partnerships to joint institutes between industry and academia. The focus of this book is on one particular model referred to herein as the integrated drug discovery and development model.

The integrated drug discovery and development platform is based on a collaborative model whereby the respective expertise of academia and industry are brought together to establish viability in early stage technologies by way of achieving proof of concept. Establishing indications of feasibility in early stage innovations will enable a more informed determination of the technology's potential and attract investment partners to take it through to commercialization. Currently, there are several public research organizations that have adopted the integrated drug discovery and development platform (referred to collectively herein as

---

[27]   CEO Council for Growth, *Identifying Opportunities to Connect Universities with Industry for Regional Economic Development* (2007).

[28]   Sean Ekins, Chris L. Waller, Mary P. Bradley, Alex M. Clark, and Antony J. Williams, *Four Disruptive Strategies for Removing Drug Discovery Battlements*. DRUG DISCOVERY TODAY, 18(5), 265–271 (2013) and Ismael Rafols, Michael M. Hopkins, Jarno Hoekman, Josh Siepel, Alice O'Hare, Antonio Perianes-Rodríguez, and Paul Nightingale, *Big Pharma, Little Science? A Bibliometric Perspective on Big Pharma's R&D Decline*. TECHNOLOGICAL FORECASTING AND SOCIAL CHANGE, 81, 22–28 (2014).

integrated drug discovery organizations, to be discussed in greater detail in Chapter 2). These integrated drug discovery organizations have each created an international network of affiliate and partner institutions to support project development by offering access to state of the art facilities, equipment, and resources, as well as technical expertise and business acumen in order to facilitate the translation of basic research into new medicines. The question is whether the current European legal framework supports a drug discovery and development model based on achieving proof of concept through collaborative partnership between industry and academia, as represented by the integrated drug discovery organization.

C. DO THE EXISTING LEGAL REGIMES SUPPORT THE INTEGRATED DRUG DISCOVERY MODEL OF DEVELOPMENT?

Drug research and development is flanked by three regulatory systems: patent law, competition law, and the drug regulation system (i.e. the European Medicines Agency and United States Food & Drug Administration). Many different factors have an interconnected influence on the social, economic, and legal dynamics that affects the pharmaceutical industry and drug discovery and development process. For example, because the cost of pharmaceutical R&D accounts for an ever greater proportion of public expenditure, governments have had to increasingly scrutinize budgets for funding drug discovery and development. This in turn affects industry practices, such as strategic use of intellectual property rights and pricing policies to ensure profitability.[29] And, this in turn affects regulator practices to ensure patients' right to health by pricing pharmaceutical products lower so that patients can have reasonable access to medicines. In other words, the triangulation of competition policy, patent policy, and drug regulation gives rise to a dynamic whereby government wants to foster innovation by providing incentives to industry through granting intellectual property rights while ensuring there are mechanisms and policy tools in place to help control anticompetitive use of such intellectual property rights.[30] Because of this 'give with one

---

[29]   See for example Himanshu Gupta, Sresh Kumar, Sraoj K. Roy, and Ram S. Gaud, *Patent Protection Strategies*. JOURNAL OF PHARMACY AND BIOALLIED SCIENCES, 2(1), 2–7 (2010).

[30]   A potential conflict can arise from intervention under competition law to prevent the emergence of monopolies by limiting the exploitation of state granted

hand, take with the other' dynamic, it is understandable why parties to the drug development process need to be cautious of the potential legal consequences and pitfalls that may arise from participating in the integrated drug discovery model of drug discovery and development.[31]

The European Union clearly recognizes the importance of funding proof of concept. With a budget of €20 million for 2015, the European Research Centre (ERC) has agreed to contribute an additional €150,000 per grant to existing ERC grant holders for the purpose of establishing proof of concept for research arising from ERC-funded projects.[32] The stated objective of the additional grant is to support the development of a commercialization strategy of ERC-funded research to attract investors by preparing a 'package' that demonstrates, among other things, viability of the technology and the intellectual property protection strategy. In 2011, a £180 million catalyst fund was made available for the purpose of establishing proof of concept so that early stage research can proceed to clinical development.[33] Soon thereafter, the UK Medical Research Council (MRC) and the University of Dundee announced new funding of

---

exclusive rights provided under patent law. However, the underlying objective of both patent and competition law is to ensure 'dynamic competition' or innovation efficiency achieved through encouraging invention, development, and commercialization of new products for the benefit of the public. See for example Joseph F. Brodley, *The Economic Goals of Antitrust: Efficiency, Consumer Welfare, Technological Progress.* NEW YORK UNIVERSITY LAW REVIEW, 62, 1020 (1987) at 1025.

[31] The misconceived view of equating patent rights to economic monopolies give rise to an oversimplified analysis of license agreements under competition law by neglecting the beneficial effects of patents in terms of dynamic competition. Consequently, inventors can potentially be 'punished' under competition law, which would have the effect of discouraging innovation because the incentives guaranteed under patent law can be undermined by competition law. See for example Michael A. Carrier, *Unraveling the Patent-Antitrust Paradox.* UNIVERSITY OF PENNSYLVANIA LAW REVIEW, 761–854 (2002) at 763–764 and Steven D. Anderman and John Kallaugher, *Technology Transfer and the New EU Competition Rules: Intellectual Property Licensing after Modernisation.* OXFORD UNIVERSITY PRESS ON DEMAND (2006).

[32] See ERC Proof of Concept Grant (accessible at https://erc.europa.eu/proof-concept). Launched in 2011, the ERC 'Proof of Concept' funding initiative is intended to fund high risk/high gain research to ensure full exploitation of the ideas it funds and is intended to bridge the gap between research and the earliest stage of marketable innovation.

[33] At the 2011 FT Global Pharmaceutical and Biotechnology Conference, Prime Minister David Cameron specifically recognized the backlog of commercializable projects stuck in the 'valley of death'. See the transcript of the speech

£14.4 million over a four-year period from July 2012 to July 2016 from a consortium of six pharmaceutical companies for early stage research and proof of concept of new drug treatments.[34] Similarly in the United States, in response to a growing concern regarding the lack of drug development by the pharmaceutical industry, the government invested US$1 billion to create the National Center for Advancing Translational Sciences in 2012 to reduce the costly and time-consuming bottlenecks in the translational research.[35]

Although government funding is essential to scientific R&D, collaboration and team science is required to perform the actual R&D, so the collaborative process is not one that can be driven by government alone. The overall evolution of the economy towards a knowledge economy creates an important incentive for constant innovation and application of state-of-the-art scientific information. This very naturally brings together universities and research organizations on the one hand and industry on the other hand. There is literature to suggest that collaboration with private partners secures additional immediate funds for R&D of multiple projects and speeds up the process to commercialization.[36] Technology transfer drives economic growth and social welfare, especially in health-related technologies.[37] It is a shortcut to gaining access to promising new

---

given by Prime Minister David Cameron at the FT Global Pharmaceutical and Biotechnology Conference on December 6, 2011 at http://www.number10.gov. uk/news/pm-speech-on-life-sciences-and-opening-up-the-nhs/

[34] The companies include AstraZeneca, Boehringer Ingelheim, GlaxoSmith-Kline, Janssen Pharmaceutica NV, Merck-Serono, and Pfizer. See Medical Research Council press release dated May 16, 2012 entitled 'Academia-Pharma Collaboration Attracts £14.4 million Funding in the UK to Accelerate Drug Discovery' (accessible at http://www.mrc.ac.uk/news/browse/academia-pharma-collaboration-attracts-144-million-funding-in-the-uk-to-accelerate-drug-discovery/).

[35] See www.ncats.nih.gov

[36] See for example Markus Perkmann, Valentina Tartari, Maureen McKelvey, Erkko Autio, Anders Brostrom, Pablo D'Este, Riccardo Fini, Aldo Geuna, Rosa Grimaldi, Alan Hughes, Stefan Krabel, Michael Kitson, Patrick Llerena, Francesco Lissoni, Ammon Salter, and Mauricio Sobrero, *Academic Engagement and Commercialization: A Review of the Literature on University-Industry Relations.* RESEARCH POLICY, 42(2), 423–442 (2013).

[37] See Rai et al., *supra* note 8. In the drug discovery and development context, any technology transfer platform between university and industry must simultaneously provide financial benefit to the industry partner and promote the interests of public sector researchers. Intellectual property may need to be 'used creatively to secure efficient pathways across the gap that separates upstream research from downstream products – a gap so economically perilous that it has

discoveries, and that is why governments encourage and promote international collaborations for the development of innovations.[38] To ensure and promote international collaborations, many of the developed countries have focused on providing recommendations and guidelines to universities and public research organizations to develop intellectual property policies to manage intellectual property rights arising from collaborative efforts. For example, in a 2008 Commission Recommendation on the Management of Intellectual Property in Knowledge Transfer Activities and Code of Practice for Universities and Other Public Research Organizations (the 'Recommendation'), the European Commission specifically recognized the need to develop policies and guidelines for public research organizations to "effectively exploit publicly-funded research results with a view to translating them into new products and services" through public/private collaborations.[39] The purpose of the Recommendation was to set out 'clear and uniform recommendations and practices that ensure equitable and fair access to intellectual property generated through international research collaborations'.[40]

An unintended consequence of such international collaborations is the potential for competitive conflict which may arise with respect to the intellectual property rights associated with a project that the industry partner may subsequently acquire rights to. Specifically, the collaboration relationship may inadvertently give rise to a violation of competition law due to anticompetitive or exclusionary conduct, such as but not limited to exclusivity agreements with industry partners, grant back restrictions, and refusal to license to third parties. Furthermore, although the bringing together of complementary skills and assets in a collaboration between industry and integrated drug discovery organizations may facilitate innovation by enhancing efficiency and reducing expenditure, the number and ability of potential market actors to enter the market may be limited by such collaboration. Intellectual property law and competition law are intended to be complementary and share the same objective – that is to

---

earned the "valley of death" moniker'. If the collaboration generates a large number of efficacious drugs, the public becomes the ultimate beneficiary.

[38] See for example Drew Gertner, Joanne Roberts and David Charles, *University-industry Collaboration: A CoPs Approach to KTPs.* JOURNAL OF KNOWLEDGE MANAGEMENT, 15(4), 625–647 (2011).

[39] Commission Recommendation, European Commission, *Management of Intellectual Property in Knowledge Transfer Activities and Code of Practice for Universities and other Public Research Organizations*, Brussels (C(2008) 1329) at 2.

[40] Ibid.

promote innovation, competition, and economic efficiency to the benefit of consumer welfare. However, the *exercise* of intellectual property rights may be considered anticompetitive under certain circumstances.

The tension between intellectual property law and competition law is especially great in the pharmaceutical context where companies often push the use of intellectual property rights to their limits in an attempt to maximize profits.[41] Patents essentially confer monopoly power in the pharmaceutical industry as they are used to gain and maintain an exclusive market share.[42] This in turn attracts criticism from the public of drug companies abusing their monopoly power afforded by patents at the expense of consumer welfare and fair competition.[43] Competition law should rightfully be used to curtail abuses of intellectual property rights when they have clearly been exercised beyond their scope. The question is when does legitimate assertion of intellectual property rights become an abuse in the eyes of competition law? When does competition law cross the invisible line and impinge on the right of exclusive use granted by patent law, thereby eliminating or substantially decreasing the incentives for innovation? The pharmaceutical industry has long maintained that patents are crucial to the financial viability of continued R&D. For instance, four months after Lipitor came off patent in November 2011, generic drug maker Ranbaxy Laboratories became the leading seller of the medication and Lipitor's worldwide sales dropped by 59% in 2012.[44]

---

[41] See for example, Ron A. Bouchard, *Patently Innovative: How Pharmaceutical Firms Use Emerging Patent Law to Extend Monopolies on Blockbuster Drugs* (Elsevier 2012) and Lara J. Glasgow, *Stretching the Limits of Intellectual Property Rights: Has the Pharmaceutical Industry Gone Too Far?* IDEA 41(2), 227 (2001).

[42] Rebecca S. Eisenberg, *Patents, Product Exclusivity, and Information Dissemination: How Law Directs Biopharmaceutical Research and Development.* FORDHAM LAW REVIEW, 72, 477 (2003).

[43] For example, see Glasgow, *supra* note 41, who states: 'Perhaps nowhere is this tension more obvious than in the pharmaceutical industry where intellectual property rights are pushed to their limits in an attempt to maximize profits on popular brand name drugs'. See also Cristian Timmermann and Hank van den Belt, *Intellectual Property and Global Health: From Corporate Social Responsibility to the Access to Knowledge Movement.* LIVERPOOL LAW REVIEW, 34(1), 47–73 (2013) who argued that the realities of the intellectual property system may mean that urgently needed medicines will not be developed at all because they are not profitable, that the existing medicines will not be suitable for countries with a precarious health infrastructure, or treatment of diseases that are prevalent in poorer regions may be ignored.

[44] See Pfizer's fourth-quarter and full-year 2012 results (accessible at http://www.pfizer.com/files/investors/presentations/q4performance_012913.pdf).

Without patents, industry could not survive in the costly and risky business of drug development. Similarly, many universities and public research organizations support patents because they need patents to protect the technology they license to industry in exchange for royalties to support continued R&D.[45] Given the nature of drug discovery and development, it is understandable that industry wants strong intellectual property protection as an incentive for taking the risk to develop early stage discoveries and be rewarded for their innovation should development lead to commercialization. However, improvement innovators need access to the intellectual property of the original innovator to develop improvements for follow-on innovation. The nature of technology-driven industries is such that an innovator will likely be both a licensor (of improved intellectual property) and a licensee (of an earlier innovation which improved intellectual property is based on). Without a balance of intellectual property law and competition policy, a potential hold-up may be created because complex technologies depend on technological inputs from prior innovators. To what extent should competition authorities limit lawfully obtained intellectual property rights in order to encourage innovations based on improvements of protected technologies?

---

[45]   Johan Bruneel, Pablo d'Este, and Ammon Salter, *Investigating the Factors that Diminish the Barriers to University-industry Collaboration.* RESEARCH POLICY, 39(7), 858–868 (2010). Universities are increasingly proactive in seeking IP protection to manage their collaborations with industry. Over the past thirty years, universities have grown to become economic actors through the rise of university technology transfer offices and their licensing activities. Such efforts have contributed to the commercial focus of universities to create and protect valuable IP for exploitation and financial gain. For example, according to WIPO's records on international patent filings in 2011, US universities are the most prolific international patent filers among higher education institutions worldwide, accounting for 30 of the top 50 institutions. However, from the university researcher's perspective, there is conflicting evidence for and against university patenting, exacerbating the difference across universities in terms of financial resources and research freedom. For example, see Lee Davis, Maria T. Larsen, and Peter Lotz, *Scientists' perspectives concerning the effects of university patenting on the conduct of academic research in the life sciences.* THE JOURNAL OF TECHNOLOGY TRANSFER, 36(1), 14–37 (2011); Valentina Tartari and Stefano Breschi, *Set Them Free: Scientists' Evaluations of the Benefits and Costs of University-Industry Research Collaboration,* INDUSTRIAL AND CORPORATE CHANGE, 21(5), 1117–1147 (2012); Ani Gerbin and Mateja Drnovsek, *Determinants and Public Policy Implications of Academic-Industry Knowledge Transfer in Life Sciences: A Review and a Conceptual Framework.* THE JOURNAL OF TECHNOLOGY TRANSFER, 1–98 (2015).

After being urged to compete, innovate, and become a solution to the drug discovery and development problem, should participants to collaborative R&D be penalized if they gain market power through legitimate competition? There is literature that supports the position that a company should not be punished for simply being innovative and more efficient than their competitors since this would be detrimental to competition and consumer welfare in the long run.[46] Furthermore, given that competition policy is meant to protect competition as opposed to competitors, it is generally accepted that 'competition on the merits' allows a company to force a rival company out of the market or discourage their entry or expansion so long as its conduct is lawful.[47] One way to reduce the conflict between competition policy and intellectual property law in the drug discovery and development context is to define a clear boundary ex-ante that specifically acknowledges and considers the particular dynamics of the pharmaceutical industry and the nature of drug discovery and development so that participants in the collaborative R&D process know in advance what is permissible. Given that competition policy is largely case law driven, whereas intellectual property law has historically been set in legislation and regulatory rule making, any adaptation of the legal system to proactively address the unique and changing circumstances of the pharmaceutical industry should be done at the competition law level, which enjoys greater flexibility.

D. THE INTERSECTION OF COMPETITION LAW AND INTELLECTUAL PROPERTY LAW

One of the first obstacles is how the law will regard and interpret the relationship between public research organizations and industry for the

---

[46] Steven Anderman, 'Innovation, IPRs, EU Competition Law: Cross Currents in the EU/US Debate' in Ariel Ezrachi (ed), *Research Handbook on International Competition Law* (Edward Elgar Publishing 2012); Marcus Glader, *Innovation Markets and Competition Analysis*: *EU Competition Law and US Antitrust Law. New Horizons in Competition Law and Economics* (Edward Elgar Publishing 2006).

[47] OECD Policy Brief, *What is Competition on the Merits?* June 2006 (accessible at http://www.oecd.org/competition/mergers/37082099.pdf). However, this concept is quite unclear in the pharmaceutical sector. See Damien Geradin, *The Uncertainties Created by Relying on the Vague 'Competition on the Merits' Standard in the Pharmaceutical Sector: The Italian Pfizer/Pharmacia Case.* JOURNAL OF EUROPEAN COMPETITION LAW & PRACTICE, 5(6), 344–352 (2014).

purposes of conducting drug discovery and development. Is the collaboration a research agreement or a transfer of technology for further development? From a competition law perspective, how will the relationship be characterized and which regulation and/or block exemption applies? The overarching question is to what extent does the application of competition law to the integrated drug discovery and development model consider or promote innovation. In other words, do the intellectual property and competition law frameworks support the integrated drug discovery and development model by satisfying the respective objectives of academia (i.e. maintaining traditional university integrity to make publically funded research available to the benefit of society) and industry (i.e. incentivizing and ensuring economic feasibility to justify investment and participation in the collaboration).

The literature indicates that the EU and a number of universities have come to realize that technology transfer can be an attractive source of income to fund the ever-increasing costs of basic research.[48] Contrary to

---

[48] See for example Goldie Blumenstyk, *Universities Report $1.8 Billion in Earnings on Inventions in 2011.* THE CHRONICLE OF HIGHER EDUCATION (2012) (accessible at http://chronicle.com/article/University-Inventions-Earned/ 133972/). In the EU context, Katholieke Universiteit Leuven reported €63.2 million in annual licensing income, generated from around 600 active patent families with close to 90% of those patent families being commercially exploited from contracts with over 2,000 companies. KU Leuven has a proven track record in transferring and translating research into valuable economic activity. See article entitled *KU Leuven – Prestigious University Fosters Innovation-Driven Economy.* THE EUROPEAN TIMES (2014) (accessible at http://www.european-times.com/countries/ku-leuven/). Max Planck Innovation reported €22.5 million in revenue from licensing income and 92 license agreements in 2013 (see http://www.max-planck-innovation.de/en/technology_transfer/successful_track_ record/licensing/). The European Commission has argued that while European research institutions are good at producing academic research outputs, they are not as successful as universities in the United States in translating and commercializing the research – the so-called 'European Paradox' – which is largely due to a less systematic and professional management of knowledge and intellectual property by European universities. See European Commission, *Improving Knowledge Transfer between Research Institutions and Industry across Europe – Embracing Open Innovation – Implementing the Lisbon Agenda* (2007). The literature generally acknowledges that a 'European Paradox' indeed does exist but questions the extent of and the reason for the European underperformance in commercializing publicly funded research. See for example Annamaria Conti and Patrick Gaule, *Is the US Outperforming Europe in University Technology Licensing: A New Perspective on the European Paradox.* RESEARCH POLICY, 40, 123–135 (2011); Neus Herranz and Javier Ruiz-Castillo, *The End of the 'European Paradox'.* SCIENTOMETRICS, 95(1) 453–464 (2013). One of the

years past, some universities today seem to play an increasing role in and operate on the market in several ways: firstly, they deliver research services to industry via collaboration arrangements; secondly, they operate on the technology market by licensing and assigning their inventions and associated intellectual property rights to third parties; and thirdly, they establish new companies, typically referred to as spin-off companies, which are usually research-intensive small and medium-sized enterprises active in high-tech markets. The commercial nature of these activities carried out by universities gives rise to some interesting and challenging legal questions. One of the issues thus far not widely examined is the impact of competition law on universities and public research organizations, such as integrated drug discovery organizations, operating on the marketplace. At first blush, collaboration agreements between industry and public research organizations do not appear to fall within the scope of Article 101 Treaty of the Functioning of the European Union (TFEU) because there is unlikely to be a limitation on competition. Firstly, public research organizations and industry are most probably not competitors on any market, given the difference in the nature of their respective activities. Secondly, industry is likely the only party to commercialize the results of any successful collaboration, given that industry is the only player in the innovation process that makes products derived from basic research available to and for the benefit of the public. Public research organizations typically have as their mission the carrying out of research 'for the sake of knowledge' and disseminating the results of that research via publications and education. Conversely, a company wishes to use the knowledge it creates or otherwise obtains rights to, in an exclusive manner, to obtain a competitive advantage over other companies in the relevant market. How could an agreement between two entities with such different aims ever be restrictive of competition?

Upon closer inspection of the activities of some universities, such public research organizations actually participate in several markets: the market for research services and the market for the licensing of intellectual property rights, known as the 'innovation market' and the 'technology market', respectively. In a typical university–industry research collaboration, the industry partner will likely require assignment of the

---

top objectives for TTOs is to generate revenue for the university to fund research collaborations, and one of the most common incentives for researchers to engage in knowledge transfer is receiving additional funding for further research. See for example European Commission, DG Research and Innovation, *Report of the Knowledge Transfer Study 2010–2012* (RTD/Dir C/C2/2010/SI2.569045 2013).

full ownership of all results arising from the sponsored research project or some form of exclusivity to prevent competitors from benefiting from the knowledge created. From a competition law perspective, this assignment or exclusivity may not necessarily be neutral since the university concerned will likely not be able to exploit its research results by licensing them to third parties, even if the industry partner fails to commercialize the results to its fullest potential. To a certain extent, aggressive and strategic use of intellectual property rights may be compatible with the concept of 'competition on the merits',[49] but when commercial practice by intellectual property owners consists of conduct that is prohibited by competition policy as either an exclusionary or exploitative abuse or restriction on competition, competition rules can operate as a limit to the exercise of intellectual property rights.[50]

This book examines the application of Article 101(1) to collaboration agreements between industry and integrated drug discovery organizations and how it impacts innovation in the field of drug discovery and development. The research presents a new perspective on the patent–antitrust intersection, by exploring the competition law assessment of licensing agreements in the light of the economic concept of innovation, licensing efficiency and transactional hazards.

E. OBJECTIVES

The questions and issues this book will attempt to address are as follows:

(a) How do the existing applicable legal frameworks (intellectual property law and competition policy) impact collaboration between

---

[49] OECD Policy Brief, *supra* note 47 states: 'Generally, the expression "competition on the merits" implies that a dominant enterprise can lawfully engage in conduct that falls within the area circumscribed by that phrase, even if the consequence of that conduct is that rivals are forced to exit the market or their entry or expansion is discouraged'.

[50] Ibid. If the concept of competition on the merits is to be helpful, it must facilitate the task of separating out harmful, exclusionary conduct from healthy competition. Competition is on the merits when it reflects rational commercial conduct based on superior efficiency. See Renato Nazzini, *The Foundations of European Union Competition Law: The Objective and Principles of Article 102* (Oxford University Press 2012). The CJEU has established the general principle that conduct is abusive when it restricts competition by means that are inconsistent with the normal profit maximizing strategy of a non-dominant undertaking. See Case C-85/76 *Hoffmann-La Roche v Commission* [1979] ECR 461 para. 172.

integrated drug discovery organizations and private pharmaceutical companies in the context of the integrated drug discovery and development platform? In other words, can the collaboration between industry and integrated drug discovery organizations be structured in a way that is compliant with existing legal regimes?

(b)   To what extent do the existing legal frameworks consider or provide incentives to facilitate innovation in the context of collaborative drug discovery and development?

(c)   Given the policy reasons underlying intellectual property law and competition law and the nature of the pharmaceutical sector, will exclusionary conduct found in collaboration agreements between industry and integrated drug discovery organizations, such as but not limited to exclusivity agreements, refusal to license, and exclusive dealings, collectively be necessarily de jure anti-competitive?

This book has two objectives. Firstly, it will analyze how European competition rules apply to the collaboration agreements between industry and integrated drug discovery organizations with respect to the collaborative R&D component and the subsequent technology transfer component, should the collaborative R&D generate positive results. The analysis will form the foundation to assess whether such collaboration agreements give rise to anticompetitive concerns. Based on the assumption that different industries have certain inherent features that give rise to unique issues that affect the industry in question,[51] the purpose of the analysis is to: (i) identify competition law issues that arise from collaborations between industry and public research organizations engaging in collaborative drug discovery and development; and (ii) determine how the interaction between such competition issues and inherent features of the pharmaceutical industry impact the drug discovery and development process.

---

[51]   As stated in the OECD Policy Roundtable, *Competition and Regulation Issues in the Pharmaceutical Industry* (DAFFE/CLP(2000)29) 2001: 'Very few industries are as profoundly influenced by regulation as the pharmaceutical industry. The nature of demand for drugs, the identity of drugs brought to market, and the nature of competition in the drug market over time are all shaped by regulation. There are three main objectives to this regulation: securing a reward to R&D to assure a continuous flow of innovative new medications; ensuring the safety of drugs; and controlling the quantity and enhancing the quality of drug expenditures. The combined effect of this regulation is that competition takes a different form than in other industries ... However, the appropriate role for competition is not always plain. Competition advocacy in this industry requires taking a holistic view'.

Secondly, this book aims to draw implications on how the integrated drug discovery model may operate in light of the current trends on the application of competition rules. By analyzing competition issues that are typically addressed ex-post in legal cases and administrative proceedings, which are decided on a case-by-case basis and with perfect hindsight, anticompetitive concerns that arise in the pharmaceutical sector can be identified and used proactively to navigate around potential pitfalls ex-ante. Arguably, legal uncertainty is one of the greatest concerns when parties enter into any legal agreement. The ability to manage potential anticompetitive concerns ex-ante would help de-risk the already precarious process of drug discovery and development. The intention is to identify a possible framework that is compatible with the existing laws and policy to promote efficient drug development and innovation without discouraging international collaboration through the intervention of competition law.[52]

The hypothesis is that the existing competition law framework fails to consider the specific nature of the pharmaceutical sector by mandating a blanket application of general competition policy without regard to the inherent features of the industry and the risks associated with drug discovery and development.[53] If the perspective of competition law is

---

[52]   Steven Anderman, *EC Competition Law and Intellectual Property Rights in the New Economy.* ANTITRUST BULLETIN, 47, 285 (2002), where it is implied that regulation of IPRs by competition policy may not be appropriate in high-technology sectors. According to Anderman, high technology markets are characterized by competition for the market (instead of in the market), and market leadership may be dependent on the exercise of IPRs, meaning dominance may be inevitable but also temporary because of self-regulation when new innovations enter the market. Following such argument, competition law may be over-reactive to the dynamics of the pharmaceutical industry if consideration is not given to the nature of the industry.

[53]   Some scholars have argued that recent reviews of some regulatory frameworks have seen sector-specific measures being scaled back and general competition law measures gaining a more prominent role. See for example Natascha Freund and Ernst-Olav Ruhle, *The Evolution from Sector-specific Regulation towards Competition Law in EU Telecom Markets from 1997 to 2011: Different Effects in Practical Implementation.* In 22nd European Regional Conference of the International Telecommunications Society (IT2011), Budapest, 18–21 September 2011. However, proponents of sector-specific rules have argued that general competition law enjoys a hierarchical priority over sector-specific rules but lacks the breadth of objectives expressed by sector regulation. In the context of the Internal Energy Market, it has been suggested that 'sector rules should have a functional priority regarding their implementation as lex specialis and constitute the context for any potential application of competition law … The

limited to viewing the collaboration agreements with a market-centric focus, then competition law fails to consider how such agreements help overcome problems associated with the innovation process, such as de-risking transactional hazards to facilitate the commercialization of new products. Protecting healthy competition must also include protecting agreements that incentivize collaboration and commercialization which form an essential part of the innovation process. As stated in the final report by the European Commission on the financing of biopharmaceutical product development in Europe:

> [T]he European Commission should recognize the unique structural characteristics of the biopharmaceutical sector (capital-intensive, long time to market, high risk of failure) by considering sector-specific policy measures targeting the special needs of the biopharmaceutical sector. Such sector-specific measures would constitute a new approach in European industrial policy (compared to the current horizontal approach) that could successfully support the future development, innovative capacity and competitiveness of the European biopharmaceutical sector.[54]

---

model proposed by the research emphasizes prioritization of sector-specific rules, use of competition rules as an interpretative tool, limitation of their independent application to cases where sector regulation fails and even then after taking into consideration sector specific context and acceptance of dynamic competition as an orientating framework', Michael D. Diathesopoulos, *Competition Law and Sector Regulation in European Energy Market after the Third Energy Package: Hierarchy and Efficiency* (University of Cambridge Faculty of Law Research Paper 2012), at 1 and 101. As indicated in the Pharma Sector Report, *supra* note 1, there are unique competition law issues that arise in the pharmaceutical context that require attention, which may provide the basis for supporting the need for sector-specific competition rules.

[54] Danish Technological Institute for the European Commission, DG Enterprise and Industry, *Study on the Competitiveness of the European Biotechnology Industry. The Financing of Biopharmaceutical Product Development in Europe – Final Report* (October 2009) Copenhagen Brussels (http://ec.europa.eu/DocsRoom/documents/1416/attachments/1/translations/en/renditions/pdf). Other highly innovative industry sectors such as software and telecommunications that rely on patents and rapid innovation to remain competitive have their own sector-specific regulations. See EU Competition Law Rules Applicable to Antitrust Enforcement Volume III: Sector Specific Rules Situation as at 1st July 2013, Luxembourg, Publications Office of the European Union, 2013 (accessible at http://ec.europa.eu/competition/antitrust/legislation/handbook_vol_3_en.pdf).

F. METHODOLOGY

If one accepts the premise that legal research involves the finding, interpretation, application, and/or critique of law and legal rules 'in context' (i.e. the law is not and cannot be applied with perfect neutrality),[55] then legal dogmatics alone as a methodology cannot answer questions of what law and policy should be. It needs to be supported by, for example, the social sciences, to provide a more holistic perspective on the way the law operates in a defined context. Legal studies are increasingly becoming less doctrinal and more interdisciplinary.[56] Whether the incorporation of insights from various disciplines in the study of law is considered part of the 'normal science' in doctrinal law or whether it constitutes a 'new' interdisciplinary or multidisciplinary approach to legal research is debatable. As a result, the methodological approach will not be limited to the traditional analysis of legal issues alone.[57]

---

[55]   Emmerson H. Tiller and Frank B. Cross, *What is Legal Doctrine?* NORTHWESTERN UNIVERSITY LAW REVIEW, 100(1), 517–534 (2006) at 522.

[56]   See for example, Jan M. Smits, *Law and Interdisciplinarity: On the Inevitable Normativity of Legal Studies.* CRITICAL ANALYSIS OF LAW, 1, 1 (2014); Richard A. Posner, *The Decline of Law as an Autonomous Discipline: 1962–1987.* HARVARD LAW REVIEW, 100, 761 (1987); Brian Z. Tamanaha, *Law as a Means to an End: Threat to the Rule of Law* (Cambridge University Press 2006) at 151; Jack M. Balkin, *Interdisciplinarity as Colonization.* WASHINGTON & LEE LAW REVIEW, 53, 949–970 (1996), which stated: 'interdisciplinary scholarship is now an expected part of a serious scholar's work at most of the elite law schools. ... Because these schools generally are looked up to as leaders of academic fashion and because they produce most of the new law professors, one would think that the future of interdisciplinary scholarship looks exceedingly bright'. However, the interdisciplinary approach to the study of law has also been widely criticized. See for example Jan A. Smits, *The Mind and Method of the Legal Academic* (Edward Elgar Publishing 2012); and Irma J. Kroeze, *Legal Research Methodology and the Dream of Interdisciplinarity.* POTCHEFSTROOME ELEKTRONIESE LAW JOURNAL, 16(3), 35–65 (2013); Shai Lavi, *Turning the Tables on 'Law and ...': A Jurisprudential Inquiry into Contemporary Legal Theory.* CORNELL LAW REVIEW, 96, 811 (2010).

[57]   As stated by Smits, *supra* note 56, traditional jurisprudence takes the investigation of the normative meaning as its main focus. It achieves its goal through the interpretation of legal texts. Because the law is increasingly being studied by economists, philosophers, psychologists, and representatives from

i. Socio-legal Approach

The overall analysis of this book will be carried out through a socio-legal perspective to study how the law interfaces with society within a defined context in which the law operates.[58] In the context of drug discovery and development, the socio-legal approach helps assess and understand the relationship and dynamic interaction between public interests of society (driven by health and welfare), private interests of industry (driven by commercial interests), and the resulting impact law has on society as well as the influence society has on shaping the law. Legitimacy of the law depends both on the consistency and coherence of legal concepts and on its responsiveness to the social context in which the law operates. There is an opportunity in this book to look at the issues from the perspective of a legal practitioner as well as a researcher and combine both empirical and theoretical viewpoints that reflect the way the law interacts with the social environment.[59] This allows the legal system to be understood from the perspective of wider political, economic, and social structures within which the law forms and operates so the system itself and its purpose may be challenged from an exogenous standpoint.[60] Compared to employing mainstream traditional doctrinal methods to the study of law,[61] a socio-legal perspective allows research in law to be conducted

---

other disciplines, the social sciences emphasize positive or empirical characteristics of legal phenomena. What it focuses on is not the normative meaning of legal texts but the reality of law to help clarify different positions on what the law ought to be.

[58] See for example Sally Wheeler and Phil A. Thomas, 'Socio-Legal Studies' in David J. Hayton (ed.), *Law's Future(s)* (Hart Publishing 2002) at 271. See also Philip A. Thomas, 'Socio-Legal Studies: The Case of Disappearing Fleas and Bustards' in Philip A. Thomas (ed.), *Socio-Legal Studies* (Dartmouth Publishing Company 1997). Because drug discovery and development has social welfare, economic, and political implications for society as a whole, all of which have the potential to shape the development of law and legal process, the subject matter lends itself to such an approach. See for example Alain Pottage, *The Socio-legal Implications of the New Biotechnologies.* ANNUAL REVIEW OF LAW AND SOCIAL SCIENCE, 3, 321–344 (2007).

[59] Reza Banakar, *Reflections on the Methodological Issues of the Sociology of Law.* JOURNAL OF LAW AND SOCIETY, 27, 273–295 at 273 (2000).

[60] Reza Banakar and Max Travers, 'Introduction in Theory and Method in Socio-Legal Research' in Reza Banakar and Max Travers (eds), *Theory and Method in Socio-legal Research* (Hart Publishing 2005).

[61] Terry Hutchison and Nigel Duncan, *Defining and Describing What We Do: Doctrinal Legal Research.* DEAKEN LAW REVIEW, 17(1), 83–119 (2012) at 102.

from a humanistic and social scientific standpoint as a means to understand the law as a reflexive social institution as opposed to merely being a system of inflexible rules and doctrines.[62] Such a perspective supplements conventional legal doctrines and sources such as case law and legal rules and regulations with an anthropological element, which helps situate and frame the law for a more nuanced analysis that reflects changing societal needs and norms.[63]

ii. Proactive Law

Rather than conducting a legal analysis of competition issues alone, this book will proactively explore how the legal environment that impacts the pharmaceutical sector relates to the integrated drug discovery and development model in a broader socio-economic framework. Instead of perceiving law as being a constraint that needs to be reactively complied with, a proactive approach to considering and anticipating what legal issues may arise ex-ante will have a greater likelihood of facilitating a more efficient and effective drug discovery and development model. As an analogy, the law as we currently know it is reactive, like taking insulin therapy for diabetes. Preventive law is like taking prophylactics to delay the progression of diabetes, and proactive law is like adopting lifestyle changes to reduce the chances of the onset of diabetes. The proactive approach can be applied to drug discovery and development as a way to align and articulate various stakeholders' interests with legal policy objectives as a way to de-risk the process. Competition law analysis needs to be transparent and predictable so that market participants can organize their business efficiently and have the confidence to cooperate and invest, especially when the burden is on the market actors to assess the legality of their practices.

iii. Legal Dogmatics

Legal dogmatics has been defined as 'the science of investigating the objective meaning on positive legal order' and 'a system of statements

---

[62]   Banakar and Travers, *supra*, note 60.

[63]   Anne Griffiths, 'Using Ethnography as a Tool in Legal Research: An Anthropological Perspective' in Reza Banakar and Max Travers (eds), *Theory and Method in Socio-Legal Research* (Hart Publishing 2006) 113–131.

about the valid law'.[64] It is typically used to interpret, clarify and evaluate, reformulate, or predict the development of valid legal norms.[65] Legal interpretation requires rationality and acceptability, which can be achieved by analyzing and interpreting statutes, rulings of courts and authorities, policy statements and relevant sector inquiries and reports. In the area of intellectual property right related competition law, anti-competitive conduct is usually analyzed on a case-by-case basis in judgments and decisions of the court and competition authorities. How-ever, decisions relating to the pharmaceutical industry relevant to this particular inquiry are few and far between. The application of com-petition law to collaboration agreements and associated licensing arrangements is an area of law that has only been addressed for a relatively short period of time by secondary legislation through Commis-sion Regulations.[66] Consequently, case law is practically non-existent and older cases apply an out-of-date style of economic analysis,[67] especially in light of the recent reforms to competition law that adopt a more economic style of analysis.[68] Turning to decisions, guidelines, and

---

[64] Enrico Pattaro. *A Treatise of Legal Philosophy and General Jurisprudence: Volume 4: Scienta Juris, Legal Doctrine as Knowledge of Law and as a Source of Law* (Springer Science & Business Media 2007)

[65] Aulis Aarnio, *Reason and Authority – A Treaty on the Dynamic Paradigm of Legal Dogmatics* (Cambridge University Press 1997).

[66] Commission Regulation (EEC) No 2349/84 of 23 July 1984 on the application of Article 85(3) of the Treaty to certain categories of patent licensing (Patent Licensing Block Exemption) [1994] OJ L 219/15; Commission Regu-lation (EC) No 240/96 of 31 January 1996 on the application of Article 85(3) of the Treaty to certain categories of technology transfer agreements (Regulation 240/96) [1996] OJ L31/21; Commission Regulation (EC) 772/2004 of 27 April 2004 on the application of Article 81(3) of the Treaty to categories of technology transfer agreements (TTBER) [2004] OJ L 123/11; Commission Regulation (EC) No 2659/2000 of 29 November 2000 on the application of Article 81(3) of the Treaty to categories of research and development agreements; Commission Regulation (EC) No 1217/2010 of 14 December 2010 on the application of Article 101(3) of the Treaty on the Functioning of the European Union to certain categories of research and development agreements.

[67] What was considered a restriction of competition thirty years ago may not be regarded as restriction of competition today. For example, Case 320/87, *Kai Ottung v Klee & Weilbach A/S and Thomas Schmidt A/S* [1989] ECR 1177 and Case 65/86 *Bayer AG and Maschinenfabrik Hennecke GmbH v Heinz Süllhöfer* [1988] ECR 5249, which found that royalty payments put licensees at a competitive disadvantage and thus may restrict competition.

[68] Commission Regulation No 316/2014 on the application of Article 101(3) of the Treaty on the Functioning of the European Union to categories of

statements made by the Commission, the authoritative value and the legal effects of such soft law instruments may be questioned as they by nature cannot be legally binding. Commission decisions essentially restate interpretations from case law but also include the Commission's own interpretation of the law as well as the facts in particular sectors and/or under certain circumstances. As such, their validity and binding effect on the courts is questionable. Although soft law does not have the character of a binding rule of law, it nevertheless creates a legitimate expectation of a rule of conduct or practice that should be followed unless justifiable reasons are given since otherwise the principles of equality of treatment would be infringed.[69]

iv. Law and Economics

Because competition law and intellectual property law regulate economic activities and incentives to innovate, the integrated drug discovery model clearly lends itself to economic analysis.[70] With economic efficiency as one of its core objectives, competition law clearly recognizes the values underlying economic concepts and can benefit from the reasoning and insights of economic theory.[71] An economic perspective will give insight into market-based issues to explain the intersection between competition law, intellectual property law, and commercialization in the context of the

---

technology transfer agreements, OJ 2014 L93/17 ('TTBER') came into force on March 21, 2014 and Commission Regulation No 1217/2010 on the application of Article 101(3) of the Treaty on the Functioning of the European Union to categories of research and development agreements, OJ 2010 L335/36 (the 'R&D Regulation') came into force December 14, 2010.

[69]   Case 148/73 *Raymond et Marie-Thérèse Louwage v Commission of the European Communities* [1974] ECR 81, para 12.

[70]   Competition law deals with markets, implying a natural link to economic theory. See Giorgio Monti, *EC Competition Policy* (Cambridge University Press 2007); Alina Kaczorowska, *European Union Law* (Routledge 2011).

[71]   Courts and the Commission decisions frequently use reasoning based on economic theory in conjunction with legal doctrine when applying and interpreting competition law. See for example Case 27/76 *United Brands Company and United Brands Continental BV v Commission of the European Communities* [1978] ECR 207, para 122, where the Court used economic theories to make a connection between entry barriers and sunk costs. See also joined Cases C-89/85, C-104/85, C-114/85, C-116/85, C-117/85 and C-125/85 to C-129/85, *A. Ahlström Osakeyhtiö and others v Commission of the European Communities* (*Woodpulp*), ECR [1993] I-1307, where the ECJ relied on economic analysis of the market to evaluate the Commission's assessment of an alleged concerted practice.

pharmaceutical industry. Law and economics identifies economic efficiency as its policy goal and may be seen as an expression of legal pragmatism because it challenges the claim that the law is closed to social and economic pressures.[72] Normative law and economics suggest that legal rules that generate the most social welfare are the only types of rules that should be accepted because they represent the collective interests of society as a whole.[73] However, not everyone accepts the premise that the main objective of society is to achieve more social welfare by satisfying the aggregate of individual preferences.[74] In the present context, understanding the economic rationale and effects of different licensing practices is crucial to understanding their effect on both innovation and competition. As such, economic analysis can complement traditional legal analysis of competition law.[75]

v. Empirical Research

Empirical research enables knowledge to be gained by direct interaction through systematic collection and analysis of information. Semi-structured interviews of four integrated drug discovery organizations were conducted, and collaboration agreements entered between each of the integrated drug discovery organizations and an industry partner were collected. Among other things, the agreements illustrate how collaboration with industry is structured, how intellectual property rights that arise from the collaboration are managed and commercialized, and what factors affect the selection of projects. The contractual terms of the collaboration agreements were analyzed with respect to the competition law framework. These results will be reviewed and analyzed in Chapter 6

---

[72] Richard A. Posner, *Overcoming Law* (Harvard University Press 1995).

[73] Louis Kaplow and Steven Shavell, *Fairness Versus Welfare* (Harvard University Press 2009).

[74] See Joseph W. Singer, *Normative Methods for Lawyers*. UCLA LAW REVIEW, 56, 899–904 (2008); Jan M. Smits, *The Mind and Method of the Legal Academic* (Edward Elgar Publishing 2011).

[75] Relying on economic theory alone may be problematic as economic considerations fail to consider other values and goals inherent in competition law such as market integration or the protection of SMEs. See Valentine Korah, *An Introductory Guide to EC Competition Law and Practice* (9th edn, Hart Publishing 2007). Economic analysis of the law also has its critics. Law and economics is premised on rationality and pragmatism and should that assumption fail because firms may behave differently than individuals, the predictive value of economic analysis also fails. See Richard A. Posner, *The Economic Approach to Law*. TEXAS LAW REVIEW, 53, 757 (1975).

in furtherance of the analysis on the applicability of the Regulation No 1217/2010 on the application of Article 101(3) to research and development agreements (the 'R&D Regulation')[76] and Commission Regulation No 316/2014 on the application of Article 101(3) to technology transfer agreements (the 'TTBER'),[77] and Article 101(3) exemptions to the collaboration agreement.

G. THE ROAD MAP

Having introduced the problem with respect to the current drug discovery and development process in this chapter, Chapter 2 will provide some background information on how the pharmaceutical industry functions and explain how and why traditional drug development may no longer be an efficient model. In that context, the integrated drug development model will be introduced as an alternative that fosters university–industry collaboration to de-risk the drug discovery and development process while facilitating innovation through achieving proof of concept. For the sake of comparison, Chapter 2 will briefly consider other approaches to the open innovation model and their possible role in the drug development process. Chapter 2 concludes with a summary analysis of the three drug development models (traditional technology transfer, integrated drug development, and open science) and proposes that the integrated drug development model (as a version of the triple helix model of innovation)[78] merits further investigation into whether international collaborative R&D between industry and public research organizations is supported by existing legal and regulatory frameworks.

Chapter 3 introduces the intersection between competition policy and intellectual property rights in the context of collaborative research in the pharmaceutical sector and as it relates to the drug discovery and development process. It further explores the applicability of Article 101 to the collaboration agreement that governs the relationship between industry and integrated drug discovery organizations. The main focus of this chapter is to analyze and determine whether the collaboration agreements between industry and integrated drug discovery organizations fall within the purview of Article 101. The chapter concludes with a

---

[76] R&D Regulation, *supra* note 68.
[77] TTBER, *supra* note 68.
[78] See for example Henry Etzkowitz and Loet Leydesdorff, *The Dynamics of Innovation: From National Systems and 'Mode 2' to a Triple Helix of University-Industry-Government Relations*. RESEARCH POLICY, 29(2), 109–123 (2000).

discussion of the effects of applying Article 101 to collaborative drug discovery and development and argues for sector-specific considerations, given the unique dynamics of the pharmaceutical sector.

Chapter 4 introduces the R&D Regulation and considers whether the R&D component of the collaboration agreement between integrated drug discovery organization and industry falls within the purview of the R&D Regulation. It focuses on the concept of R&D poles and how they may restrict collaborative innovation in the drug discovery and development context. The chapter concludes with an argument for the need to support collaborative R&D in drug discovery and development, despite potential restrictions on the innovation market.

Chapter 5 introduces the TTBER and considers whether the licensing aspects of the collaboration agreement between integrated drug discovery organization and industry falls within the purview of TTBER. The chapter analyzes various contractual restrictions typically found in technology transfer agreements and how such restrictions are viewed from the perspective of competition policy.

Chapter 6 analyzes the contractual terms of the collaboration agreements collected from each of the four integrated drug discovery organizations with reference to the R&D Regulation and TTBER. Analysis of Article 101(3) exemptions will also be discussed with respect to whether they apply to the collaborative agreements should the agreements not qualify for exemption under the block exemptions.

Chapter 7 summarizes the legal implications of the integrated drug discovery model and discusses various concluding remarks, observations, and comments relating to integrated drug discovery in the larger innovation framework.

2. The pharmaceutical industry and drug discovery and development models

A. IN CONTEXT: THE PHARMACEUTICAL INDUSTRY – FACTS AND FIGURES

The pharmaceutical industry is considered to be among the largest and most profitable businesses worldwide, with global sales reaching US$1 trillion in 2014 (forecasted to grow to US$1.3 trillion by 2018)[1] and 17 pharmaceutical companies on the Fortune 500 list in 2015.[2] The industry has been characterized as having a need for ongoing innovation and high intensity of R&D,[3] and intellectual property rights associated with pharmaceutical products are considered critical assets to protect innovation.[4] Recent surveys in the pharmaceutical sector indicate that an overwhelming majority of the respondents characterized patents as

---

[1] See the 2015 *CMR International Pharmaceutical R&D Factbook.*
[2] See http://fortune.com/fortune500/2015/
[3] Eurostat considers the pharmaceutical industry to be a high technology industry, which is defined on the basis of the R&D expenditures in relation to economic activities (see http://ec.europa.eu/eurostat/statistics-explained/index.php/High-tech_statistics_-_economic_data); see also International Federation of Pharmaceutical Manufacturers & Associations, *The Pharmaceutical Industry and Global Health Facts and Figures 2014.*
[4] European Commission Pharmaceutical Sector Inquiry, Final Report, July 8, 2009, at page 11 states that 'Intellectual property rights are a key element in the promotion of innovation ... it is particularly important for the pharmaceutical sector because of the necessity to address current and emerging health problems and the long life cycle of products (including long development periods). The pharmaceutical sector in the EU indeed has one of the highest investments in R&D in Europe and relies significantly on intellectual property rights to protect innovation'.

'extremely important' in 'creating a competitive advantage'.[5] Although there are many pharmaceutical companies throughout the world, the industry has been considered to be highly concentrated, with approximately 20 major pharmaceutical companies dominating the industry and accounting for nearly 66% of the pharmaceutical market worldwide.[6] However, in recent years, the industry has observed a stagnation in the number of new medicines being granted approval, which may be evidence of a decline in the productivity of pharmaceutical innovation despite significant spending on associated R&D.[7] Some have attributed this decline or plateauing as in part resulting from the high costs and high risks associated with the drug discovery and development process. As discussed in Chapter 1, the average cost of developing a new drug and bringing it to market has been estimated at over US$2.6 billion over a 10–12 year time period.[8] The high cost reflects the various challenges associated with R&D, such as sunk costs into failed projects that do not translate into commercializable medicines and challenges related to strict

---

[5]   Iain Cockburn and Genia Long, *The Importance of Patents to Innovation: Updated Cross-industry Comparisons with Biopharmaceuticals*. EXPERT OPINION ON THERAPEUTIC PATENTS, 25(7), 739–742 (2015).

[6]   EvaulatePharma, *World Preview 2015, Outlook to 2020* reported that leading pharmaceutical companies accounted for more than 53% of US pharmaceutical products. See US Bureau of the Census, *Concentration Ratios in Manufacturing Industries* (Washington). See also Anand Grover, Brian Citro, Mihir Mankad, and Fiona Lander, *Pharmaceutical Companies and Global Lack of Access to Medicines: Strengthening Accountability under the Right to Health*. THE JOURNAL OF LAW, MEDICINE & ETHICS, 40(2), 234–250 (2012) at 238.

[7]   Naci, Huseyin, Alexander W. Carter and Elias Mossialos, *Why the Drug Development Pipeline is not Delivering Better Medicines*. BRITISH MEDICAL JOURNAL h5542 (2015); Frederic M. Scherer 'Pharmaceutical Innovation' in Bronwyn H. Hall and Nathan Rosenberg (eds), *Handbook of the Economics of Technological Innovation Volume 1* (Elsevier 2010) 539–574 at 542–543. See also Ian M. Cockburn, *The Changing Structure of the Pharmaceutical Industry*. HEALTH AFFAIRS, 23(1), 10–22 (2004) at 11; Bethan Hughes, *FDA Drug Approvals: A Year of Flux*. NATURE REVIEWS DRUG DISCOVERY, 7(2), 107–109 (2009). See also Brian P. Zambrowicz and Arthur T. Sands, *Knockouts Model the 100 Best-Selling Drugs – Will They Model the Next 100?* NATURE REVIEWS DRUG DISCOVERY, 2(1), 38–51 (2003), which reported that, on average, only three drugs that act on novel targets have reached the market annually in recent years.

[8]   Asher Mullard, *New Drugs Cost US$2.6 Billion to Develop*. NATURE REVIEWS DRUG DISCOVERY, 13, 877 (2014). See also Valerie G. Koch, *Incentivizing the Utilization of Pharmacogenetics in Drug Development*. JOURNAL OF HEALTH LAW & POLICY, 15, 263 (2012) at 274.

regulatory requirements associated with obtaining market approval.[9] Available statistics indicate that only one in ten thousand chemical compounds prove to be medically effective and go on to be developed into a product; and after development, over half of those products entering phase I of clinical trials fail to advance to approval, rendering the clinical approval success rate to be approximately 10% to 12%.[10] According to another report, on average, only three drugs acting on novel targets enter the market annually.[11] R&D accounts for a significant portion of development costs, with an average of 17% and up to 40% of global sales being reinvested into further R&D.[12] Compared to other high technology industries, the annual R&D spending by the pharmaceutical industry far exceeds that of the aerospace and defense industry, the chemical industry, and the software and computer industry.[13] The high cost of R&D combined with the low number of new product approvals raises significant concerns regarding the sustainability and future health of the industry.

---

[9]   Kenneth I. Kaitin, *Deconstructing the Drug Development Process: The New Face of Innovation*. CLINICAL PHARMACOLOGY AND THERAPEU-TICS, 87(3), 356–361 (2010).

[10]   Pharmaceutical Research and Manufacturers of America, *2015 Bio-pharmaceutical Research Industry Profile*, Washington, DC: PhRMA (2015); Joseph A. DiMasi, L. Feldman, A. Seckler, and A. Wilson, *Trends in Risks Associated with New Drug Development: Success Rates for Investigational Drugs*. CLINICAL PHARMACOLOGY AND THERAPEUTICS, 87(3), 272–277 (2010); Jill A. Fisher, Marci D. Cottingham and Corey A. Kalbaugh. *Peering into the Pharmaceutical 'Pipeline': Investigational Drugs, Clinical Trials, and Industry Priorities*. SOCIAL SCIENCE & MEDICINE, 131, 322–330 (2015) and Michael Hay, David W. Thomas, John L. Craighead, Celia Economides, and Jesse Rosenthal, *Clinical Development Success Rates for Investigational Drugs*. NATURE BIOTECHNOLOGY, 32(1), 40–51 (2014).

[11]   Arti K. Rai, Jerome H. Reichman, Paul F. Uhlir, and Colin R. Crossman, *Pathways Across the Valley of Death: Novel Intellectual Property Strategies for Accelerated Drug Discovery*. YALE JOURNAL OF HEALTH POLICY, LAW AND ETHICS, 8(1), 53–89 (2008).

[12]   *2013 Biopharmaceutical Research Industry Profile*. Washington, DC: PhRMA (2013). See also Peter Eichhorn, 'General introduction on pharmaceuti-cals' in Mira Petrovic, Sandra Perez and Damia Barcelo (eds), *Analysis, Removal, Effects and Risk of Pharmaceuticals in the Water Cycle: Occurrence and Transformation in the Environment, Volume 62* (Elsevier 2013), 1–36 at 4.

[13]   Joint Research Centre, *The 2011 EU Industrial R&D Investment Score-board* (Brussels: European Commission 2011), at 32.

B. THE DRUG DISCOVERY AND DEVELOPMENT PROCESS: A BRIEF OVERVIEW

A simple overview of the drug development process will illustrate why drug discovery and development requires such significant investments. Before a new drug is developed, scientists usually start the discovery process by researching the basic mechanisms and pathways of a specific disease. For example, they may study which genes are involved in a disease of interest and look at how certain proteins contribute to the onset, progression, or maintenance of the disease in order to identify potential targets that may interact with a drug.[14] Once identified, targets are validated to demonstrate they are relevant to the disease in question before further effort is spent on determining if a drug could affect the target enough to alter the course of the disease. After a target is validated, compounds are screened to ascertain and quantify the interaction between the target and each of the compounds. From the screened compounds, lead compounds that show potential are selected to go through initial screening to determine, among other factors, toxicity, pharmacodynamics, and pharmacokinetics. Those involved in the drug development process now want researchers to provide early indications of feasibility that the lead compounds will survive initial screening before resources are invested into optimizing the lead compounds. Optimized compounds are then put through pre-clinical testing, a process that usually takes 2–3 years and is governed by Directive 27/2004/EC in Europe. Drug candidates that survive pre-clinical trials then need to be qualified for clinical trials in humans, a process which is also regulated by the aforementioned Directive and usually takes another 3–4 years. If the candidate demonstrates positive results after

---

[14] Pharmaceutical products typically work by affecting the activity of proteins, known as targets, that have been implicated in a particular disease pathway. See Michelle R. Arkin and James A. Wells, *Small-Molecule Inhibitors of Protein-Protein Interactions: Progressing Towards the Dream.* NATURE REVIEWS DRUG DISCOVERY, 3(4), 301–317 (2004). To date, only a few hundred proteins have been identified that yield therapeutically and biologically useful results, while there are an estimated 3,000 protein targets in the human genome that may potentially be susceptible to a drug. See Adrian Whitty and Gnanasambandam Kumaravel, *Between a Rock and a Hard Place?* NATURE CHEMICAL BIOLOGY, 2(3), 112–118 (2006) and Andreas P. Russ and Stefan Lampel, *The Druggable Genome: An Update.* DRUG DISCOVERY TODAY, 10(23), 1607–1610 (2005).

Phase III of clinical trials, the company applies for marketing author-
ization through the FDA in the United States and the EMA in Europe, a
process that can take up to several years. According to one study, the
breakdown of R&D expenditure into the various stages of the discovery
and development process is as follows: 27.3% devoted to pre-clinical
trials; 7.4% to Phase 1; 13.1% to Phase II; 28.5% to Phase III; 5.1% to
the approval procedure; 13.4% to Phase IV; and 5.2% to administrative
support.[15] By the time a drug is approved for the market, more than half
of the exclusivity period guaranteed under the patent system has
elapsed.

Up until the product enters the market, the company receives no
revenue because the product has not been approved for commercialization and therefore cannot generate any sales to earn any return on the
investment injected into R&D for the past 10–12 years. Long development times coupled with low success rates and lack of revenue translates
into high overall R&D costs. With significant sunk costs, no revenue, and
over half the patent term lapsed while the drug candidate goes through
the various stages of clinical trials, companies rely on various strategies
to recoup their investment and earn a profit to fund further R&D.
Although there are supplementary protection certificates to extend the
patent term, this is increasingly being challenged by generics.[16] In light
of all the challenges associated with developing a new drug, and given
that, on average, only three in ten new products generate revenues equal
to or greater than average industry R&D costs,[17] the risks industry
undertakes in drug discovery and development become more understandable. Industry argues that the promise of potentially significant profits
derived from patent rights balances against the risks of drug discovery

---

[15]   See Joseph A. DiMasi, Ronald W. Hansen, and Henry G. Grabowski, *The
Price of Innovation: New Estimates of Drug Development Costs*. JOURNAL OF
HEALTH ECONOMICS, 22(2), 151–185 (2003); Joseph A. DiMasi and Henry
G. Grabowski, *The Cost of Biopharmaceutical R&D: is Biotech Different?*
MANAGEMENT AND DECISION ECONOMICS, 28, 469–479 (2007); *2011
Pharmaceutical Industry Profile* (Washington, DC, PhRMA 2011).
[16]   For example, see *Generics Ltd v Novartis AG (UK) Ltd (T/A Myylan)*
[2012] EWCA Civ 1623 (12 December 2012) where the Court of Appeal upheld
the judgment of the High Court to revoke Novartis' supplementary protection
certification (SPC) and underlying basic patent for the drug Rivastigmine; see
also *Generics (UK) Ltd v Synaptech Inc.* Case C-427/09 (CJEU, 28 July 2011)
where the ECJ ruled that the drug Galatamine was not eligible for SPC.
[17]   Henry G. Grabowski, John M. Vernon, and Joseph A. DiMasi, *Returns on
Research and Development for 1990s New Drug Introductions*. PHARMACO-
ECONOMICS, 20(3), 11–29 (2002).

and development. Intellectual property rights are considered critical assets in the industry to protect investments in innovation and to maximize the income that can be earned from the small number of products that actually reach the market.[18] Furthermore, royalties payable to collaborative research partners such as integrated drug discovery organizations and public research organizations to fund basic research and further R&D are also dependent on profits derived from patent rights.[19]

'Blockbuster' successes, defined as products that generate annual global revenues in excess of US$1 billion, can more than repay the development costs.[20] Sales of some pharmaceutical products have far exceeded the 'blockbuster' threshold, for example, worldwide sales of Pfizer's Lipitor in 2011 before it came off patent was US$9.6 billion,[21] earning a total of US$131 billion in sales over the life of the patent.[22] AbbVie's Humira, which will come off patent in 2016, generated worldwide sales in excess of US$14 billion in 2015.[23] Despite the success stories, industry is currently undergoing a period of significant challenge because many high-revenue-generating blockbuster drugs have recently come off patent.[24] Known as the 'patent cliff', patents on drugs worth approximately US$50 billion in annual sales expired in 2012,[25] and once drugs lose patent protection, they can lose up to 90% of their

---

[18]   Henry G. Grabowski, Joseph A. DiMasi, and Genia Long, *The Roles of Patents and Research and Development Incentives in Biopharmaceutical Innovation*, HEALTH AFFAIRS, 34(2) 302–310 (2015).

[19]   Valentina Tartari and Stefano Breschi, *Set Them Free: Scientists' Evaluations of the Benefits and Costs of University-Industry Research Collaboration.* INDUSTRIAL AND CORPORATE CHANGE, 21(5) 1117–1147 (2012).

[20]   European Commission, *Pharmaceutical Sector Inquiry, Preliminary Report (DG Competition Staff Working Paper)*, 28 November 2008 at 17.

[21]   Pfizer 2011 Financial Report, at: http://www.pfizer.com/files/annualreport/2011/financial/financial2011.pdf

[22]   News Brief in NATURE REVIEWS DRUG DISCOVERY, 10, 889 (December 2011).

[23]   Abbvie *2015 Annual Report* (accessible at http://www.abbvieinvestor.com/phoenix.zhtml?c=251551&p=irol-reportsannual).

[24]   Charlotte Harrison, *The Patent Cliff Steepens.* NATURE REVIEWS DRUG DISCOVERY, 10(1), 12–13 (2011); Eric J. Topol and Nicholas J. Schork, *Catapulting Clopidogrel Pharmacogenomics Forward.* NATURE MEDICINE, 17(1), 40–41 (2011); Jack DeRuiter and Pamela L. Holston, *Drug Patent Expirations and the 'Patent Cliff'.* US PHARMACIST, 37(6) (Generic Suppl.), 12–20 (2012).

[25]   Eileen McDermott, *How to Survive the Patent Cliff.* MANAGING INTELLECTUAL PROPERTY, 216, 22 (2012).

annual sales to generics.[26] Forecasts predict that US$230 billion in sales
are at risk from patent expirations between 2013 and 2018.[27] In 2012, it
was reported that major US pharmaceutical companies lost about US$21
billion in revenue from medicines that came off patent while European
pharmaceutical companies suffered a US$10 billion loss of revenue from
medicines that came off patent in 2011.[28] The current drug discovery
pipeline is not close to replacing these values[29] and represents a real
threat to the industry's ability to sustain and grow.[30]

Without a doubt, the greatest challenge in the drug discovery and
development process is the gap between bringing potential drug candidates
out from the discovery phase and into development.[31] A collaborative
relationship between academia and industry appears to be an obvious
solution by bringing together the respective core competencies of each
party: academia is a rich source of basic research and discovery, which is
the foundation of innovation and new discoveries, and industry specializes
in clinical translational activities and procedures required to convert
early-stage research into new therapies.[32] Combined with the recent trend

[26]   DeRuiter and Holston, *supra* note 24 (2012). See also Stephen S. Hall,
Prescription for Profit. New York Times Magazine, 40–45 (March 2001)
regarding the case of Claritin, which costs $85 per month to consumers, giving
the pharmaceutical company annual sales of $2 billion during the life of the
patent. When Claritin's patent expired, the cost of generic Claritin dropped to
$10 per month.
[27]   Executive Summary of EvaluatePharma *World Preview 2013, Outlook to
2018: Returning to Growth*, which is based on data from 4,000 pharmaceutical
and biotech companies.
[28]   Standard and Poor's Rating Services, *Global Pharmaceutical Companies:
Strongest to Weakest*, Ratings Direct, December 18, 2012.
[29]   Benjamin Jardines, *Big Pharma's 2009–2013 Patent Cliff: A Comparison
of Company-level Responses and Strategic Recommendations for Pfizer, Inc. and
Eli Lilly and Company*, WRLGC (2011).
[30]   Nicoleta Tuominen, *Patenting Strategies of the EU Pharmaceutical Industry: Regular Business Practice or Abuse of Dominance.* WORLD COM-
PETITION, 35(1), 27–54 (2012).
[31]   John Hudson and Hanan F. Khazragui, *Into the Valley of Death: Research
to Innovation.* DRUG DISCOVERY TODAY, 18(13), 610–613 (2013); House of
Commons Science and Technology Committee (March 2013) *Bridging the Valley
of Death: Improving the Commercialization of Research, Eighth Report of
Session 2012–13*; Rai et al., supra note 11; Kenneth I. Kaitin, *Translational
Research and the Evolving Landscape for Biomedical Innovation.* JOURNAL OF
INVESTIGATIVE MEDICINE, 60(7), 995–998 (2012).
[32]   See Peter Lee, *Transcending the Tacit Dimension: Patents, Relationships,
and Organizational Integration in Technology Transfer.* CALIFORNIA LAW

in academia towards promoting applied research,[33] collaborative R&D between academia and industry should have the effect of facilitating the difficult transition from basic research to commercialization.

C. TRADITIONAL UNIVERSITY TECHNOLOGY TRANSFER

There is no denying the innovative capacity of university research, which continues to provide a valuable pipeline of inventions, discoveries, and breakthrough technologies. University research is largely funded by the public,[34] and should therefore be translated and returned to the benefit of society in the form of new products and services, which in turn stimulates and maintains economic growth. Over the last few decades, the position in the market of universities and public research organizations has evolved considerably.[35] Gradually, they have become more actively involved in the process of transferring technology to industry, presumably because disseminating basic research in the public domain is not the most effective way to generate and return the full benefits of innovation to the public.[36] The overall evolution of the economy towards

---

REVIEW, 100, 1503 (2012) at 1534, which stated that 'in the pharmaceutical industry, firm connectedness to the academic community, such as through collaboration and co-authoring scientific articles, is a key determinant of successful drug discovery'. See also Kenneth I. Kaitin, *21st Century Bioinnovation: Academic-Industry Partnerships are Increasingly Important in Biopharmaceutical Innovation*. PHARMACEUTICAL TECHNOLOGY, 35(6), 32 (2011); Fabio Pammolli, Laura Magazzini, and Massimo Riccaboni, *The Productivity Crisis in Pharmaceutical R&D*. NATURE REVIEWS DRUG DISCOVERY, 10(6), 428–438 (2011); Kaitin, supra note 9.

[33]   Christopher P. Milne and Kenneth I. Kaitin, *Translational Medicine: An Engine of Change for Bringing New Technology to Community Health*. SCIENCE TRANSLATIONAL MEDICINE, 1(5), 1–4 (2009).

[34]   According to the European University Association, 73% of university funding comes from public sources (as reported at the EUA 2012 Annual Conference on 'The Sustainability of European Universities', http://www.eua.be/Libraries/eua-annual-conf-2012-warwick/FINAL_Thomas_Estermann.pdf?sfvrsn=0).

[35]   Bart van Looy, Paolo Landoni, Julie Callaert, Bruno van Pottelsberghe, Eleftherios Sapsalis and Koenraad Debackere, *Entrepreneurial Effectiveness of European Universities: An Empirical Assessment of Antecedents and Trade-offs*. RESEARCH POLICY, 40(4), 553–564 (2011).

[36]   Mike Wright, Bart Clarysse, Philippe Mustar and Andy Lockett, *Academic Entrepreneurship in Europe* (Edward Elgar 2007).

a knowledge economy has created an important incentive for constant innovation and exploitation of such new technologies, which very naturally brings together academia on the one hand and industry on the other.[37] Policy changes, such as Responsible Research and Innovation, encourage collaboration between stakeholders such as universities and industry to maximize the impact of basic research through open innovation and commercialization.[38] Industry benefits from having access to cutting-edge research and discoveries, the public benefits from new innovations, government benefits from economic growth arising from commercial activity associated with successful commercialization, and academia benefits from receiving royalties to fund further R&D in light of budgetary cuts to public funding.[39] However, the process of successfully taking basic research and early stage discoveries through to product development is plagued with gaps and inefficiencies, especially in the pharmaceutical context.

Traditionally, the interface between academia and industry is managed by university technology transfer offices (TTOs) by way of license agreements that grant rights in new discoveries to third parties for further development.[40] The main justification for university ownership of patents is because of their ability to centralize, organize, and facilitate technology transfer in order to commercialize academic research for the benefit of the public.[41] It is the main role of TTOs to find industry partners

---

[37] Petra Andries and Koenraad Debackere, *Adaptation and Performance in New Businesses*. SMALL BUSINESS ECONOMICS, 29(1–2), 81–99 (2007).

[38] See Henry Chesbrough, *Open Innovation: Where We've Been and Where We're Going*. RESEARCH TECHNOLOGY MANAGEMENT, 55(4), 20–27 (2012); David Roessner, Jennifer Bond, Sumiye Okubo and Mark Planting, *The Economic Impact of Licensed Commercialized Inventions Originating in University Research*. RESEARCH POLICY, 42(1), 23–34 (2013).

[39] Joseph Friedman and Jonathan Silberman, *University Technology Transfer: Do Incentives, Management, and Location Matter?* THE JOURNAL OF TECHNOLOGY TRANSFER, 28(1), 17–30 (2003).

[40] Koenraad Debackere, *The TTO, A University Engine Transforming Science Into Innovation*, Advice Paper No. 10, League of European Research Universities (2012).

[41] The Association of University Technology Managers (AUTM) have continually published very positive data in support of the Bayh-Dole model of university–industry collaboration and technology transfer, such as increases in university patenting, licensing, and revenue to support the positive effects of the university technology transfer model, on the assumption that such metrics are indicative of social welfare gains. However, the source of such data is derived from surveys conducted by AUTM. There does not appear to be any objective data or empirical analysis to validate the social benefits of the technology

interested in acquiring rights to university research for the purpose of commercialization.[42] In order to 'sell' university research, TTOs need to assert intellectual property rights in university discoveries in order to have something proprietary to license to third parties. However, the reality is that the rate of commercialization of university inventions by TTOs is slow, mainly because TTOs have limited resources and skills required to assess and market inventions that come from all the different disciplines and faculties of a university.[43] TTOs are given the responsibility of deciding what research to protect by way of intellectual property rights. However, without the benefit of the necessary scientific or relevant expertise or know-how to evaluate and decide which innovations have potential and which do not, promising research potentially falls through the gap. TTOs also typically do not have pre-existing relationships or contacts with industry or potential licensees, especially in relation to highly innovative inventions with niche markets, making such inventions particularly difficult to market.[44] The financial consequences of missing out on opportunities to successfully commercialize a potential innovation can be quite significant. For example, in the United States, more than $1

---

transfer model, given that AUTM (and pharmaceutical companies) have a vested interest in espousing the virtues of the technology transfer model.

[42] *Turning Science into Business: Patenting and Licensing at Public Research Organisations* (OECD 2003).

[43] See P.M. Swamidass and V. Vulasa (2009) *Why University Inventions Rarely Produce Income? Bottlenecks in University Technology Transfer*. THE JOURNAL OF TECHNOLOGY TRANSFER, 34(4), 343–363, which reported that more than a third of 99 randomly selected US research universities claimed that in 2006, they failed to process more than 26% of inventions due to insufficient processing capacity and budget shortages. See also Robert E. Litan and Lesa Mitchell, *A Faster Path from Lab to Market*. HARVARD BUSINESS REVIEW, 88(1–2), 52 (2010), where the university technology transfer model is criticized as being monopolistic and has the effect of holding university researchers hostage and delaying the speed at which university-developed innovation can reach the marketplace due to the lack of capacity and limited capabilities of the university technology transfer office. By compelling university researchers to pursue the licensing opportunities of their inventions through the university technology transfer offices, researchers essentially need to wait for, and depend on, the technology transfer office to give them their attention, regardless of the researcher's own efficiency or contacts to potential industry partners.

[44] Paul M. Swamidass, and Vulasa Venubabu, *Why University Inventions Rarely Produce Income? Bottlenecks in University Technology Transfer*. THE JOURNAL OF TECHNOLOGY TRANSFER, 34(4), 343–363 (2009), which argued that highly innovative university inventions usually need to be translated

billion dollars in licensing income have been reported by universities in each fiscal year since 2003.[45]

With respect to drug discovery and development, the nature of pharmaceutical research is such that very few early stage discoveries actually deliver promising results. The process of defining leads and candidates as well as the target validation process are complex, lengthy, and unpredictable. Successful technology transfer presupposes the technology is developed to a point where third parties can assess its feasibility to determine whether the technology is worth the investment to license the intellectual property for commercialization or further R&D purposes. Without proof of concept, TTOs have an even more difficult time trying to interest potential investors to license basic research in the drug discovery space because of the lack of demonstrated viability. Furthermore, typical strategies used by TTOs in an effort to license out early stage discoveries may not be based on sound business practices, especially in the pharmaceutical field and could lead to undesirable results.[46] For example, a common criticism of university TTOs is the amount of time and resources spent on negotiating royalty/licensing fees for access to basic research in the absence of any measures to determine what a fair fee would be.[47] Without proof of concept, investing in lengthy and costly negotiations over early stage discoveries may not be the most productive and effective way to approach translation and commercialization, especially when there is a significant risk the discovery will not deliver promising results. Positional negotiations may even potentially deter collaboration if both sides hold fast to their respective positions.

---

scientifically and economically into 'investor friendly' business plans to identify or create new markets to avoid delay in the flow of university inventions to the public.

[45]   Ampere A. Tseng and Miroslav Raudensky, *Performances of Technology Transfer Activities of US Universities after Bayh-Dole Act.* JOURNAL OF ECONOMICS, BUSINESS & MANAGEMENT, 3(6), 661–667 (2015).

[46]   Karin Fisher, *Building a New Economy with Biotechnology.* THE CHRONICLE OF HIGHER EDUCATION (September 2007).

[47]   Anna Fazackerley, Martin Smith and Alex Massey, *Innovation and Industry: The Role of Universities.* POLICY EXCHANGE (2009), which noted that university technology transfer offices often control rather than facilitate interaction by attempting to maximize revenue through tough negotiations of licensing terms. As a result, they often develop a culture that is harmful to collaboration while trying to do exactly the opposite. See also Tatiana Schofield, *Critical Success Factors for Knowledge Transfer Collaborations between University and Industry.* JOURNAL OF RESEARCH ADMINISTRATION, 44(2), 38–56 (2013).

Therefore, traditional university TTOs may not be the most effective model to translate and commercialize early stage discoveries, especially in the drug discovery and development context. As established earlier, there is evidence suggesting that the private sector is hesitant about investing in and/or licensing early stage discoveries without proof of concept because it is too risky and the costs are far too high to take basic research from discovery to commercial application without proof of concept.[48] The traditional university technology transfer model therefore lacks the means to bridge the gap between early-stage academic discoveries and pre-clinical research to achieve proof of concept, which investors increasingly require in order to assess the risk and justify financial investment in new discoveries. Known as the 'Valley of Death', innovations that may be the next 'blockbuster success' could potentially languish and be left undeveloped at the early stages because of lack of funding and expertise to bring the discovery through to an investible point, both commercially and clinically.[49]

D. INTEGRATED DRUG DISCOVERY MODEL

The traditional technology transfer platform needs to be better positioned to manage industry access to university discoveries.[50] Referred to herein

---

[48]   See for example, John C. Reed, *NCATS Could Mitigate Pharma Valley of Death.* GENETIC ENGINEERING & BIOTECHNOLOGY, 31(10), 6–8 (2011), stating that 'private companies and venture capitalists are increasingly reluctant to fund the crucial early stages of preclinical development – the research necessary to "translate" promising discoveries made in laboratories into optimized candidate therapeutics ready for testing in clinical trials'.

[49]   Barry S. Coller and Robert M. Califf, *Traversing the Valley of Death: A Guide to Assessing Prospects for Translational Success.* SCIENCE TRANSLATIONAL MEDICINE, 1(10), 109 (2009); Michelle G. Habets, Johannes J. van Delden, and Annelien L. Bredenoord, *The Social Value of Clinical Research.* BMC MEDICAL ETHICS, 15(1), 66 (2014); Maureen Kelley, Kelly Edwards, Helene Starks, Stephanie M. Fullerton, Rosalina James, Sara Goering, Suzanne Holland, Mary L. Disis, and Wylie Burke, *Values in Translation: How Asking the Right Questions Can Move Translational Science towards Greater Health Impact.* CLINICAL AND TRANSLATIONAL SCIENCE, 5(6), 445–451 (2012).

[50]   See for example, Constance E. Bagley and Christina D. Tvarnø, *Pharmaceutical Public-Private Partnerships: Moving from the Bench to the Bedside.* HARVARD BUSINESS LAW REVIEW, 4, 373 (2014) at 373–374, which discusses the $230 million Accelerating Medicines Partnership in the United States, aimed at bringing together industry, academia, and government to collaborate on open-source projects designed to bridge the gap between research

as the 'integrated drug discovery platform' this model of technology transfer relies on a specialized group to pool resources and expertise and facilitate an effective collaboration between academia and industry to allow drug targets to be validated more quickly and developed cost effectively. The integrated drug discovery organization is comprised of a multi-disciplinary expert team of professionals with experience in both the academic environment as well as industry. By demonstrating hands-on knowledge and understanding of the core values of both communities, the integrated drug discovery organization has the credibility to effectively interact with and relate to industry and academia to facilitate the translation of basic research into 'fit for use' form by achieving proof of concept. These specialized skills enable the integrated drug discovery organization team to 'speak the language' of both parties and move between the worlds of science and industry.

Typically, the integrated drug discovery organization has autonomy to conduct its business but operates under the mandate of its affiliated academic institution. The core function of the integrated drug discovery organization is to provide comprehensive support services, allowing the researchers to concentrate on their scientific activities while leaving the intellectual property management, business development, legal issues, and administration to the integrated drug discovery organization. Importantly, the integrated drug discovery model requires direct and ongoing collaboration between academics and industry throughout the proof of concept phase, thereby dispelling criticisms of excluding the value and input of academics in the development process. Academics responsible for the original discovery of the innovation play an integral role in establishing proof of concept in collaboration with industry partners, and therefore have a vested interest in the outcome. Another key function of integrated drug discovery organization is to actively search and identify new drug discovery research being conducted at public research organizations with the most potential for public benefit and commercial interest to industry. Again, this requires close and direct contact with both academia and industry to effectively 'match-make' market-relevant research with industry development priorities in hopes of soliciting interest from both parties to collaborate. The premise of the integrated drug discovery platform is that both academic and industrial scientists

---

and new therapies. See also Cathy J. Tralau-Stewart, Colin A. Wyatt, Dominique E. Kleyn and Alex Ayad, *Drug Discovery: New Models for Industry–Academic Partnerships*. DRUG DISCOVERY TODAY, 14(1), 95–101 (2009) at 96–97 citing that the pharmaceutical industry also looks to university partners as a means to advance pharmaceutical innovation.

share at least one common interest, which is to improve public health, and it is this mutual desire that drives the collaboration and development of partnerships to bridge the translational gap. However, despite a shared public health commitment, significant 'cultural' obstacles' between academia and industry[51] can potentially stand in the way of a successful partnership. Academics speak the language of science and industry speaks the language of business. Academics are generally motivated by research and publication and industry is motivated by commercial interests. In other words, conflicting objectives may create reluctance among the parties to align too closely. Advantageously, the integrated drug discovery organization can reconcile the cultural gap between the parties and use the tension to stimulate collaborative research that reinforces the core missions of both communities while respecting the values and norms of both industry and academia. Recent research indicates that university–industry collaboration positively affects academic research performance in terms of patenting and publication activities.[52] Knowledge spillovers between academia and industry represent a core contribution to the advancement of academic science. Public–private collaboration in product development is not a new idea and appears to be an obvious model to explore in the context of drug discovery and development given that both academia and industry play a key role in the efficient translation of basic research to develop commercializable products. As an adapted version of the traditional technology transfer model, the integrated drug discovery platform exemplifies the role universities today can play in the economics of technology and innovation.[53]

---

[51]   Kaitin, *supra* note 9.

[52]   Bart van Looy, Marina Ranga, Julie Callaert, Koenraad Debackere, and Edwin Zimmermann, *Combining Entrepreneurial and Scientific Performance in Academia: Towards a Compounded and Bi-directional Matthew-Effect.* RESEARCH POLICY, 33(3), 425–441 (2004); Bart van Looy, Julie Callaert and Koenraad Debackere, *Publication and Patent Behavior of Academic Researchers: Conflicting, Reinforcing or Merely Co-existing?* RESEARCH POLICY, 35(4), 596–608 (2006).

[53]   Dominique Foray, *The New Economics of Technology Policy* (Edward Elgar 2009).

E. INTEGRATED DRUG DISCOVERY ORGANIZATIONS

Currently, there are several active integrated drug discovery organizations. These include the Centre for Drug Research and Development (CDRD) in Vancouver, British Columbia, representing the Canadian Centre of Excellence in Commercialization and Research; the Lead Discovery Centre (LDC), representing the Max Planck Institutes in Germany; the Centre for Drug Design and Discovery (CD3), representing Katholieke Universiteit Leuven in Belgium; and MRC Technology (MRCT), representing the Medical Research Council in the UK. A network of the aforementioned organizations enable sharing and open access to resources in order to further streamline the drug development process. A key problem with the traditional drug discovery process is that all the relevant parties in the process tend to work in parallel, identifying similar or identical target molecules while remaining unaware that the compounds may have already been tested and discarded by another organization. The network attempts to reduce this duplication through sharing of information.

Integrated drug discovery organizations can bridge the commercialization and translational gap between drug discovery and private investment by employing a cost-efficient collaboration and development model based on leveraging existing networks, facilities, and infrastructure to create partnerships between academia and industry. Industry participating in the collaboration can benefit from having access to international and national research expertise and state of the art facilities and equipment while working on projects in an innovation-focused environment. Researchers will have access to expertise and resources to advance their research to the next stage. Royalties due to integrated drug discovery organizations through successful collaborations would significantly diminish the demand on government to fund drug discovery and development.

i. Centre for Drug Research and Development (Canada)

The Centre for Drug Research and Development (CDRD) is an independent, non-profit organization with a focus on bridging the gap between academic discoveries in the health sciences and the development of new medicines to treat human disease.[54] Created as a joint effort between

---

[54] http://www.cdrd.ca/

government, industry, and academia, CDRD developed a drug development and commercialization platform, based on achieving proof of concept, to advance innovative health technologies from early stage research through to the pre-clinical stage. CDRD works with a network of national and international university TTOs and public research organizations to identify early stage academic research projects worth taking through to proof of concept. In essence, basic research identified as being a potential project may be brought into CDRD as a project for further research and development. Specifically, CDRD will help the academic principal investigator (PI) by assembling a team of experts to devise a detailed project plan of critical experiments required to validate the basic research and discovery that can then be used to attract private investment or interest in commercialization. In general, the project plan involves several cycles of experimentation, each cycle lasting six to nine months, with well-defined project milestones. If the project fails to meet certain milestones within the defined time frame, no further resources will be invested into the project as a means to minimize loss. Typically a project will need to proceed through two to four cycles before being considered validated. Any and all originating intellectual property rights relating to the PI's research and discovery remains with the PI and his/her affiliated institution (in accordance with the institution's intellectual property policy) and the PI will continue to have control over the research project.

ii. Centre for Drug Design and Discovery (Belgium)

The Centre for Drug Design and Discovery (CD3) at the Katholieke Universiteit Leuven (KU Leuven) is a project group that manages an investment fund dedicated to translating university research in the small molecule space into more useable results for further development by pharmaceutical companies into new medicines. CD3 achieves this by providing expertise and financial resources and applying them to the pool of basic knowledge, innovation, and technology originating from the university and associated spin-off companies. CD3 thereby bridges the gap between academic research and industry and fulfills its mandate 'to fully apply the expertise of universities and small companies for the validation of innovative targets and the discovery of novel drug-like compounds'.[55]

CD3 is established within KU Leuven Research and Development (LRD), which is KU Leuven's TTO and the entity that enters into license

---

[55] http://www.cd3.eu/

agreements with third parties on behalf of KU Leuven. In 2007, KU Leuven founded The Centre for Innovation and Stimulation of Drug Discovery (CISTM), which is an independent non-profit entity. CISTM conducts drug discovery projects approved by CD3 pursuant to a service contract with KU Leuven. CD3 will also contract third-party contract research organizations (CROs) to provide necessary expertise. In 2006, CD3 secured its first round of funding of €8 million from the European Investment Fund (EIF) and LRD and received a further €16 million in 2010. Both the EIF and LRD have an expectation of return on investment, which is specifically set out in the funding agreement and reflected in the make-up of the Investment Committee. CD3 was involved in the development and commercialization of six of the top 50 blockbuster drugs.

iii. Lead Discovery Centre (Germany)

The Lead Discovery Centre GmbH (LDC) was founded in 2008 and is an independent enterprise established by Max Planck Innovation (MPI), the technology transfer organization responsible for connecting research arising from all the institutes of the Max Planck Society (MPS) with industry.[56] LDC is largely funded by MPS and was founded to advance small molecule basic research into the development of commercially viable and medically valuable products by demonstrating proof of concept in early stage discoveries. Structured as an independent limited liability company with an entrepreneurial outlook, LDC collaborates with research institutions, universities, and industry to transform promising early-stage projects into pharmaceutical leads. Through its various strategic partnerships and relationships, LDC can leverage the scientific excellence at MPS research institutes and other universities to facilitate the collaboration between academic project owners and industry to translate early stage projects into marketable assets. Licensing income generated through industry collaborations are reinvested into LDC for future R&D projects and LDC expects to be self-funded in the next 10–12 years.

iv. Medical Research Council Technology (MRCT) (UK)

MRCT is a UK-based technology transfer organization that was originally responsible for commercializing intellectual property rights on

---

[56] http://www.lead-discovery.de/de/

discoveries and inventions owned by the Medical Research Council (MRC).[57] The MRC is a publically funded government organization that supports medical sciences research and is made up of 27 units, 26 centers, and three institutes. MRC owns the intellectual property rights on discoveries derived from such units, centers, and institutes, and commercializes the inventions through MRCT. Today, MRCT works with MRC-funded research as well as with universities, medical research charities, and pharmaceutical and biotechnology organizations around the world in order to gain access to the best science. Established in 2000 as a charity to identify commercially viable opportunities to progress publically funded research, MRCT has its own laboratories and scientists who carry out applied research to advance basic science to proof of concept in order to bridge the gap between basic medical research and commercial application. Licensing income is then reinvested and applied for further medical research.

F. OPEN INNOVATION MODEL OF DRUG DISCOVERY AND DEVELOPMENT

Like the integrated drug discovery platform, the open innovation model of drug discovery and development advocates the benefits of collaboration, but some models criticize intellectual property as being 'a key culprit in the decline of innovation'.[58] The models that criticize intellectual property rights define open innovation as 'the sourcing and leveraging of expertise wherever it can be found and the sharing of knowledge, intellectual property and information as freely as possible'.[59] For example, the collaborative open innovation approach proposed by the Structural Genomics Consortium at the University of Oxford proposes a restriction on asserting intellectual property rights until early clinical

---

[57]   http://www.mrctechnology.org/
[58]   Michele Boldrin and David K. Levine, *The Case Against Patents*. THE JOURNAL OF ECONOMIC PERSPECTIVES, 27(1), 3–22 (2013); Thomas Senderovitz, *How Open Innovation COULD Reinvigorate the Pharmaceutical Industry with Fresh R&D Opportunities*. EXPERT REVIEW OF CLINICAL PHARMACOLOGY, 2(6), 585–587 (2009).
[59]   Kenneth A. Getz and Kenneth I. Kaitin, *Open Innovation: The New Face of Pharmaceutical Research and Development*. EXPERT REVIEW OF CLINICAL PHARMACOLOGY, 5(5), 481–483 (2012).

trials show promising results.[60] Under this model, pharmaceutical companies would only be allowed to compete after candidates are deemed safe and potentially effective. By making all data on prospective drug candidates freely available to others up until early clinical stages, parties will no longer work in parallel, unaware of compounds that have already been tested and discarded.[61] Conspicuously, the model fails to address how industry participation would be incentivized and whether such openness is feasible, having regard to the industry's interests and necessary involvement in translation and commercialization processes.

The core idea of open innovation is to reduce barriers that restrict access to knowledge and technology[62] and foster the exchange of information from diverse external sources, such as collaborative R&D.[63] Supporters of open innovation explain and espouse the virtues of collaboration to increase R&D innovation and productivity through the sharing of expertise and intellectual property to create synergies and superior products.[64] Some of these concepts are also embodied in the integrated drug discovery model, namely, the leveraging of expertise and knowledge from different sources as a means to increase efficiency, reduce cost and duplication efforts, and share risk. However, this type of open innovation introduces challenges to the drug discovery and development innovation process, particularly with respect to the management of intellectual property rights.[65] There is much debate as to whether

---

[60]   Daniel Cressey, *Traditional Drug Discovery Model Ripe for Reform.* NATURE NEWS, 47(7336), 17–18 (2011).

[61]   Ibid.

[62]   See for example, Linus Dahlander and David M. Gann, *How Open is Innovation?* RESEARCH POLICY, 39(6), 699–709 (2010).

[63]   See for example, Keld Laursen and Ammon Salter, *Open for Innovation: The Role of Openness in Explaining Innovation Performance Among U.K. Manufacturing Firms.* STRATEGIC MANAGEMENT JOURNAL, 27(2), 131–150 (2006); Eelko K. Huizingh, *Open Innovation: State of the Art and Future Perspectives.* TECHNOVATION, 31(1), 2–9 (2011).

[64]   See for example, Joel West, Ammon Salter, Wim Vanhaverbeke and Henry Chesbrough, *Open Innovation: The Next Decade.* RESEARCH POLICY, 43(5), 805–811 (2014); Getz and Kaitin *supra* note 59.

[65]   Paavo Ritala and Pia Hurmelinna-Laukkanen, *Incremental and Radical Innovation in Coopetition – The Role of Absorptive Capacity and Appropriability.* JOURNAL OF PRODUCT INNOVATION MANAGEMENT, 30(1), 154–169 (2013); Keld Laursen and Ammon Salter, *The Paradox of Openness: Appropriability, External Search and Collaboration.* RESEARCH POLICY, 43(5), 867–878 (2014).

intellectual property rights promote innovation.[66] Some scholars have suggested that the free exchange of knowledge seems inconsistent and conflicts directly with intellectual property protection,[67] while others argue for the importance of intellectual property rights for enabling knowledge transfer.[68] The reconstruction of R&D costs for the development of the rotavirus vaccine known as RotaTeq and Rotarix has been cited as evidence that the costs and risks of drug development can be remarkably low up until the final phases of clinical trials and that investments can be recovered within the first 18 months of commercialization.[69] Opponents contend that patents are the life-blood of the drug discovery and development process.[70] Academia would be deprived of

---

[66]   See for example, Cassandra M. Sweet and Dalibor S.E. Maggio, *Do Stronger Intellectual Property Rights Increase Innovation?* WORLD DEVELOPMENT, 66, 665–677 (2015); Boldrin and Levine., *supra* note 58; Seokkyun Woo, Pilseong Jang, and Yeonbae Kim, *Effects of Intellectual Property Rights and Patented Knowledge in Innovation and Industry Value Added: A Multinational Empirical Analysis of Different Industries.* TECHNOVATION, 43, 49–63 (2015).

[67]   Miriam Bentwich, *Changing the Rules of the Game: Addressing the Conflict between Free Access to Scientific Discovery and Intellectual Property Rights.* NATURE BIOTECHNOLOGY, 28(2), 137–140 (2010); Wei Hong and John P. Walsh, *For Money or Glory? Commercialization, Competition, and Secrecy in the Entrepreneurial University.* THE SOCIOLOGICAL QUARTERLY, 50(1), 145–171 (2009); Julien Pénin, Caroline Hussler, and Thierry Burger-Helmchen, *New Shapes and New Stakes: A Portrait of Open Innovation as a Promising Phenomenon.* JOURNAL OF INNOVATION ECONOMICS, 1, 11–29 (2011).

[68]   Stuart J. Graham and David C. Mowery, 'The Use of Intellectual Property in Software: Implications for Open Innovation' in Henry W. Chesbrough, Wim Vanhaverbeke, and Joel West (eds), *Open Innovation: Researching a New Paradigm* (Oxford University Press 2006) 109–133; Francesco Sandulli and Henry W. Chesbrough, *The Two Faces of Open Business Models.* SSRN Working Paper Series No. 1325682 (2009); Jeroen P.J. De Jong, Tarmo Kalvet, and Wim Vanhaverbeke, *Exploring a Theoretical Framework to Structure the Public Policy Implications of Open Innovation.* TECHNOLOGY ANALYSIS & STRATEGIC MANAGEMENT, 22(8), 877–896 (2010); Kaisa Henttonen, Pia Hurmelinna-Laukkanen, and Paavo Ritala, *Managing the Appropriability of R&D Collaboration.* R&D MANAGEMENT, 46(1), 145–158 (2015).

[69]   Donald W. Light, *Advanced Market Commitments: Current Realities and Alternate Approaches* (Amsterdam, the Netherlands, HAI Europe/Medico International Publication 2009).

[70]   Sander Kern and Rik van Reekum, *The Use of Patents in Dutch Biopharmaceutical SME: A Typology for Assessing Strategic Patent Management Maturity.* NEW TECHNOLGY-BASED FIRMS IN THE NEW MILLENIUM, 9, 131–149 (2012); Marcia Angell and Arnold S. Relman, *Patents, Profits &*

royalties and the industry would carry a heavy investment burden with very little assurance of financial return.[71] The ability to exclude others to maintain a competitive edge and maximize return on investment is what allows pharmaceutical companies to exist and continue to fund R&D.[72]

An open innovation model in the drug discovery and development that embraces open science at the expense of intellectual property assumes that the relevant players (industry and academia) are ready, willing, and able to depart from the deeply rooted traditions and adopt an altruistic and philanthropic approach to freely sharing information and discoveries. Open science, defined as 'a practice in which the scientific process is shared completely and in real time', may not necessarily lead to innovation because the application of scientific knowledge requires the involvement of various stakeholders, each with their own motivations to participate in the innovation process. Most academics are trained to work by themselves or within their research group and protect their findings until they are ready to be published. Even when results are ready for publishing, academics have been known to hold back on fully divulging findings for personal reasons, such as preserving the ability to seek funding for further related research.[73] Industry is inherently financially motivated and intellectual property rights are their greatest asset. As such, an open innovation drug discovery and development model that is premised on the relevant stakeholders' willingness to freely and openly share knowledge without preserving proprietary rights will unlikely entice academia, industry, and government to collaborate because of the lack of incentive to induce investments of the time, money, and intellectual capital required to introduce new innovations.

Other forms of open innovation in drug discovery and development have adopted a more conciliatory approach to intellectual property. For example, the Wellcome Trust defines open innovation as 'the process of innovating with others for shared risk and reward to produce mutual

---

American Medicine: Conflicts of Interest in the Testing & Marketing of New Drugs. DAEDALUS, 131(2), 102–111 (2002); *Contrasting European and U.S. Patent Laws: Issues for the Pharmaceutical Industry*. Wiley Handbook of Current and Emerging Drug Therapies (2007).

[71]   Cressey, *supra* note 60.

[72]   Wiley Handbook, *supra*, note 70.

[73]   Patrick Andreoli-Versbach and Frank Mueller-Langer, *Open access to data: An ideal professed but not practiced*. RESEARCH POLICY, 43(9), 1621-1633 (2014); Marie Thursby, Jerry G. Thursby, Carolin Haeussler, and Lin Jiang, *Do academic scientists share information with their colleagues? Not necessarily* (2009) http://www.voxeu.org/article/why-don-t-academic-scientists-share-information-their-colleagues?

benefits' and their position on intellectual property is that 'there is a spectrum of intellectual property "openness" between the two poles' to balance commercial value with benefit to public health.[74] There is an express acknowledgment that a 'too open' approach to intellectual property can negatively affect the rewards that drive competitive research and private investment and can lead to a free-rider problem.[75] There is a recognition that protecting innovation might be unavoidable and the value of 'openness' needs to be compromised in practice to protect commercial interests in order to engage the expertise of industry. This form of open innovation advocates for a flexible approach to intellectual property, enabling the parties to negotiate and design intellectual property strategies aligned with their respective interests and objectives,[76] which essentially describes the integrated drug discovery model. The reality is that translation of knowledge acquired by basic research into applicable tools and technologies often requires the expertise of industry and resources of other stakeholders. Public equity of benefit cannot be realized if research cannot be commercialized due to economic unfeasibility or inability to assert intellectual property rights.

G. REMARKS: THE CURRENT LANDSCAPE

An understanding of the pharmaceutical industry and drug discovery development process is essential to understanding: (i) why the integrated drug discovery model is needed; (ii) how it attempts to address the problems associated with the traditional drug discovery development model; and (iii) why it is essential to assess the impact and interaction

---

[74] *Shaping the Future of Open Innovation: A Practical Guide for Life Sciences Organisations* (The Wellcome Trust 2014), 14.

[75] Ibid. See also Richard C. Levin, *A New Look at the Patent System.* AMERICAN ECONOMIC REVIEW, 76(2), 199–202 (1986); Richard R. Nelson, *The Role of Knowledge in R&D Efficiency.* QUARTERLY JOURNAL OF ECONOMICS, 97, 467–8 (1982); Rebecca S. Eisenberg and Richard R. Nelson, *Public vs Proprietary Science: A Fruitful Tension?* DAEDALUS, 131(2), 89–91 (2002); Tuija Luoma, Jaakko Paasi, and Katri Valkokari, *Intellectual Property in Interorganisational Relationships – Findings from an Interview Study.* INTERNATIONAL JOURNAL OF INNOVATION MANAGEMENT, 14(3), 399–414 (2010).

[76] Jackie Hunter, *Is the Pharmaceutical Industry Open for Innovation?* DRUG DISCOVERY WORLD, 9–14 (2010), which argued that parties can tailor contractual terms to achieve comfort in their ability to control the use and potential loss of IPRs.

between intellectual property law and competition policy on the integrated drug discovery platform. From a 'big picture' perspective, the socio-economic environment created by a three-way tension between government, industry, and public interests sets the stage for the challenges the current drug discovery and development process faces. Scholars have often commented on what appears to be a constant conflict between government and the pharmaceutical industry regarding the pricing of drugs.[77] When drugs are priced too high, access by patients, as well as their right to health, may be undermined.[78] When priced too low, the pharmaceutical industry has less money to invest in the R&D required to bring new medicines to market.[79] Due to the increasing burden on government to allocate more and more of the national budget to fund healthcare, government has adopted a variety of policy tools to help cap the rise of drug prices and therefore health care expenditure.[80] A cascading effect results in a three-way tension: (i) the government wants to control the healthcare budget by capping drug prices but needs to

---

[77]   Conflicts can arise between pricing of new drugs and launch lags. See Patricia M. Danzon and Andrew J. Epstein, *Effects of Regulation on Drug Launch and Pricing in Interdependent Markets.* ADVANCES IN HEALTH ECONOMICS AND HEALTH SERVICES RESEARCH, 23, 35–71 (2012). Conflict can also arise between pricing and reimbursement policies governing orphan drugs in different countries, creating differences in access and utilization of orphan drugs. See Steven Simoens, *Pricing and Reimbursement of Orphan Drugs: the Need for More Transparency.* ORPHANET JOURNAL OF RARE DISEASES, 6(42), 1–8 (2011). Because pharmaceutical pricing and reimbursement systems differ significantly between member states, this can give rise to parallel import issues. See Mattias Ganslandt and Keith E. Maskus, *Parallel Imports and the Pricing of Pharmaceutical Products: Evidence from the European Union.* JOURNAL OF HEALTH ECONOMICS, 23(5), 1035–1057 (2004).

[78]   Patricia M. Danzon and Adrian Towse, *Differential Pricing for Pharmaceuticals: Reconciling Access, R&D and Patents.* INTERNATIONAL JOURNAL OF HEALTH CARE FINANCE AND ECONOMICS, 3(3), 183–205 (2003).

[79]   Joseph A. DiMasi and Henry G. Grabowski, 'R&D Costs and Returns to New Drug Development: A Review of the Evidence'. *The Oxford Handbook of the Economics of the Biopharmaceutical Industry*, Oxford University Press, Oxford (2012) at Chapter 2, 21–46.

[80]   See for example, Silvia M. Ess, Sebastian Schneeweiss, and Thomas D. Szucs, *European Healthcare Policies for Controlling Drug Expenditure.* PHARMACOECONOMICS, 21(2), 89–103 (2003); Giuseppe Carone, Christoph Schwierz, and Ana Xavier, *Cost-containment Policies in Public Pharmaceutical Spending in the EU.* EUROPEAN ECONOMY (2012); Ivan Moreno-Torres, Jaume Puig-Junoy, and Josep M. Raya, *The Impact of Repeated Cost Containment Policies on Pharmaceutical Expenditure: Experience in Spain.* THE EUROPEAN JOURNAL OF HEALTH ECONOMICS, 12(6), 563–573 (2011).

incentivize industry (i.e. through the patent system) to continue to produce drugs; (ii) industry needs to make a profit in order to continue to drive innovation and develop life-saving medicines, but the lack of financial support from government will lead industry to be more conservative about their risk assessment and investment in R&D; and (iii) given the aging population, consumers expect access to medicines at the lowest prices possible, especially since their tax dollars indirectly fund drug discovery and development through publically funded research. Government price control schemes may reduce the price of pharmaceuticals but they may not necessarily lead to a reduction in government expenditures. Decreasing the price of a drug means the government pays less, consumers have greater access to medicines at a lower cost, but industry will recoup less of the costs invested to bring a new drug to the market. If industry cannot survive, there will be fewer new drugs available and government will have to step in to deal with the social and economic consequences.[81] As such, an argument can be made that government should play a greater role in ensuring the health of the pharmaceutical industry by creating a favorable environment to foster drug discovery and development.[82]

The 'valley of death' has attracted much commentary at academic, industry, and government levels and is beyond the scope of this book to explore exhaustively.[83] Because the pharmaceutical sector is dependent on developing and maintaining a pipeline of viable innovative technologies, promising early stage discoveries will likely have a greater

---

[81]   See EFPIA, *The Pharmaceutical Industry in Figures* (2010).

[82]   Bhaven N. Sampat and Frank R. Lichtenberg, *What Are the Respective Roles of the Public and Private Sectors in Pharmaceutical Innovation?* HEALTH AFFAIRS, 30(2), 332–339 (2011). Government funding plays an indirect role by funding basic underlying research that forms the foundation for the drug discovery process in almost half of the drugs approved. Studies have found that direct government funding can benefit the development of innovative new drugs. See also Paul Feldstein, *Health Care Economics* (Cengage Learning 2011), Chapter 2 'The Role of Government in Health and Medical Care'.

[83]   See for example, Christopher A. Lipinski, *The Anti-Intellectual Effects of Intellectual Property.* CURRENT OPINION IN CHEMICAL BIOLOGY, 10(4), 380–383 (2006); Ian M. Cockburn, *The Changing Structure of the Pharmaceutical Industry.* HEALTH AFFAIRS, 23(1), 10–22 (2004) at 10; U.S. Food and Drug Administration, *Innovation or Stagnation: Challenge and Opportunity on the Critical Path to New Medical Products* (2004); Fredric J. Cohen, *Macro Trends in Pharmaceutical Innovation.* NATURE REVIEWS DRUG DISCOVERY, 4(1), 78–84 (2005); Robert F. Service, *Surviving the Blockbuster Syndrome.* SCIENCE (New York, NY), 303(5665), 1796 (2004).

chance of reaching the market if academic researchers collaborate with industry partners to develop basic research into commercializable products. By involving an intermediary such as university TTOs or integrated drug discovery organizations, academic researchers can interface with one organization to handle the aspects of the commercialization process he/she is unfamiliar with and focus instead on conducting R&D. By entering into collaborations between integrated drug discovery organizations and industry, publically funded research has a greater likelihood of reaching the market at a faster rate through pooled resources, shared risk, and a reduction in duplication efforts.

The question is how does competition policy impact collaborations between integrated drug discovery organizations and highly innovative and R&D intensive industries such as the pharmaceutical industry.[84] Successful collaborations between integrated drug discovery organizations and industry can give rise to benefits for both industry (by way of competitive advantage) and the public (by way of creating new life-saving therapies).[85] However, downstream application of research arising from the collaboration may be contractually restricted.[86] In the pharmaceutical context, exclusivity is often required by industry in order to secure rights to any revenue that may arise from successful development as a means to recoup R&D costs. This however raises concerns about the impact of patenting on academic goals and access to publically funded research results. Patents may become a barrier for researchers to access basic science and the research tools required for further research.[87] This in turn increases costs and discourages follow-on R&D, which is further exacerbated by the ongoing criticism of overbroad patents in the pharmaceutical field.

---

[84]   The pharmaceutical industry is a highly innovative and R&D intensive industry, characterized by: a high rate of technological change compared to most other industries; the vital role of R&D due to the high rate of technological change; high barriers to market entry; uncertain outcomes of R&D despite significant investment; and displacement of leading technology with new technology. See John T. Lang, *European Community Antitrust Law: Innovation Markets and High Technology Industries.* FORDHAM INTERNATIONAL JOURNAL, 20, 717 (1997).

[85]   Bagley and Tvarnø, *supra* note 50 at 383.

[86]   Jerome H. Reichman and Paul F. Uhlir, *A Contractually Reconstructed Research Commons for Scientific Data in a Highly Protectionist Intellectual Property Environment.* LAW & CONTEMPORARY PROBLEMS, 66(1/2), 315–462 (2003) at 320.

[87]   See for example Ian Ayres and Gideon Parchomovsky, *Tradable Patent Rights.* STANFORD LAW REVIEW, 863–894 (2007).

There is no doubt that the development and commercialization of new medicines by pharmaceutical companies has brought substantial public health benefits, such as improved quality of life and increased longevity. However, innovation comes at a substantial cost in terms of time, money, and intellectual capital. Adequate incentives must be made available in order to motivate researchers and industry to devote the time and money to conduct the necessary R&D to develop new pharmaceutical products. Without proper incentives, industry will have no reason to engage in collaborative R&D with academia, given the risks involved in the drug discovery and development process, including low success rates, substantial time delays to enter the market, as well as the considerable financial commitment required to see the project through to commercialization. R&D costs constitute a high entry barrier, making industry players hard to replace if they cannot survive in the market, which means there will be fewer pharmaceutical companies to develop and bring new products to market.[88] In response to the commercial realities of drug discovery and development, companies have increasingly employed strategic uses of intellectual property rights to increase or maintain their competitive edge. Such strategies are usually adaptations of accepted and common commercial practices within the law: patenting technology, acquiring patent portfolios of already developed technologies, securing revenue from royalties, and licensing are all part of the legitimate exercise of entrepreneurial imagination to derive income. However, some strategies attract the scrutiny of competition law to ensure that certain strategic uses of intellectual property rights do not extend beyond the legally permissible scope. In the pharmaceutical industry, patent flooding (filing numerous patents on trivial variants of an original innovation) is a common strategy used to stave off competition by creating a defensive wall around a core technology. Sometimes, the strategy is used for the purposes of delaying third-party entry into the market after the initial patent lapses. Such behavior will have an effect on competition, but in order to successfully translate upstream research into potential new drugs, new models of R&D and commercialization should be considered.[89] The reality is that drug discovery and development require the involvement of both academia and industry because none of the individual players have all the

---

[88]   Alfonso Gambardella, Luigi Orsenigo, and Fabio Pammolli, *Global Competitiveness in Pharmaceuticals: A European Perspective*. Office for Official Publications of the European Communities (2001).

[89]   See for example, Rai et al., *supra* note 11 at 4, citing that companies must fundamentally review R&D business models and exploit new strategies for re-establishing core drug discovery expertise.

necessary skills and resources to discover and develop pharmaceutical products independently. There is no denying the financial motive of industry. However, as a 'quid pro quo' for making life-saving products available for the benefit of public health, efficient and effective translation of publically funded research through university/industry collaborations is a necessity that should mitigate a certain level of criticism and discontent relating to commercialization.

3. Intellectual property rights and competition law in collaborative drug discovery and development between industry and integrated drug discovery organizations

A. FOSTERING INTERNATIONAL COLLABORATIONS

Studies indicate that innovation, as measured by R&D expenditure, has a significant positive effect on output and productivity.[1] Although an increase in R&D expenditures alone will not guarantee greater productivity, OECD data supports the general conclusion that firms that invest in knowledge are more likely to produce new technologies for commercialization.[2] In the past, R&D-based innovations were largely conducted in-house by R&D-intensive industries,[3] including but not limited to the pharmaceutical industry. In other words, innovation was traditionally more likely to be localized in R&D-intensive firms where innovation was conducted internally and where the R&D expenditure of such firms was

---

[1]   See Mosahid Khan and Kul B. Luintel, *Sources of Knowledge and Productivity: How Robust is the Relationship?* OECD STI Working Papers (2006); Chiara Criscuolo, Jonathan E. Haskel, and Matthew J. Slaughter, *Global Engagement and the Innovation Activities of Firms.* INTERNATIONAL JOURNAL OF INDUSTRIAL ORGANIZATION, 28(2), 191–202 (2010); Rinaldo Evangelista and Antonio Vezzani, *The Economic Impact of Technological and Organizational Innovations: A Firm-level Analysis.* RESEARCH POLICY, 39(10), 1253–1263 (2010); OECD, *Innovation in Firms* (OECD 2010); OECD, *Open Innovation in Global Networks* (OECD 2009); and Jose M. Benavente and Rodolfo Lauterbach, *Technological Innovation and Employment: Complements or Substitutes?* EUROPEAN JOURNAL OF DEVELOPMENT RESEARCH, 20(2), 318–329 (2008).

[2]   OECD, *Measuring Innovation – A New Perspective* (OECD 2010).

[3]   Jan Fagerberg, Martin Scrholec, and Bart Verspagen, 'Innovation and Economic Development' in Browyn Hall and Nathan Rosenberg (eds), *Handbook of the Economics of Innovation* (North Holland 2010), Volume 2, 833–872.

largely invested in employing highly educated people to perform such innovation. Today, with the emphasis in economic literature on universities and public research organizations as an essential source of knowledge,[4] companies are increasingly looking to collaborate with academia in search for new innovations to commercialize.[5] The transformation from the traditional internal innovation process to a more collaborative innovation process seems to be motivated by industry's increasing desire to seek knowledge and skills beyond their own core competencies in order to enlarge their capabilities and enhance their assets.[6] As a part of this shift in the innovation paradigm, there appears to be evidence of an intensification of investment in innovation at a global level[7] and an increase in international collaborations.[8] For example, available data on co-patent filings at the United States Patent and Trademark Office as well as at the European Patent Office indirectly suggest an increase in collaborations (based on the assumption that collaborative R&D will result in patenting, and the increase in patent applications that identify

---

[4]   See WIPO Economics & Statistics Series, *2011 World Intellectual Property Report: The Changing Face of Innovation*, Chapter 4 Harnessing Public Research for Innovation – The Role of Intellectual Property, Box 4.1: The economic impact of publicly funded research at 141–142 and Ricardo J. Caballero and Adam B. Jaffe, 'How High are the Giants' Shoulders: An Empirical Assessment of Knowledge Spillovers and Creative Destruction in a Model of Economic Growth' in Jean O. Blanchard and Stanley Fischer (eds), *NBER Macroeconomics Annual* (The University of Chicago Press 1993) Volume 8, 15–86.

[5]   Richard R. Nelson, *The Market Economy, and the Scientific Commons*. RESEARCH POLICY, 33(3), 455–471 (2004). R&D conducted by universities and public research organizations account for a substantial share of total R&D. See also OECD, Research and Development Database (2011).

[6]   Cathy J. Tralau-Stewart, Colin A. Wyatt, Dominique E. Kleyn and Alex Ayad, *Drug Discovery: New Models for Industry–Academic Partnerships*. DRUG DISCOVERY TODAY, 14(1), 95–101 (2009) at 96–97.

[7]   Claims that innovation is increasingly international and collaborative in nature seem to be supported by evidence and available data. See Bruce S. Tether and Abdelouahid Tajar, *The Organisational-Cooperation Mode of Innovation and Its Prominence Amongst European Service Firms*. RESEARCH, 37(4), 720–739 (2008) and *UNESCO Science Report 2010* (UNESCO 2010).

[8]   See James Wilsdon, *Knowledge, Networks and Nations: Global Scientific Collaboration in the 21st Century* (The Royal Society 2011). Combined with increased mobility and internationalization of business R&D, such factors positively influence the international transfer of knowledge. See Jakob Edler, Heide Fier, and Christoph Grimpe, *International Scientist Mobility and the Locus of Knowledge and Technology Transfer*. RESEARCH POLICY, 40(6), 791–805 (2011).

two or more applicants may be a reflection of an increase in R&D collaborations), with a majority of recent filings in the areas of pharmaceutical, biotechnology, and chemical materials.[9] Despite the limitations of the available data, there is general consensus in the literature[10] that there is an increase in: (i) national and international collaboration in innovation;[11] (ii) R&D partnerships in certain sectors including the pharmaceutical sector;[12] (iii) R&D outsourcing and contract research to public research organizations;[13] and (iv) the number of patent co-inventors from different countries on the same patent application.[14]

Collaborative research between academia and industry may be motivated by strategic reasons or to improve efficiency.[15] More specifically in drug discovery and development, collaborations between industry and integrated drug discovery organizations with complementary assets or skills offer several benefits: improved R&D efficiency by sharing in the accumulated knowledge and experiences (including failures) to facilitate joint problem solving;[16] the cost of underinvested projects with potential

---

[9]   Koenraad DeBacker, Vladmir Lopez-Bassols, and Catalina Martinez, *Open Innovation in a Global Perspective – What do Existing Data Tell Us?* OECD STI Working Paper (2008). However, there is some disagreement in the literature as to how accurately sectoral patterns of co-patenting reflect the extent of collaborative R&D. See WIPO Economics & Statistics Series, *2011 World Intellectual Property Report: The Changing Face of Innovation*, Chapter 3, Balancing Collaboration and Competition at 112–113.

[10]   WIPO Economics & Statistics Series, *2011 World Intellectual Property Report: The Changing Face of Innovation*, Chapter 1 'The Changing Face of Innovation' at 44.

[11]   UNESCO report, *supra* note 7.

[12]   John Hagedoorn and Nadine Roijakkers, *Inter-firm R&D Partnering in Pharmaceutical Biotechnology since 1975: Trends, Patterns, and Networks*, RESEARCH POLICY, 35(3), 431–446 (2006).

[13]   OECD (2009), *supra* note 1.

[14]   OECD, *The OECD Innovation Strategy: Getting a Head Start on Tomorrow* (OECD 2010); WIPO, *World Intellectual Property Indicators* (WIPO 2010). However, the relevance of considering patents with multiple inventors from different countries as an indicator of international R&D collaboration has been questioned. See Anna Bergek and Maria Bruzelius, *Are Patents with Multiple Inventors from Different Countries a Good Indicator of International R&D Collaboration? The Case of ABB.* RESEARCH POLICY, 39(10), 1321–1334 (2010).

[15]   WIPO, *supra* note 9.

[16]   Benjamin F. Jones, *The Burden of Knowledge and the 'Death of the Renaissance Man': Is Innovation Getting Harder?* REVIEW OF ECONOMIC STUDIES, 76(1), 283–317 (2009). If knowledge accumulates as technology

can be shared through collaboration; efficiency gains from sharing costs associated with access to laboratories, equipment, and materials, as well as ancillary services such as technical specialists, administrative support, and technicians, that may otherwise be too high for one party to assume; and, of specific relevance to the pharmaceutical industry where successful commercialization typically comes at the cost of repeated R&D failures, collaborations spread the development risk and allow both industry and integrated drug discovery organizations to pursue multiple projects, including riskier undertakings.[17] Through collaboration, the benefits of publicly funded research can be maximized because the combined efforts of the parties may lead to the translation of basic research into useful products for commercialization.[18] Understandably, policymakers want to bolster the effectiveness of commercializing innovations derived from publicly funded research.[19]

---

advances, then collaborating with other parties can save innovators the time and commitment required to attain and build up knowledge by leveraging others' experience instead of building up knowledge internally.

[17]   Pursuing multiple projects increases the probability that at least one successful project will help compensate for the cost of the unsuccessful projects. Advantageously, even unsuccessful projects have value. Knowledge derived from unsuccessful projects can help target successful outcomes in future projects by avoiding duplication of failed efforts.

[18]   Government-funded research usually enables academics to freely conduct 'blue-sky' research without worrying about business considerations, such as the commercial application of the research. See Paula E. Stephan, 'The Economics of Science' in Browyn Hall and Nathan Rosenberg (eds), *Handbook of the Economics of Innovation* (North Holland 2010), Volume 1, 217–273. The economic impact of academic research on business innovation indicates a positive effect on productivity by stimulating private R&D but not a direct contribution to economic growth. James D. Adams, *Fundamental Stocks of Knowledge and Productivity Growth.* JOURNAL OF POLITICAL ECONOMY, 98(4), 673–702 (1990); Kul B. Luintel and Mosahid Khan, *Basic, Applied and Experimental Knowledge and Productivity: Further Evidence.* ECONOMICS LETTERS, 111(1), 71–74 (2011); and Paul A. David and Bronwyn H. Hall, *Property and the Pursuit of Knowledge: IPR Issues Affecting Scientific Research.* RESEARCH POLICY, 35(6), 767–771 (2006).

[19]   Dominique Foray and Francesco Lissoni, 'University Research and Public-Private Interaction' in Bronwyn Hall and Nathan Rosenberg (eds), *Handbook of the Economics of Innovation* (North Holland, 2010), Volume 1, 275–314; Richard E. Just and Wallace E. Huffman, *The Economics of Universities in a New Age of Funding Options.* RESEARCH POLICY, 38(7), 1102–1116 (2009). Dissemination of publicly funded research in the public domain is no longer seen as sufficient to generate the full benefits of the research. Bart van Looy, Paolo Landoni, Julie Callaert, Bruno van Pottelsberghe, Eleftherios Sapsalis and

Government and policymakers play a key role in and can have a direct impact on the innovation process. In addition to implementing policy initiatives and strategies to promote collaboration between industry and academia as a means to facilitate the translation of publically funded research into new products, as key stakeholders in the innovation process, governments can also directly fund research[20] and provide incentives to parties who invest in innovation (such as by way of intellectual property protection). However, because government funding for university R&D has declined over the years[21] and the process of obtaining research grants has become increasingly competitive with a greater emphasis on supporting research that will create societal impact,[22] there is literature suggesting that universities have come to realize that the transfer of technology can be an attractive extra source of income to fund the ever-increasing costs of basic research.[23] The increasing trend of university–industry collaborations is evidenced by the creation of the 'Responsible Partnering Initiative' to facilitate collaborative research and knowledge transfer between academia and industry.[24] Studies also indicate an intensification of knowledge-driven interactions between universities and industry in the

---

Koenraad Debackere, *Entrepreneurial Effectiveness of European Universities: An Empirical Assessment of Antecedents and Trade-offs*. RESEARCH POLICY, 40(4), 553–564 (2011).

[20] On average, government funding is responsible for about 53% of total R&D and as the country's income decreases, government funding approaches 100%, especially in the health and agricultural sectors. See UNESCO Report, *supra* note 7.

[21] See for example, Philip G. Altbach, Liz Reisberg, and Laura E. Rumbley. *Trends in Global Higher Education: Tracking an Academic Revolution*, World Conference on Higher Education (2009); Marek Kwiek, *Knowledge Production in European Universities: States, Markets, and Academic Entrepreneurialism* (Peter Lang 2012).

[22] See for example, Daniel J. Howard and Frank N. Laird, *The New Normal in Funding University Science*. ISSUES IN SCIENCE AND TECHNOLOGY, 30(1), 71 (2013); Giuseppe Veltri, Alexander Grablowitz, and Fulvio Mulatero, *Trends in R&D Policies for a European Knowledge-based Economy*, EC JRC Scientific and Technical Reports (2009).

[23] Gail Edmondson, Lori Valigra, Michael Kenward, Richard L. Hudson, and Haydn Belfield, *Making Industry-University Partnerships Work: Lessons from Successful Collaborations*. Science Business Innovation Board (2012); Younhee Kim, *The Ivory Tower Approach to Entrepreneurial Linkage: Productivity Changes in University Technology Transfer*. THE JOURNAL OF TECHNOLOGY TRANSFER, 38(2), 180–197 (2013)

[24] http://www.eua.be/

recent past.[25] As set out in the 2007 European Commission Communication entitled *Improving knowledge transfer between research institutions and industry across Europe: embracing open innovation – implementing the Lisbon agenda*, the Directorate-General for Science and Research and Directorate-General for Enterprise and Industry stated:

> European universities and other research institutions are equally realising their changing role in the globalized economy and have undertaken interesting initiatives … In order to remain attractive, they will need to open up to business and international collaboration, which may also help leverage new funds. Sharing knowledge in particular through R&D collaborations with business – while a potential source of income for research institutions – may well give an important boost to both quantity and quality of the research undertaken.[26]

Changes in the innovation landscape will likely have the effect of compelling market participants to adapt their business strategies in order to remain competitive. However, any successful adaptations will require the parties to be alive to the legal policies that govern and impact innovation. Specifically, collaborations between industry and academia may give rise to complex issues arising from the management of innovation, intellectual property, and competition.[27] Under what circumstances, if any, can collaborative R&D and licensing of intellectual property between public research organizations and industry be enjoined

---

[25]   Bart Clarysse, Mike Wright, Johan Bruneel, and Aarti Mahajan, *Creating Value in Ecosystems: Crossing the Chasm between Knowledge and Business Ecosystems.* RESEARCH POLICY, 43(7) 1164–1176 (2014); Carolin Plewa, Nisha Korff, Claire Johnson, Gregory Macpherson, Thomas Baaken, and Giselle Camille Rampersad, *The Evolution of University–Industry Linkages – a framework.* JOURNAL OF ENGINEERING AND TECHNOLOGY MANAGEMENT, 30(1), 21–44 (2013).

[26]   Commission Communication, *Improving knowledge transfer between research institutions and industry across Europe: embracing open innovation – implementing the Lisbon agenda* (COM 182, 2007).

[27]   Valentine Korah, *Collaborative Joint Ventures for Research and Development where Markets are Concentrated: The Competition Rules of the Common Market and the Invalidity of Contracts.* FORDHAM INTERNATIONAL LAW JOURNAL, 15(2), 248–302 (1991) which states '[b]usinessmen and politicians tend to believe that any collaboration to innovate must either be neutral or increase competition. … The Commission has tended to stress the negative aspects of collaboration in those industries where few firms are capable of substantial research efforts'. See also WIPO Report, *supra* note 9 which states '[f]irms must weigh the efficiency gains from sharing efforts and knowledge against the risks that partners may act opportunistically'.

on the basis of competition policies? For example, R&D collaborations can be used by industry as a means to lower its R&D costs to bring new drugs to the market cost effectively, but the collaborations can also be used for less altruistic purposes, such as tying up leading research partners in a particular field or delaying the introduction of new technologies to extend the market life of existing technologies.[28] Is it the intention of the R&D Regulation to provide a blanket exemption from competition policy to all collaborations between industry and research institutes, academic bodies, or 'undertakings which supply research and development as a commercial service'?[29] Can the parties of a university–industry collaboration agree to restrict the licensing of resulting intellectual property to all third parties without attracting the scrutiny of competition authorities? Evaluating the competitive effects of specific collaborative agreements can be challenging, especially in the drug discovery and development context where new technologies and their impact on the market are uncertain. For the same reason, economic research is not likely to be able to provide universal guidance on the balance between optimal social and market outcomes because the incentives and benefits for collaboration are highly specific to the technology and dynamics of the industry it relates to.

Policymakers also need to play a role in assessing the effectiveness of existing policies and, where necessary, adapt them to the changes in the innovation landscape or find the most adequate framework to support the commercialization of publicly funded research. Because most universities are principally publically funded, it is imperative that the same public authorities that support and encourage university research activities also provide a legal environment that facilitates the transfer of publically funded research to the market for the benefit of the public. In order to avoid running afoul of competition policy, industry and public research organizations need to understand how to structure their collaboration and management of intellectual property rights. As stated by Louis Berneman, Past President of the Association of University Technology Managers:

---

[28] Luis M.B. Cabral, *R&D Cooperation and Product Market Competition.* INTERNATIONAL JOURNAL OF INDUSTRIAL ORGANIZATION, 18(7), 1033–1047 (2000); Tomaso Duso, Lars-Hendrik Röller, and Jo Seldeslachts, *Collusion through Joint R&D: An Empirical Assessment.* REVIEW OF ECONOMICS AND STATISTICS, 96(2), 349–370 (2014).

[29] WIPO Report, *supra* note 9 at 109, which states '[p]olicymakers are eager to encourage the efficient introduction of new technologies, favoring cooperation; however, they must guard against harmful anticompetitive practices'.

The question is not whether universities should forge closer ties to industry through partnerships and collaborations. Nor is the question whether universities should play an active role in promoting economic development. Rather, today, the relevant question is '*how*' universities should do so. Different universities will define and preserve academic core values differently and adopt differing strategies and tactics in the 'innovation enterprise.' All universities will seek to structure collaborations that provide companies with the competitive advantage they seek while preserving core academic values. Companies, investors, and entrepreneurs are urged to understand and accept that these core values must be preserved. Industry partners must accept universities' obligation to publish research results and educate students with minimal confidentiality restrictions. Companies are also urged to accept university ownership of IP and work with us to collaborate on patent prosecution. Companies must not seek to restrict access to research tools that need to be made broadly accessible. Companies should pay at least the government-negotiated rate for indirect cost recovery. Companies must understand that individual and institutional conflicts of interest and commitment must be managed to preserve the public's confidence in the academic research enterprise. Finally, companies, investors, and entrepreneurs must grant to universities and our faculties an opportunity to participate in the wealth our discoveries help engender. The two worlds – university and industry – can be bridged. In fact, their widely divergent missions and institutional obligations (public vs. private interests) can be complementary, synergistic, and beneficial to all.[30]

B. THE FAULT LINE BETWEEN COMPETITION POLICY AND INTELLECTUAL PROPERTY LAW

The pharmaceutical industry sits on the fault lines between a number of competing policy objectives: intellectual property policy, competition policy, health and safety regulation, and social welfare, and the interaction between these objectives shape and influence the market and the practices of industry.[31] In brief, industry players involved in R&D and innovation seek patent protection to secure their exclusive position in the

---

[30] Louis Berneman *University-Industry Collaborations: Partners in Research Promoting Productivity and Economic Growth*. RESEARCH MANAGEMENT REVIEW, 13(2), 28–37 (2003) at 36 (emphasis added).

[31] Simon Priddis and Simon Constantine, 'The Pharmaceutical Sector, Intellectual Property Rights, and Competition Law in Europe' in Steven Anderman and Ariel Ezrachi (eds), *Intellectual Property and Competition Law: New Frontiers* (Oxford University Press 2011) at 241.

market to protect their profits.[32] The competition authority, which serves the well-being of the market and consumers, has the ability to restrict the exercise of patent rights to ensure market rivalry. The dubious balance between patent rights and competition policy is further complicated by the highly regulated and government influenced environment in which the pharmaceutical industry operates. On the one hand, government intervenes under its public safety mandate through agencies such as the FDA in the US and the EMA in the EU, which regulate the approval, efficacy, and registration of pharmaceutical products. On the other hand, government intervenes under its social welfare mandate by: (i) facilitating and encouraging generic market entry once a product has come off patent; (ii) influencing or setting prices for prescription drugs; and (iii) determining which products will be reimbursed in full or in part under national health schemes. As the largest purchaser of pharmaceuticals, government decisions and actions have a significant and direct economic impact on the industry.[33] As owners of intellectual property adopt more aggressive commercial strategies in their exploitation of intellectual property rights,[34] regulatory authorities have adapted in

---

[32]   See Nicoleta Tuominen, *Patenting Strategies of the EU Pharmaceutical Industry: Regular Business Practice or Abuse of Dominance*. WORLD COMPETITION, 35(1), 27–54 (2012). Industry further claims that 'the patent system balances the interests of the inventor with the broader interests of society at large' because patents enable inventors to eliminate 'free riders' while allowing society to benefit from the knowledge of the inventor.

[33]   See for example Benjamin Zycher, *The Human Cost of Federal Price Negotiations: The Medicare Prescription Drug Benefit and Pharmaceutical Innovation*, Manhattan Medical Institute Medical Progress Report, No. 3, (2006). Medicare is the largest purchaser of prescription medicines in the US. Medicare's significant purchasing power enables it to negotiate large price discounts, which can be translated into savings for taxpayers but reduces the return on investment to the pharmaceutical industry, which in turn may then reduce the funds for the necessary R&D for new innovations. Although there is criticism that this effect would not be significant, the data suggests that the price reduction demanded by Medicare would reduce industry R&D investment by approximately US$5.6–11.6 billion per year. See also Directorate General for Internal Policies, Economic and Scientific Policy Department, *Differences in Costs of and Access to Pharmaceutical Products in the EU* (Study, PE 451.481, 2011). In the EU where Member States have the primary role in providing health care, Member State spending on pharmaceuticals varies significantly. Member State governments take a strong role in regulating national pharmaceutical markets and prices, which also varies across Member States.

[34]   See European Commission Pharmaceutical Sector Inquiry, Final Report, July 8, 2009 with respect to the 'tool box' of strategies employed by industry

response to their interpretation of competition law concepts such as relevant market, market power, and the definition of abuse in an effort to maintain the balance.[35] In this section, the focus will be on how competition policy interacts with patent rights with respect to innovation from an economics perspective in the drug discovery and development context. To understand why and what leads to tension between these two systems, this section examines the different theories that underlie competition law and patent law. This interaction will form the basis of a theoretical framework that will be used in subsequent chapters to analyze and evaluate different licensing arrangements and restraints found in collaborative drug discovery and development agreements. Given the shortage of studies examining competition policy and patent licensing from an economic perspective in the drug discovery and development context, this book attempts to contribute to the existing literature by providing a novel examination of how these elements interact with the integrated drug discovery model and the particular dynamics of the pharmaceutical sector.

Understanding how patent protection and competition policy affect innovative behavior has long been a fertile field in research.[36] It is generally accepted that growth in worldwide R&D expenditure and the shift towards more applied research have led to a surge in patent applications.[37] In earlier literature, patent rights were thought to be inherently anticompetitive by nature because exclusivity prevented others

---

deemed to be potentially problematic from a competition policy point of view, for example, with respect to the anticompetitive intent of industry in obtaining and maintaining patents and the resulting exclusionary and negative effect on innovation.

[35]   Communication from the Commission, *Executive Summary of the Pharmaceutical Sector Inquiry Report,* (COM 351, 2009).

[36]   Steven D. Anderman and John Kallaugher, *Technology Transfer and the New EU Competition Rules: Intellectual Property Licensing after Modernisation.* OXFORD UNIVERSITY PRESS ON DEMAND (2006); Valentine Korah, *Intellectual Property Rights and the EC Competition Rules* (Hart Publishing 2006); Valentine Korah, *Technology Transfer Agreements and the EC Competition Rules* (Clarendon Press 1996); Valentine Korah, *Patent Licensing and EEC Competition Rules Regulation 2349/84* (ESC Publishing 1985).

[37]   Jérôme Danguy, Gaétan de Rassenfosse, and Bruno van Pottelsberghe de la Potterie, *On the Origins of the Worldwide Surge in Patenting: An Industry Perspective on the R&D–Patent Relationship.* INDUSTRIAL AND CORPORATE CHANGE, 23(2), 535–572 (2014) and Samuel Kortum and Josh Lerner, *What is Behind the Recent Surge in Patenting?* RESEARCH POLICY, 28(1), 1–22 (1999) observed that IP rights are being used more intensively to protect technologies and as defensive mechanisms.

from using the technology, therefore, limiting competition.[38] One may argue that patent ownership of key technologies for which few substitutes exist can lead to concentrated markets and restrict competition. In concentrated markets, consumers have less product choice and there would be insufficient competitive pressure to innovate. On the other hand, one can also argue that patents incentivize innovation by preventing free-riding.[39] The disclosure requirement enables improvement inventions and the temporary nature of exclusive rights granted induces continuing innovation to maintain a competitive edge. As a trade-off for incentivizing innovation, a certain amount of restriction should therefore be tolerated. However, the sole right to exploit does not mean market forces are allowed free rein or that the scope of patent rights should be unconstrained.[40] One of the main purposes of competition law continues to be the regulation of the exercising of intellectual property rights.[41]

---

[38] See for example Willard K. Tom and Joshua A. Newberg, *Antitrust and Intellectual Property: From Separates Spheres to Unified Field.* ANTITRUST LAW JOURNAL, 66(1), 167–229 (1997) at 171; Dina Kallay, *The Law and Economics of Antitrust and Intellectual Property* (Edward Elgar Publishing 2004) at 8; Louis Kaplow, *The Patent-Antitrust Intersection: A Reappraisal.* HARVARD LAW REVIEW, 1813–1892 (1984) at 1817.

[39] The Commission has acknowledged that 'without effective means of enforcing intellectual property rights, innovation and creativity are discouraged and investment diminished'. See Council Directive 2004/48/EC, of 29 April, 2004, on the enforcement of intellectual property rights, OJ L 195/16–25, recital 3.

[40] In *Consten & Grundig*, the Court made a key distinction between the existence and exercise of IPRs, implying there is a line between permissible and impermissible exercise of IPRs. See joined Cases 56 and 58–64, *Établissements Consten S.à.R.L. and Grundig-Verkaufs-GmbH v Commission of the European Economic Community*, ECR [1966] 429. The distinction was further elaborated in *Deutsche Grammophon Gesellschaft v Metro-SB-Grossmärkte GmbH* Case 78/70 [1971] ECR 487.

[41] See Valentine Korah, *The Interface Between Intellectual Property and Antitrust: The European Experience.* ANTITRUST LAW JOURNAL, 69(3), 801–839 (2002) at 801. Although the inherent tension between competition policy and intellectual property appears to be apparent, it has been recognized as simplistic and wrong. See for example, Tom et al., *supra* note 38 on the 'marked reduction in antitrust hostility toward intellectual property' in the US in the last 50 years; Ioannis Lianos, *Competition Law and Intellectual Property Rights: Is the Property Rights Approach Right?* CAMBRIDGE YEARBOOK OF EUROPEAN LEGAL STUDIES, 8, 153 (2005); Vivien Rose and David Bailey, 'EU Competition Law and its Territorial Reach' in Vivien Rose and David Bailey (eds), *Bellamy & Child European Union Law of Competition* (7th edn, Oxford University Press 2013). See also Communication from the Commission, *A Single*

Although patents are not presumed to automatically grant market power resulting in economic monopolies, the *use* of patent rights in certain circumstances may give rise to competition concerns.

Over time, the attitude towards patent law and competition policy became more tolerant.[42] Although patents are not presumed to automatically grant market power resulting in economic monopolies, the *use* of patent rights in certain circumstances may give rise to competition concerns.[43] In the drug discovery and development context, it is generally accepted that patent law plays a key role in incentivizing the creation of new pharmaceutical products by granting a time-limited exclusivity that is intended to be compensatory in nature.[44] The exclusive right provided

---

Market for Intellectual Property Rights. Boosting Creativity and Innovation to Provide Economic Growth, High Quality Jobs and First Class Products and Services in Europe (COM 287, 2011) at 6. The EC states that 'rigorous application of competition rules' could counterbalance intellectual property policy based on strong protection and enforcement of intellectual property rights. See also Communication from the Commission, *An Industrial Property Rights Strategy for Europe* (COM 465/3, 2008) at 2 and 9.

[42]   See for example, Michael Lehmann, *The Theory of Property Rights and the Protection of Intellectual and Industrial Property*. INTERNATIONAL REVIEW OF INDUSTRIAL PROPERTY AND COPYRIGHT LAW, 16(5), 525–540 (1985), which stated 'industrial property rights may be viewed as competitive restrictions which can actively serve the advancement of competition in a modern industrial society, so that in truth, a logical connection and no contradiction exists between the monopolistic intangible property rights and protection of the institution of competition'. However, in hardcore cases, conflict between IPRs and competition policy remains. For example, see the Court of First Instance interim decision in Case T-184/01 R *IMS v Commission* ECR [2001] page II-3193 paragraph 144. '[T]he characterization of the refusal to license at issue in the present proceedings as abusive turns, prima facie, on the correctness of the Commission's interpretation of the case-law concerning the scope of the exceptional circumstances. It is this case-law which explains the clearly special situations in which the objective pursued by Article [102] may prevail over that underlying the grant of intellectual property rights.

[43]   A balance has to be struck between promoting innovation and dynamic competition and maintaining market rivalry in a way that reflects the policy goals of both competition law and patent law. Nancy T. Gallini and Michael Trebilcock, 'Intellectual Property Rights and Competition Policy: A Framework for Analysis of Economic and Legal Issues' in Robert D. Anderson and Nancy T. Gallini (eds), *Competition Policy and Intellectual Property Rights in the Knowledge-Based Economy* (University of Calgary Press 2002), Chapter 2, 17–61 at 18.

[44]   Ish Khanna, *Drug Discovery in Pharmaceutical Industry: Productivity Challenges and Trends*. DRUG DISCOVERY TODAY, 17(19), 1088–1102

by patent law is essential to ensure continued investment in R&D in the pharmaceutical industry.[45] One study concluded that an estimated 65% of the drugs on the market would not have been developed at all absent patent protection.[46] A similar study cited that up to 90% of pharmaceutical inventions would not have been developed without patents.[47] Patent rights therefore play an essential role in the innovation process, especially in highly innovative industries such as the pharmaceutical industry. This 'incentive effect' has generally been explained by the argument that the prospect of monopoly profits induces innovation,[48]

(2012); Carlos M. Correa, *Ownership of Knowledge: The Role of Patents in Pharmaceutical R&D*. BULLETIN OF THE WORLD HEALTH ORGANIZATION, 82(10), 784–787 (2004); Rebecca S. Eisenberg, *Patents, Product Exclusivity, and Information Dissemination: How Law Directs Biopharmaceutical Research and Development*. FORDHAM LAW REVIEW, 72, 477 (2003). See also Wesley M. Cohen, Richard R. Nelson and John P. Walsh, *Protecting their Intellectual Assets: Appropriability Conditions and Why US Manufacturing Firms Patent (or Not)* (National Bureau of Economic Research 2000), asserting that patents are more effective in the pharmaceutical industry than in most other industries.

[45] See the remarks of J. Thomas Rosch, Commissioner, Federal Trade Commission, *The Role of Static and Dynamic Analysis in Pharmaceutical Antitrust* at the Fifth Annual In-House Counsel Forum on Pharmaceutical Antitrust (18 February 2010) (http://www.ftc.gov/speeches/rosch/100218pharma antitrust.pdf): 'Thus it appears that patent protection may stimulate innovation in the pharmaceutical industry to a far greater degree than in other industries. This is not entirely surprising, given the large upfront costs and degree of risk developing a new product and the relative ease of copycat products'. Also see the Recital 2 of Council Regulation (EEC) No 1768/92 of 18 June 1992 concerning the creation of a supplementary protection certificate for medicinal products: 'Whereas medicinal products, especially those that are the result of long, costly research will not continue to be developed in the Community and in Europe unless they are covered by favourable rules that provide for sufficient protection to encourage such research'.

[46] Roy Levy, *FTC Bureau of Economics Staff Report – The Pharmaceutical Industry: A Discussion of Competitive and Antitrust Issues in an Environment of Change* (Diane Publishing 1999).

[47] Edwin Mansfield, *Patents and Innovation: An Empirical Study*. MANAGEMENT SCIENCE, 32(2), 173–181 (1986).

[48] Joseph A. Schumpeter, *Capitalism, Socialism and Democracy* (Routledge 2013). See also Rebecca Eisenberg, *Patents and the Progress of Science: Exclusive Rights and Experimental Use*. THE UNIVERSITY OF CHICAGO LAW REVIEW, 56(3), 1017–1086 (1989) at 1037; Mark A. Lemley, *A New Balance Between IP and Antitrust*. SOUTHWESTERN JOURNAL OF LAW & TRADE IN THE AMERICAS, 13, 237 (2007) at 241.

suggesting that the exclusivity associated with patent rights alone will induce investments for R&D. This 'Schumpeter theory' takes a long-term vision of the market and argues that short-term anticompetitive effects should not be corrected even if the market does not function optimally for a period of time because ongoing innovation will eventually correct the market.[49] For example, when Viagra became available in 1998, it dominated the market with 92% of global market sales in 2000.[50] In 2003, after enjoying a five-year monopoly position, competing products such as Cialis entered the market and Viagra's market share gradually dropped to 52% by 2008.[51] As such, Schumpeter believed that monopolists would lead to more innovation.[52] Schumpeter did not believe there was a role for competition law if the standard of an optimal market is achieving 'perfect competition'.[53] Because the theory identifies innovation as the driving force behind introducing new products and processes, it is often viewed in the literature as one of the most appropriate economic theories to apply to the highly innovative nature of drug discovery and development.[54]

---

[49]   Schumpeter, ibid., at 83. See also Mariateresa Maggiolino, 'The Economics of Antitrust and Intellectual Property Rights' in Steven D. Anderman and Ariel Ezrachi (eds) *Intellectual Property and Competition Law: New Frontiers* (Oxford University Press 2011) at 84.

[50]   Alison Keith, *The Economics of Viagra.* HEALTH AFFAIRS, 19(2), 147–157 (2000).

[51]   Guy David and Sara Markowitz, *Side Effects of Competition: The Role of Advertising and Promotion in Pharmaceutical Markets.* National Bureau of Economics Research (2011).

[52]   Schumpeter, *supra* note 48; Sanghoon Ahn, *Competition, Innovation and Productivity Growth: A Review of Theory and Evidence*, OECD Working Paper (2002) .

[53]   See for example Michael A. Carrier, *Resolving the Patent-Antitrust Paradox through Tripartite Innovation.* VANDERBILT LAW REVIEW, 56(4), 1046 (2003), arguing that protecting innovation should be the primary goal of competition policy and that all practices that are necessary for innovation, even if there is a limitation of competition in the markets, should be permitted.

[54]   Because of the highly innovative nature of the pharmaceutical industry, an assessment of anticompetitive behavior within the sector would lend itself well to an analysis based on dynamic competition. Illustrative literature on the role of dynamic versus static competition in competition law and highly innovative industries can be found, for example, in Gregory Sidak and David J. Teece, *Dynamic Competition in Antitrust Law.* JOURNAL OF COMPETITION LAW AND ECONOMICS, 5(4), 581–631 (2009) and Douglas H. Ginsburg and Joshua D. Wright, *Dynamic Analysis and the Limits of Antitrust Institutions.* ANTITRUST LAW JOURNAL, 78(1), 12–48 (2012) .

Another line of argument suggests the application of competition law to protect market rivalry, which creates the competitive pressure necessary to motivate innovation among rivals to achieve a competitive advantage in the market.[55] This 'Arrow theory' argues that competitive markets provide stronger incentives for innovation than the promise of future monopoly profits.[56] This principle is arguably demonstrated in the *Microsoft* case[57] where the courts leveled the playing field to encourage potential market entrants to innovate.[58]

Another school of thought is that competition law should primarily protect consumer welfare and only intervene in exceptional circumstances to achieve economic efficiency or if consumers are harmed.[59] Essentially, the 'Chicago School' believes that the market is inherently self-correcting and that market forces will eventually induce behavior resulting in total welfare.[60] The belief in free markets and economic efficiency also means the Chicago School views collaboration and licensing agreements as parties taking the initiative to achieve efficiency through legitimate methods of competition. As such, intervention by competition law should be minimized unless it can be shown that such

---

[55] Luc Peeperkorn, *IP Licenses and Competition Rules: Striking the Right Balance.* WORLD COMPETITION, 26(4), 527 (2003) at 532–533. This is based on Arrow's argument that those who enjoy a monopoly position are less likely to incur the cost of innovating new technologies that will replace their existing technology. See Kenneth Arrow, 'Economic Welfare and the Allocation of Resources for Invention' in *The Rate and Direction of Inventive Activity: Economic and Social Factors* (Princeton University Press 1962) 609–626.

[56] Paul Belleflamme and Cecilia Vergari, *Incentives to Innovate in Oligopolies.* THE MANCHESTER SCHOOL, 79(1), 6–28 (2011).

[57] Case T-201/04 *Microsoft Corp. v Commission of the European Communities (Microsoft)*, ECR [2007] page II-03601.

[58] Christos Genakos, Kai U. Kuhn and John van Reenen, *The European Commission Versus Microsoft: Competition Policy in High-tech Industries*, CENTREPIECE, 12(1), 2–7 (2007).

[59] See for example, Robert H. Lande, *The Rise and (Coming) Fall of Efficiency as the Ruler of Antitrust.* THE ANTITRUST BULLETIN, 33, 429 (1988) at 438–439; Michael S. Jacobs, *Essay on the Normative Foundations of Antitrust Economics.* NORTH CAROLINA LAW REVIEW, 74, 219 (1995) at 228; Richard A. Posner, *The Chicago School of Antitrust Analysis.* UNIVERSITY OF PENNSYLVANIA LAW REVIEW, 127(4), 925–948 (1979) at 928.

[60] Herbert Hovenkamp, *Antitrust Policy after Chicago.* MICHIGAN LAW REVIEW, 84(1) 213–284 (1985) at 226–227.

efforts would create negative effects on the market.[61] In other words, competition policy plays a corrective role in protecting and regulating innovation by intervening in defined circumstances to strike a balance between market rivalry and patent rights.[62] Arguably, this principle is demonstrated in the *IMS Health* case[63] where the court engaged in balancing innovation incentives with protection of competition in an effort to protect consumer welfare and follow-on innovation, explicitly stating that there is a role for competition law to intervene in extreme cases.

Aside from financial incentives, patent rights can be seen as a means to facilitate collaboration and induce R&D investment by allowing the parties with the best knowledge of a particular market or technology to make decisions on how to manage the risks and protect their innovation.[64] In other words, the transactional function of patents (as opposed to the proprietary rights) can itself be seen as an incentive to facilitate collaboration by providing a system by which the parties can organize collaborative R&D in a manner that is most efficient based on their

---

[61]   Posner, *supra* note 59 at 930–931; Frank H. Easterbrook, *Workable Antitrust Policy*. MICHIGAN LAW REVIEW, 84(8), 1696–1713 (1986); Frank H. Easterbrook, *Limits of Antitrust*. TEXAS LAW REVIEW, 63(1), 1–40 (1984).

[62]   Janusz A. Ordover, *Economic Foundations and Considerations in Protecting Industrial and Intellectual Property*. ANTITRUST LAW JOURNAL, 53(3), 503–518 (1984). Arguably, the *IMS* and *Microsoft* cases are examples where the court explicitly engaged in balancing innovation incentives with protection of competition in an effort to protect consumer welfare and follow-on innovation. Case law suggests that there is a role for competition law to intervene in extreme cases. Case T-201/04 *Microsoft Corp. v Commission of the European Communities* (*Microsoft*), ECR [2007] page II-03601 and Case C-418/01, *IMS v NDC Health* (*IMS*), ECR [2004] I-5039.

[63]   Case C-418/01, *IMS v NDC Health* (*IMS*), ECR [2004] I-5039.

[64]   William M. Landes and Richard A. Posner, *The Economic Structure of Intellectual Property Law* (Harvard University Press 2009); James Langenfeld, *Intellectual Property and Antitrust: Steps Toward Striking a Balance*. CASE WESTERN RESERVE LAW REVIEW, 52, 91 (2001) at 93. Because parties never have perfect information when entering into a collaboration, uncertainties and information asymmetries manifest themselves as transaction costs when parties use best efforts to negotiate agreements governing their relationship. See Paul L. Joskow, *Transaction Cost Economics, Antitrust Rules and Remedies*. JOURNAL OF LAW, ECONOMICS AND ORGANIZATION, 18(1), 95–116 (2002) at 96 and Herbert Hovenkamp, *Harvard, Chicago, and Transaction Cost Economics in Antitrust Analysis*, THE ANITRUST BULLETIN, 57(3), 613–662 (2012).

unique knowledge of industry dynamics.[65] As such, the intervention of competition law can have a negative effect on innovation by making it unpredictable, and therefore more costly, to engage in collaborative R&D.[66] This 'transactional cost theory' believes that intervention by competition law to limit or take away the exclusivity granted by patent law will likely have a negative effect on innovation if competition policy can undermine the purpose of patent law.[67] The ex-post intervention by competition law appears to introduce an 'external system' of regulation, values, and rationale to the exercise of intellectual property rights, thereby giving rise to legal uncertainty.[68] However, such an argument assumes that the balancing of interests made under patent law are the same or similar to the balancing that would be made under competition law. In the context of licensing, any balancing made under patent law is incapable of contemplating the manner in which license agreements may be used to restrict competition. Therefore, it only seems logical to accept that competition law at least plays a role in regulating licensing agreements.[69] In the integrated drug discovery and development context, the collaborative R&D and subsequent licensing of successful project results contribute to the innovation process by making pharmaceutical products

---

[65]   Nancy T. Gallini and Suzanne Scotchmer, 'Intellectual Property: When is it the Best Incentive System?' in Adam B. Jaffe, Josh Lerner, and Scott Stern (eds), *Innovation Policy and the Economy* (MIT Press 2002) Volume 2, 51–78 at 51; Bronwyn H. Hall and Dietmar Harhoff, *Recent Research on the Economics of Patents*, National Bureau of Economic Research (2012).

[66]   The parties' ability and freedom to manage the risks and uncertainties of a relationship, as well as the costs associated with doing so, can negatively affect the cost benefit of licensing technology and thus affect the parties' willingness to enter into a collaborative relationship. See John W. Schlicher, *Some Thoughts on the Law and Economics of Licensing Biotechnology Patent and Related Property Rights in the United States*. JOURNAL OF THE PATENT AND TRADEMARK OFFICE SOCIETY, 69, 263 (1987) at 266–267.

[67]   Alison Jones and Brenda Sufrin, *EU Competition Law: Text, Cases, and Materials* (Oxford University Press 2014) Chapter 1 at 31.

[68]   See Ilkka Rahnasto, *Intellectual Property Rights, External Effects and Antitrust Law: Leveraging IPRs in the Communications Industry* (Oxford University Press 2003); Thorsten Käseberg, *Intellectual Property, Antitrust and Cumulative Innovation in the EU and the US* (Bloomsbury Publishing 2012).

[69]   Nancy T. Gallini and Michael Trebilcock, 'Intellectual Property Rights and Competition Policy: A Framework for Analysis of Economic and Legal Issues' in Robert D. Anderson and Nancy T. Gallini (eds), *Competition Policy and Intellectual Property Rights in the Knowledge-Based Economy* (University of Calgary Press 2002) at 331.

available that would otherwise not be on the market. As such, competition law has a role in protecting the agreements governing the collaboration. By reducing the transactional hazards associated with creating the relationship between industry and integrated drug discovery organizations, discoveries have a greater likelihood of being translated into products for the benefit of the public. However, transactional efficiencies may give rise to competitive concerns. Because licensing agreements are characterized by high transaction costs, the incorporation of restrictive clauses and clauses to manage future events may be used to offset risks.[70]

The European Commission clearly recognizes that competition law and intellectual property law work in a complementary manner to benefit consumer welfare by ensuring the efficient allocation of economic resources and encouraging investment in R&D, thereby promoting innovation.[71] Intellectual property law protects technological advances and the profits derived therefrom as a reward for innovating and as a means to recoup investments incurred. Competition law keeps market power granted by intellectual property rights in check to a certain extent so as not to discourage R&D investment and ongoing advances in technology. The key issue is to determine where the equilibrium lies between innovation and healthy competition in the market.

---

[70]   Richard E. Caves, Harold Crookell, and Peter Killing, *The Imperfect Market for Technology Licenses.* OXFORD BULLETIN OF ECONOMICS AND STATISTICS, 45(3), 249–257 (1983); Deepak Somaya, Youngjun Kim, and Nicolas S. Vonortas, *Exclusivity in Licensing Alliances: Using Hostages to Support Technology Commercialization.* STRATEGIC MANAGEMENT JOURNAL, 32(2), 159–186 (2011).

[71]   Communication from the Commission, *Guidelines on the application of Article 101 of the Treaty on the Functioning of the European Union to technology transfer agreements*, Official Journal C89, 28.03.2014, 3-50 (hereinafter referred to as 'TTBER Guidelines') at paragraph 7, which states that intellectual property law and competition law both 'share the same basic objective of promoting consumer welfare and an efficient allocation of resources. Innovation constitutes an essential and dynamic component of an open and competitive market economy. Intellectual property rights promote dynamic competition by encouraging undertakings to invest in developing new or improved products and processes. So does competition by putting pressure on undertakings to innovate. Therefore, both intellectual property rights and competition are necessary to promote innovation and ensure competitive exploitation thereof'.

C. INTRODUCTION TO ARTICLE 101: ANTICOMPETITIVE AGREEMENTS

Since strategic collaborations between integrated drug discovery organizations and industry are brought about by means of agreements, from a competition law perspective, Article 101 is the principal instrument for regulating the collaboration agreements. When an integrated drug discovery organization and an industry partner enters into an agreement to carry out research and development for the purpose of achieving proof of concept, and ultimately, to facilitate commercialization of a pharmaceutical product, does such an agreement fall into the scope of Article 101 of the TFEU?

Article 101(1) (previously known as Article 81 of the EC Treaty) prohibits agreements between undertakings that have as their object or effect the prevention, restriction, or distortion of competition between Member States within the common market. Any such agreement shall be void under Article 101(2), unless the agreement falls within one of the exceptions set out in Article 101(3). Article 101 scrutinizes the contractual terms included in an agreement between two undertakings that may give rise to competition concerns, whereas Article 102 (as described in greater detail in Chapter 7) is concerned with the way intellectual property rights are used during exploitation. Within the scope of Article 101 are several block exemptions. Broadly speaking, the purpose of the block exemptions is to define certain categories of agreements that satisfy the conditions of Article 101(3) so as to qualify for an exemption from Article 101(1) if the agreement fulfills the list of conditions set out in the block exemption. The R&D Regulation provides self-assessment factors on how parties may collaborate on R&D without violating competition law. As described in greater detail in Chapter 4, the R&D Regulation sets out the circumstances where R&D agreements may be exempt, even if they contain provisions relating to the transfer of technology, so long as the assignment or license is not the primary object of the agreement but merely incidental and necessary to carry out the R&D. If the licensing component in the agreement is not considered incidental to the object of the agreement, as in the present case where the collaborative drug discovery and development agreement includes commercialization options such as a separate but related licensing arrangement, TTBER sets out the basis for exemption of agreements relating to the transfer of technology under prescribed circumstances. As described in greater detail in Chapter 5, agreements that fulfill the conditions laid down in TTBER benefit from the safe harbor.

Agreements that fall outside the scope of the R&D Regulation or TTBER are not, however, presumed to be contrary to Article 101 and could still qualify for individual exemption on the basis of Article 101(3).[72] Although competition policy tolerates some contractual limitations in respect of intellectual property rights, if the anticompetitive effects of a restriction outweighs its pro-competitive effects or if the restriction falls into a category known as hardcore restrictions, such circumstances can give rise to competition concerns and will not be tolerated.

D. APPLICABILITY OF ARTICLE 101(1)

The first consideration is the legal qualification of the collaboration agreement between integrated drug discovery organizations and industry to determine whether such collaborations fall within the scope of Article 101, which reads as follows:

1. The following shall be prohibited as incompatible with the internal market: all agreements between undertakings, decisions by associations of undertakings and concerted practices which may affect trade between Member States and which have as their object or effect the prevention, restriction or distortion of competition within the internal market, and in particular those which:
    (a) directly or indirectly fix purchase or selling prices or any other trading conditions;
    (b) limit or control production, markets, technical development, or investment;
    (c) share markets or sources of supply;
    (d) apply dissimilar conditions to equivalent transactions with other trading parties, thereby placing them at a competitive disadvantage;
    (e) make the conclusion of contracts subject to acceptance by the other parties of supplementary obligations which, by their nature or according to commercial usage, have no connection with the subject of such contracts.
2. Any agreements or decisions prohibited pursuant to this Article shall be automatically void.
3. The provisions of paragraph 1 may, however, be declared inapplicable in the case of any agreement or category of agreements between undertakings; any decision or category of decisions by associations of undertakings; or any concerted practice or category of concerted practices,

---

[72]   This two-part analysis is confirmed by the General Court's ruling in Case T-328/03 *O2 (Germany) GmbH & Co. OHG v Commission* [2006] ECR page II-1231 at paragraph 71.

which contributes to improving the production or distribution of goods or to promoting technical or economic progress, while allowing consumers a fair share of the resulting benefit, and which does not:

(a) impose on the undertakings concerned restrictions which are not indispensable to the attainment of these objectives;

(b) afford such undertakings the possibility of eliminating competition in respect of a substantial part of the products in question.

i. What is an 'Undertaking'?

The term 'undertaking' is not defined in the TFEU but has been interpreted in various decisions to mean an entity that carries out an 'economic activity'.[73] Following such a definition, a pharmaceutical company clearly engages in commercial 'economic activity'[74] and qualifies as an undertaking. However, does an integrated drug discovery organization carry out 'economic activity'? The purpose of defining the term 'undertaking' is to determine whether competition rules apply to certain entities and whether the activities of such entities are a result of independent conduct.[75] These issues become less clear when public bodies are involved because an entity may be an undertaking for the

---

[73]   See *Federación Nacional de Empresas de Instrumentación Científica, Médica, Técnica y Dental (FENIN) v Commission of the European Communities*, Case T-319/99, where the CFI found 'Whilst an entity may wield very considerable economic power, even giving rise to a monopsony, it nevertheless remains the case that, if the activity for which that entity purchases goods is not an economic activity, it is not acting as an undertaking for the purposes of Community competition law and is therefore not subject to the prohibitions laid down in Articles 81(1) EC and 82 EC'. Similarly, in *Höfner and Elser v Macrotron GmbH* (1991) ECR I-1979, Case C-41/90, the ECJ held that 'the concept of an undertaking encompasses every entity engaged in an economic activity, regardless of the legal status of the entity or the way in which it is financed'. This was also supported in Case C-244/94 *Fédération Française des Sociétés d'Assurances and Others v Ministère de l'Agriculture et de la Pêche* (1996) ECR I-4013 at paragraph 14. Note that the EEA Agreement defines an undertaking as 'any entity carrying out activities of a commercial or economic nature', Article 1 of Protocol 22.

[74]   An activity is economic in nature when it involves 'offering goods or services on the market'. See for example Case C-35/96 *Commission v Italy* [1998] ECR I-3851, [1998] 5 CMLR 889, paragraph 36; Case T-513/93 *CNSD v Commission* [2000] ECR II-180, [2000] 5 CMLR 614, paragraph 36.

[75]   Rose and Bailey, *supra* note 41.

purpose of some of its activities but not for others, depending on the nature of the activity being scrutinized.[76]

Traditionally, the role of public research organizations such as universities has been to facilitate the development of knowledge and dissemination of ideas for the purpose of advancing education. However, in today's knowledge intensive society, universities have become key institutions in the generation and dissemination of knowledge, with a direct impact on social and economic development. Many universities today have a technology transfer office (TTO) whose role is to identify research and technological developments and devise strategies to exploit them to ensure their accessibility to a wider range of users. As such, the activities of TTOs and integrated drug discovery in supplying research and development as a commercial service may be considered 'economic activities'. The literature supports a functional approach to construing whether an entity is an undertaking,[77] taking into account its actions, the context in which it operates, and the purpose and effect of its activities.[78] According to the ECJ, the offering of goods or services on the market[79] or activity that can be carried out by an undertaking to make a profit constitutes 'economic activity', regardless of whether the entity in fact makes a profit or if it is set up for an economic purpose and regardless of how it is financed.[80] The ECJ specifically recognized the need to

---

[76]   See for example the Opinion of AG Jacobs in Case C-264/01 *AOK Bundeverband* [2004] ECR I-2493, [2004] 4 CMLR 1261 at paragraph 25 where a functional approach to the definition of undertaking was adopted.

[77]   For example, see Case C-475/99, *Firma Ambulanz Glöckner v Landkreis Südwestpfalz* [2001] ECR I-8089, paragraph 72 and Case C-49/07, *Motosykletis-tiki Omospondia Ellados NPID (MOTOE) v Elliniko Dimosio* [2008] ECR I-4863, paragraph 25. Furthermore, in the Opinion of Advocate General Francis Jacobs in joined cases C-264/01, C-306/01, C354/01, and C-355/01 *AOK Budesverband and Others v Ichthyol-Gesellschaft Cordes and Others*, delivered May 22, 2003 at paragraph 25: '... the Court's general approach to whether a given entity is an undertaking within the meaning of the Community competition rules can be described as functional, in that it focuses on the type of activity performed rather than on the characteristics of the actors which perform it, the social objectives associated with it, or the regulatory or funding arrangements to which it is subject in a particular Member State. Provided that an activity is of an economic character, those engaged in it will be subject to Community competition law'.

[78]   Case C-159 & 160/91, *Poucet and Pistre*, joined cases, [1993] ECR I-637.

[79]   Case C-205/03 *FENIN v Commission* (11/07/2006) ECR I-6295, para. 25.

[80]   See Case C-41/90, *Höfner and Elser v Macrotron GmbH* [1991] ECR I-1979 where the Court of Justice said 'in the context of competition law ... the

consider the nature of activities carried out by a public body to determine if it is economic in nature in order to justify the application of competition rules.[81] As such, case law seems to suggest that the focus of the assessment is therefore on the *nature* of the particular activity, not the nature of the organization that undertakes the activity, whether it is a publically funded or not-for-profit entity.

In the case of the Centre for Drug Research and Development (CDRD), Ventures is the for-profit entity that enters the strategic collaboration agreement with industry to facilitate the commercialization of the drug development projects, while CDRD (a not-for-profit entity) facilitates the actual R&D. The nature of the activities carried out by Ventures include the negotiation and licensing of the successful pre-validated drug development projects resulting from the efforts of CDRD and the in-licensing of technologies from industry and other research institutions to further develop and commercialize such technologies jointly. Since Ventures is offering and supplying a service for profit (by way of future royalties), Ventures will likely be considered an under-taking under Article 101(1) because of the commercial nature of its activities (and its nature as a for-profit organization, despite being publically funded). As such, any collaboration agreement between industry and Ventures will likely be subject to the scrutiny of Article 101. The 'effects doctrine'[82] of jurisdiction means that Article 101 applies to all undertakings situated inside the EU and to those based elsewhere if the anticompetitive effects are felt within the EU. As such, Article 101 could apply to international collaborations between CDRD and an industry partner in the EU.[83]

---

concept of an undertaking encompasses every entity engaged in economic activity, regardless of its legal status or the way in which it is financed'. This test has been affirmed and applied in many subsequent cases such as Case T-513/93, *Consiglio Nazionale degli Spedizionieri Doganali v Commission* [2000] ECR II-1807, para 36; Cases C-189/02P, etc., *Dansk Rørindustri v Commission* [2005] ECR I-5425, [2005] 5 CMLR 796, para 112.

[81]   Case C-343/95 *Diego Cali & Figli Srl v Servizi Ecologici Porto di Genova SpA (SPEG)* (1997) ECR I-547.

[82]   See for example, European Commission Directorate-General for Competition, *Glossary of Terms Used in EU Competition Policy* (2002). The effects doctrine was embraced by the Court of First Instance of 25.3.1999 in Case T-102/96, *Gencor Ltd v Commission* [1999] ECR, p. II-0753, at paragraphs 89–92.

[83]   As long as the agreement or concerted practice is implemented within the internal market, an undertaking situated outside the internal market is still an undertaking for the purposes of Article 101(1). See for example Cases 89/95,

The Centre for Drug Design and Discovery (CD3) is a project group within KU Leuven Research and Development (LRD), which is the legal entity that enters into collaboration and licensing agreements with industry partners. More specifically, LRD enters into the agreements on behalf of the university. The fact that a university is entrusted with a public service task does not exclude it from the application of competition rules. Where a university is acting as an entity to fulfill a public function, such as to provide tertiary education, the Commission has noted that universities are not to be considered to be engaging in economic activity, and are therefore not undertakings for the purpose of competition rules.[84] However, universities engage in many different activities other than providing tertiary education, some of which are commercial in nature.[85] As such, a university may be considered an undertaking in respect of its activities that are economic in nature. If the activity in question could, even in principle, be carried out by a private undertaking for profit, then the university can be classified as an undertaking.[86] Given that the activities of LRD include delivering research services (a task that CROs perform for a fee) and/or licensing technology to industry, it would appear that LRD will also be considered an undertaking for the purposes of Article 101(1).

Similar to the analysis with respect to CDRD and Ventures, because the Lead Discovery Centre (LDC) is structured as a limited liability company and because its activities include providing drug development and project management services to help early stage research in pharmaceutical leads reach proof of concept, it is also likely to fall within the purview of Article 101(1). However, with respect to the projects funded wholly by the Max Planck Fund, an argument can be made that the

---

etc., *Ahlstrom Osakeyhtio v Commission ('Wood Pulp I')* [1988] 4 CMLR 901 paragraphs 12–13.

[84] Commission, *Community framework for state aid for research and development and innovation* (OJ C 323/01, 2006) at Article 3.1.1.

[85] The difficulty in assessing the nature of activity carried out by the State or State entity is described as '… the Court is entering dangerous territory, since it must find a balance between the need to protect undistorted competition on the market and respect for the powers of the Member States. The power of the State, which is exercised in the political sphere is subject to democratic control. A different type of control is imposed on economic operators acting on a market; their conduct is governed by competition law'. See Case C-205/03P *FENIN v Commission* [2006] ECR I-6295, [2006] 5 CMLR 559 Opinion of A.G. Maduro, paragraph 26.

[86] See Case C-41/90, *Höfner and Elser v Macrotron GmbH* [1991] ECR I-1979.

nature of LDC's activities for such projects is merely an exercise of the powers mandated by the fund to carry out State prerogatives, namely, to conduct basic research.[87] As discussed in Chapter 2, the biggest funder of LDC is the Max Planck Fund, which is a public source of funding. Projects receiving financial support from the Max Planck Fund are only permitted to pursue basic research activity and not applied activity. The exercise of 'public functions' is not deemed to constitute economic activity, even if there is a commercial aspect to the activity in question.[88] In other words, as long as the activities of LDC on a project funded by the Max Planck Fund are an integral part of and in keeping with the given mandate approved by the public authority, the actions of the LDC should not be construed as activities of an economic nature.[89] As noted above, the exercise of certain 'public powers' by an entity does not prevent other activities carried out by the same entity from being subject to competition law.

With respect to Medical Research Council Technology (MRCT), as an independent charity with a mandate to ensure technological progress in human health and medical research, it is arguable that the nature of the activities of MRCT is that of a public function. Historically, MRC (the predecessor of MRCT) was a publically funded organization dedicated to research relating to the improvement of human health. Over the years, MRC evolved into playing a commercial liaison role through its laboratory-based technology transfer operation and its office-based patenting and licensing activities, thereby forging ties with industry. Since the creation of MRCT as an integrated drug development organization, MRCT now receives funding from MRC and royalties from prior successful projects to work with industry and academic partners to translate scientific discoveries into commercial products. As such, it would appear that the scope of MRCT's activities have evolved into being economic in nature and therefore are considered an undertaking for the purposes of Article 101(1).

---

[87] In Case C-113/07PSELEX *Sistemi Integrati v Commission* [2009] ECR I-2207, [2009] 4 CMLR 1083, paragraph 102, the Court of Justice held that it is not necessary for the activity concerned to be essential or indispensable to achieving the public function before it is treated as ancillary to that public function; what matters is that the activity is connected with that function.

[88] See *Diego* case, *supra* note 81.

[89] Case C-364/92 *SAT Fluggesellschaft v Eurocontrol* [1994] ECR I-43, paragraph 28.

ii.   Does the Collaboration Agreement Affect Trade?

The Commission guidelines on the concept of effect on trade as it relates to Articles 81 and 82 (currently Articles 101 and 102) explain that the effect on trade must be appreciable for the purpose of Article 101(1).[90] Trade relates to all economic activities relating to goods, as well as services,[91] and the ECJ has held that trade could be affected by an agreement if it has a direct or indirect, or actual or potential effect on the flow of trade between Member States.[92] In other words, it is sufficient to demonstrate that the agreement is *capable* of affecting trade without needing to demonstrate whether trade between Member States has actually been affected.[93] As stated by the ECJ in *Windsurfing International Inc. v Commission:*

> Community law on competition applies to agreements between undertakings, which may affect trade between Member States. Only if the agreement as a whole is capable of affecting trade is it necessary to examine which are the clauses of the agreement, which have as their object or effect a restriction or distortion of competition. In a case such as the present one in which there is no doubt as to the significance of the agreements at issue for trade between Member States, it is therefore unnecessary to examine whether each clause restricting competition, taken in isolation, may affect intra-community trade.[94]

iii.   'Prevention, Restriction or Distortion of Competition'

The final consideration is whether the agreement between industry and integrated drug discovery organizations 'have as their object or effect the prevention, restriction or distortion of competition within the internal market' in the manners set out in Article 101(1)(a) to 101(1)(e). The

---

[90]   Commission Notice, *Guidelines on the effect on trade concept contained in Articles 81 and 82 of the Treaty* (OJ C101/07, 2004).

[91]   See for example *Reuter/BASF*, OJ 1976 L254/40, [1976] 2 CMLR D44, relating to the provision of consulting services by an individual, and Cases C-180/98 to C-184/98 *Pavel Pavlov and Others v Stichting Pensioenfonds Medische Specialisten* [2000] ECR I-6451, [2001] 4 CMLR 30 with respect to the supply of professional services, such as specialist medical services, all of which have been held to be 'trade' for the purposes of Article 101(1).

[92]   *Consten & Grundig, supra* note 40 at 341. See also Case 42/84 *Remia and others v Commission* (1985) ECR 2545, paragraph 22.

[93]   Case C-219/95 P *Ferriere Nord v Commission* (1997) ECR I-4411 at paragraph 19.

[94]   Case 193/83 *Windsurfing International Inc. v Commission* (1986) ECR 611 at paragraphs 96 and 97.

concept of restriction of competition is controversial and continues to be widely debated among scholars.[95] The analysis of the distinction between 'object or effect' is typically difficult because most agreements, especially those that are commercial in nature, usually restrict competition in some manner but enhance it in others.[96] An object to restrict competition limits the analysis to the agreements and its content, while the effects analysis considers the subjective intent of parties.[97] The approach taken by the ECJ has been to analyze the agreement in its legal and economic context by determining the purpose of the agreement.[98] If an agreement is not designed to be restrictive,[99] then its effect must be considered in its economic and legal context. This applied specifically to situations where the absence of the restraint would lead to no rivalry at all on the market; for example, if without the restraint (such as exclusivity) the distributor would not have accepted the agreement and no

---

[95]   See for example, Renato Nazzini, *Article 81 EC between Time Present and Time Past: A Normative Critique of 'Restriction of Competition' in EU Law.* COMMON MARKET LAW REVIEW, 43(2), 497–536 (2006); Jan Peeters, *The Rule of Reason Revisited: Prohibition on Restraints of Competition in the Sherman Act and the EEC Treaty.* THE AMERICAN JOURNAL OF COMPARATIVE LAW, 37(3), 521–570 (1989); Valentine Korah, *The Rise and Fall of Provisional Validity: The Need for a Rule of Reason in EEC Antitrust.* NORTH WESTERN JOURNAL OF INTERNATIONAL LAW AND BUSINESS, 3, 320 (1981) at 346; O. Odudu, *Interpreting Article 81(1): Demonstrating Restrictive Effect. European Law Review*, 26(4), 379–390 (2001).

[96]   Rose and Bailey, *supra* note 41.

[97]   Case C-209/07 *Competition Authority v Beef Industry Development Society and Barry Brothers*, ECR [2008] I-8637, paragraph 21, which argued that it is not enough to establish that there is merely a potential restriction of competition. There must be a certain economic impact.

[98]   Case 56/65 *Société La Technique Minère v Maschinenbau Ulm* (1966) ECR 235, (1966) CMLR 357, where the ECJ adopted an economic approach by holding that a market analysis was necessary to determine whether the agreement in question was restrictive to competition. The ECJ also found that the granting of exclusive rights of sale did not 'by their very nature' restrict competition within the meaning of Article 81(1) and that the purpose of the agreement must be considered in the economic context in which it is to be applied. Similarly in joined Cases 96-102, 104, 105, 108, and 110/82 *NV IAZ International Belgium and others v Commission* (1983) ECR 3369, it was held that restrictions by object are identified by examining the terms of the agreement, as drafted, in the legal and economic context in which the specific agreement was concluded, and by the conduct of the parties.

[99]   In *Consten & Grundig*, *supra* note 40, the Court held that if an anticompetitive object can be established, there is no need to evaluate the actual effects of the agreement, even if these would constitute pro-competitive effects.

product would have entered the market.[100] Subsequent case law appears to have adopted the effects test analysis by undertaking economic analysis in individual cases in the form of a market evaluation.[101]

Adopting an economic analysis approach to the agreement between industry and integrated drug discovery organizations, the collaboration does not normally contemplate exploitation by both parties. Only the industry partner will exploit the results of the collaboration in exchange for royalties back to the integrated drug discovery organization. As such, the collaboration agreement will typically not include clauses that could lead to concerns regarding price fixing (Article 101(1)(a)), limitations of output (Article 101(1)(b)), or market partitioning (Article 101(1)(c)). In fact, the difference in the respective activities of integrated drug discovery organizations and industry are such that they are unlikely to be considered competitors in any product market (the competitive relationship between integrated drug discovery organizations and industry will be discussed in greater detail in Chapter 5 in the context of TTBER). The mission of integrated drug discovery organizations is generally to engage in R&D for the purpose of advancing basic research to proof of concept so as to facilitate commercialization. On the other hand, industry is generally in the business of producing and selling pharmaceutical products. Consequently, at first blush, there does not seem to be any competition to be limited. It would seem inconceivable that an agreement between two undertakings with such different missions can be restrictive of competition.

However, the collaboration agreement typically includes clauses that affect how the research results are to be commercialized. For example, the industry partner typically insists on an exclusive license of the results arising from the research project it funded. Depending on the scope of the license with respect to field of use and degree of market power,[102]

---

[100]   Case 56/65 *Société La Technique Minière v Maschinenbau Ulm* (1966) ECR 235, (1966) CMLR 357.

[101]   Joined Cases T- 374/94, T-375/94, T-384/94 and T-388/94 *European Night Services and others v Commission of the European Communities (European Night Services)*, [1998] ECR p. II-3141 and Case C-234/89 Judgment of the Court of 28 February 1991, *Stergios Delimitis v Henninger Bräu AG (Delimitis)*, ECR [1991] I-935.

[102]   In Case 56/65 *Société Technique Minière v Maschinenbau Ulm* [1966] ECR 235, 249, [1966] CMLR 357, 375, the Court of Justice found an exclusive right of sale does not have the object of restricting competition where the exclusive right is necessary for the penetration of a new area by an undertaking. However, in Case T-374/94. etc., *European Night Services v Commission* [1998] ECR II-3141, [1998] 5 CMLR 718, the Commission found that in circumstances

from a competition law perspective, the exclusive license may not be neutral since the integrated drug discovery organization will no longer be able to exploit its research results by licensing them to third parties, including possible competitors of the industry partner. The Court of Justice has held that in order to find a restriction of competition by object, it is not necessary to establish that final consumers are deprived of the advantages of effective competition in terms of supply or price.[103] In other words, the application of Article 101(1) does not require only a direct link to protecting the interests of society but also indirectly through protecting the competitive structure of the market.[104]

E. ARTICLE 101(3) EXEMPTION

The criteria for exempting the prohibition in Article 101(1) are set out in Article 101(3) and can be applied to any agreement regardless of the industry sector concerned.[105] In summary, Article 101(3) includes four cumulative conditions: (i) economic benefit; (ii) consumer benefit; (iii) indispensability; and (iv) no elimination of competition, all of which must be satisfied in order for the exemption to apply.[106] The Commission issued Guidelines on the application of Article 101(3) of the Treaty (the 'Guidelines')[107] as well as an EC report entitled '*Practical methods to assess efficiency gains in the context of Article [101(3)]*' to set out its views and rationale on the application of Article 101(3) in 'typical'

---

of granting an exclusive right, it is necessary to consider the effect of the agreement by analyzing the economic context in which the undertakings operate as well as the actual structure of the market.

[103] Cases C-501/06P, etc. *GlaxoSmithKline Services v Commission* [2009] ECRI-9291, [2010] 4 CMLR 50, paragraph 63.

[104] See for example, Case C-234/89 *Delimitis v Henninger Brau* [1991] ECR I-935, [1992] 5 CMLR 210.

[105] Case T-111/08 *Matra Hachette v Commission* [1994] ECR II-595 paragraph 85; see also Case T-168/01 *GlaxoSmithKline Services v Commission* [2009] ECR I-9291, [2010] 4 CMLR 50, paragraph 233; Case T-111/08 *Mastercard v Commission*, judgment of 24 May 2012 paragraph 199.

[106] An early case establishing this principle is *Consten & Grundig, supra* note 40. Commission decisions showing the application of this principle include Case T-65/98 *Van den Bergh Foods Ltd v Commission (Van den Bergh)* [2003] ECR II-4653, paragraph 137; COMP/38606 *Groupement des Cartes Bancaires*, Decision of 17 October 2007 at paragraph 502.

[107] Communication from the Commission, *Guidelines on the application of Article 101(3)* (OJ C101/97, 2004) (hereinafter referred to as 'Article 101(3) Guidelines').

scenarios.[108] While the Guidelines provide general policy and structure on the assessment of restriction of competition from the Commission's perspective, the Courts by way of case law may override soft law should there be a conflict or difference in interpretation.[109] Consequently, uncertainty may arise when attempting to determine what is binding law whenever there are contradictions between the Commission's view in the Guidelines and any conflicting case law.

The General Court has held that it is only within the specific framework of Article 101(3) that the pro- and anticompetitive aspects of a restriction of competition may be weighed.[110] Article 101(1) should assess whether contractual obligations of an agreement give rise to anticompetitive effect, and if they do Article 101(3) should assess whether the clauses are necessary to perform the agreement. The burden of proof falls on the party claiming the benefit of the Article 101(3) to establish satisfaction of all four criteria.[111] Article 101(3) applies as long as all four conditions are cumulatively fulfilled, and ceases to apply when that is no longer the case, and is therefore sensitive to material changes in facts,[112] so there is an ongoing obligation on the parties to assess for compliance. However, where the benefits of an agreement cannot be

---

[108]   European Commission Directorate-General for Enterprise and Industry, *Practical Methods to Assess Efficiency Gains in the Context of Article 81(3) of the EC Treaty* (Final Report, 2006).

[109]   See for example, paragraph 939 of joined Cases T-191/98, T-212/98 to T-214/98, *Atlantic Container Line AB and Others v Commission of the European Communities*, ECR [2003] II-3275 where the Commission's analysis of the elimination of competition was overruled by the General Court by finding the test could not be interpreted to mean that every time a dominant undertaking is party to an agreement which appreciably restricts competition, that agreement cannot benefit from an exemption under Article 101(3). This overrules paragraph 127 of Commission Notice, *Guidelines on the applicability of Article 81 of the EC Treaty to vertical restraints* (OJ C130/01, 2010) (hereinafter referred to as 'Vertical Guidelines'), stating that if one of the parties to the agreement is dominant, it automatically leads to a finding that no exemption can be given. Compare paragraph 939 in *Atlantic Container* and paragraph 127 of Vertical Guidelines.

[110]   Case T-65/98 *Van den Bergh Foods v Commission* [2003] ECR II-4653, [2004] 4 CMLR 14 paragraph 106.

[111]   Any finding that an agreement demonstrates efficiencies within the meaning of Article 101(3) '… must be founded on a detailed, robust and compelling analysis that relies in its assumptions and deductions on empirical data and facts'. See COMP/34579 *Mastercard* decision of 19 December 2007 paragraph 732.

[112]   Article 101(3) Guidelines, *supra* note 107, paragraphs 44–45.

achieved without considerable investment, the length of time required to ensure a proper return on investment is necessarily an essential factor to be taken into account.[113]

Whether an agreement fulfills the conditions set out in Article 101(3) requires individual assessment, except where agreements include hard-core restrictions (as set out in various block exemptions), which are usually deemed not likely to fulfill all the conditions of exemption.[114] Unilateral conduct, such as refusal to supply, can also be a reason why an agreement may not benefit from Article 101(3) exemption, if, on balance, the disadvantages to competition outweigh the benefits from the agreement.[115] Not all restrictive agreements concluded by a dominant undertaking necessarily constitute an abuse of a dominant position.[116] The possibility that an agreement would enable an undertaking to acquire a dominant position and empower it to subsequently commit an abuse under Article 102 does not preclude the application of Article 101(3),[117] but Article 101(3) will not apply if the agreement affords the undertaking the possibility of eliminating competition in respect of substantial part of the products in question. Qualifying for Article 101(3) exemption does not necessarily prevent application of Article 102[118] but does indirectly bar (in the absence of material change in facts) from a finding that the same agreement constitutes abuse under Article 102.

---

[113] Case T-374/94 *European Night Services v Commission* [1998] ECR II-3141, [1998] 5 CMLR 718, paragraphs 230–231 where the court annulled the exemption granted for eight years when the financing of the project was arranged over 20 years.

[114] Article 101(3) Guidelines, *supra* note 107, paragraph 46; TTBER Guidelines, *supra* note 71, paragraph 37.

[115] Refusal is part of the circumstances surrounding the application of the agreement and must therefore be taken into account when balancing the benefits from the agreement with the disadvantages to competition. See Cases 25 & 26/84 *Ford v Commission* [1985] ECR 2725, [1985] 3 CMLR 528 paragraph 33; Case T-208/01 *Volkswagen v Commission* [2004] ECR II-5141, [2004] 4 CMLR 727 paragraph 51.

[116] Commission decision *Whitbread*, OJ 1999 L88/26, [1999] 5v CMLR 118 paragraphs 155–170.

[117] *Matra Hachette v Commission*, *supra* note 105, paragraphs 124 and 154.

[118] Case C-310/93P *BPB Industries and British Gypsum v Commission* [1995] ECR I-865, [1997] 4 CMLR 238 paragraph 11.

i. Promote Technical and Economic Progress: Economic Benefit Test

The economic benefit test requires that the restrictive clauses objectively create some form of efficiency, such as improving production or distribution of goods, reducing costs, or promoting technical or economic progress.[119] In the *GSK* case, the Court of Justice held that the benefit or improvement must be an appreciable objective advantage of such a character as to compensate for the disadvantages caused by the agreement in the field of competition.[120] In other words, subjective reasons for the agreement that benefits the parties of the agreement cannot in and of themselves fulfill the economic benefit condition,[121] but efficiency gains will likely justify the application of Article 101(3)[122] and should be assessed within the context of the relevant market.[123] The General Court has found that Article 101(3) does not require a specific link with the relevant product market in which competition is restricted.[124] In certain cases, consideration should also be given to advantages arising from the agreement for other markets on which the agreement might have beneficial effects.[125] However, the benefits claimed must directly result from

---

[119]   Case 45/85 *Verband der Sachversichere v Commission* [1987] ECR 405, [1988] 4 CMLR 264 paragraph 58 and Article 101(3) Guidelines, *supra* note 107 at paragraph 48 state that agreements which contribute to improving the provision of services have been held to fulfill the criteria of Article 101(3). The Article 101(3) Guidelines also state that the benefits claimed for an agreement should be substantiated so that the following can be verified: the nature of the claimed efficiencies; the link between the agreement and the efficiencies; the likelihood and magnitude of each claimed efficiency; and how and when each claimed efficiency would be achieved. See paragraphs 51–58.

[120]   See for example joined Cases C-501/06 P, C-513/06 P, C-515/06 P, and C-519/06 P *GlaxoSmithKline Services Unlimited v Commission of the European Communities* [2009] ECR I-9291, paragraph 92. See also Article 101(3) Guidelines *supra* note 107 at paragraph 49 and *Consten & Grundig, supra* note 40.

[121]   Ibid., *Consten & Grundig*.

[122]   Article 101(3) Guidelines, *supra* note 107, paragraph 48.

[123]   Article 101(3) Guidelines *supra* note 107, paragraph 43. In other words, the *nature* of the benefits affects whether the restrictive clause directly relates to provision of the benefit.

[124]   *GSK* case, *supra* note 120 at paragraph 248. See also case T-213/00 CMA *CGM v Commission* [2003] ECR II-2913, [2003] 5CMLR 268, where the General Court indicated at paragraphs 225–227 that it is not even necessary to define the relevant market before applying the first three criteria of Article 101(3).

[125]   *GSK* case, ibid.

the agreement[126] and the benefits must outweigh the negative effects, even if a causal link can be difficult to establish – especially in the case where the benefit relates to the economic conditions of the industry or sector as a whole or where the benefit is not directly related to a specific contractual restriction.[127] The Court of Justice in *GSK* held that it is sufficient for the Commission, on the basis of the arguments of causal link and evidence in its possession, to conclude that an agreement is likely to create appreciable objective advantages so long as the benefits are greater than the disadvantages.[128] The Court of Justice further ruled that an appreciable objective advantage of the agreement should be analyzed as a whole and does not presuppose that all the additional profits flowing from an agreement had to be invested in research and development.[129] In other words, the claimed benefits could relate to the market generally and as a whole and not necessarily compensate in the area for which the negative features relate.

Other forms of benefits such as cost efficiencies may result from economies of scale and from economies of scope.[130] Avoiding duplication of costs, where cooperation enables increased production, the public must receive a fair share of the benefit from the increased efficiencies.[131] In other words, cost savings to the undertakings do not necessarily translate into public benefit unless prices can be lowered, because cost savings may be wholly internalized or appropriated by the parties. Qualitative efficiencies, such as higher quality or new products or improvements being introduced more quickly or at lower costs,[132] or the

---

[126]   Case T-19/91 *Vichy v Commission* [1992] ECR II-415, paragraph 93 and Article 101(3) Guidelines, *supra* note 107 at paragraph 54. However, requiring that the restrictive clause be directly related to the claimed benefit is essentially an assessment of necessity, which is the criterion for the requirement of indispensability.

[127]   Case T-65/98 *Van den Bergh Foods Ltd v Commission* [2003] ECR II-4653, paragraphs 139–143 where the General Court held that an exclusivity clause did not result in an objective advantage that was not severable from the exclusivity. In other words, the court required a causal link between the efficiency enhancing effects of the agreement and restrictive clauses. See also Case 45/85 *Verband der Sachversicherer e.V. v Commission of the European Communities* [1987] ECR 405, paragraphs 60–61.

[128]   *GSK* case, *supra* note 120 at paragraph 93.

[129]   Ibid.

[130]   Article 101(3) Guidelines, *supra* note 107, paragraphs 64–68.

[131]   Case 26/76 *Metro v Commission* [1977] ECR 1875 paragraph 43.

[132]   See for example, Commission decision, *Pasteur Mérieux – Merck*, OJ 1994 L309/1 paragraphs 83 and 85.

more rapid dissemination of advanced technology,[133] can also constitute 'appreciable objective advantages'. In an industry where innovation is an important dimension of competition and where R&D costs are generally funded from income rather than loans, restrictions that optimize income through price discrimination may exceptionally benefit from exemption under Article101(3).[134] Analysis under Article 101(3) arising from horizontal agreements involves the identification of the complementary skills and assets that are combined as a result of the agreement and evaluating whether the resulting efficiencies are such that the conditions of Article 101(3) are met.[135] As such, collaboration agreements may bring together different capabilities that allow parties to produce better products more efficiently and cost effectively, thereby shortening the time for those products to reach the market and leading to a wider dissemination of knowledge at a lower cost.

ii. Consumers Must Receive a Fair Share of the Benefits

An objectively appraised fair share of the economic benefits must be passed on to the consumer.[136] Whether such benefits can be achieved by means other than the contractual restrictions is to be assessed in relation to the indispensability of the restrictions.[137] Consumers include all users of the goods or services concerned in all the relevant markets, meaning the parties do not need to establish that every consumer group receives a benefit, nor that the final consumer receives a net increase in welfare.[138] However, an argument of economic or production efficiency may not

---

[133]   Commission decision, *Olivetti-Digital*, OJ 1994 L309/24 at paragraph 30.

[134]   Case T-168/01 *GSK Services v Commission* [2006] ECR II-2969, [2006] 5 CCMLR 1589.

[135]   Communication from the Commission, *Guidelines on the applicability of Article 101 of the Treaty on the Functioning of the European Union to horizontal co-operation agreements* (OJ C11/01, 2011) (hereinafter referred to as 'Horizontal Guidelines') at paragraphs 51 and 141–146.

[136]   Case C-238/05 *Asnef-Equifax, Servicios de Información sobre Solvencia y Crédito, SL v Ausbanc* [2006] ECR I-11125, paragraphs 67–71. See also the Office of Fair Trading discussion note, *Article 101(3) – A discussion of narrow versus broad definition of benefits* (OFT roundtable, 2010) at paragraphs 5.1–5.16 and A.18–A.23. See also Article 101(3) Guidelines, *supra* note 107, paragraph 88.

[137]   *Matra Hachette v Commission*, *supra* note 105, paragraph 122.

[138]   Horizontal Guidelines, *supra* note 135, paragraph 84. See also Case C-238/05 *Asnef-Equifax, Servicios de Información sobre Solvencia y Crédito, SL v Ausbanc* [2006] ECR I-11125 at paragraph 70.

necessarily translate into benefits to consumers to compensate for any loss caused by the restriction of competition. In other words, agreements with positive long-term effects may not satisfy the consumer benefit requirement.[139] The Guidelines provide guidance on situations where restrictive effects are relatively limited and the efficiencies are substantial (i.e. a detailed analysis is not necessary as it is likely that a fair share of the cost savings will be passed on to consumers) and if the restrictive effects are substantial and the cost savings are relatively insignificant (i.e. a detailed analysis is not necessary as it is very unlikely that any benefit will be passed to the consumer).[140] However, careful analysis of the consumer benefits are required if the agreement gives rise to both significant pro-competitive and anticompetitive effects.[141]

As discussed above, cost efficiencies may constitute an economic benefit but the parties must be able to demonstrate that such efficiencies have been or are likely to be passed on to consumers, taking into account the characteristics and structure of the market, the nature and magnitude of the efficiency gains, and the magnitude of the restriction of competition.[142] The court and commission evaluates the extent of the benefit and compares it with the importance of the restriction of competition.[143] Any such assessment requires value judgment[144] and case law has held that new or improved products and expanded ranges of products and

---

[139]   Phedon Nicolaides, *The Balancing Myth: The Economics of Article 81(1) & (3)*. LEGAL ISSUES OF ECONOMIC INTEGRATION, 32(2), 123–145 (2006) at 124.

[140]   Article 101(3) Guideline, *supra* note 107, paragraphs 90–92.

[141]   See COMP/38287 *Telenor/Canal +/Canal Digital*, decision of 29 December 2003, paragraph 231, where the Commission indicated merely that certain cost efficiencies were not unlikely to translate into price advantages for consumers in the face of tight competition existing in the market (albeit a market characterized by duopoly).

[142]   Article 101(3) Guidelines, *supra* note 107, paragraphs 95–101. However, it may be difficult to prove that consumers will receive a benefit as it is difficult to assess and the Guidelines provide no guidance on what level of value will be considered adequate compensation to consumers. See Nicolaides, *supra* note 139 at 137.

[143]   See Commission decision *BT-MCI*, OJ 1994 L 223/36 [1995] 5 CMLR 285 at paragraph 55, where the Commission remarked in particular that the new services to be provided would enable large companies to 'operate more effectively on a global scale and to better compete with their global as well as with their EU and EEA competitors'.

[144]   Article 101(3) Guidelines, *supra* note 107, paragraph 103.

services satisfy the condition of benefit.[145] The fact that there are some consumers who may not derive a benefit from the restrictive agreement or are disadvantaged as a result does not preclude the second condition from being fulfilled: it is the beneficial nature of the effect on consumers generally in the relevant markets that has to be considered.[146]

iii. Indispensability of Restrictions

The parties must show that the restrictions are reasonably necessary to achieve the economic benefits claimed and cannot be attained by other less restrictive means.[147] The evaluation must however consider the particular market conditions facing the parties.[148] The Commission will not second guess the business judgment of the parties and will intervene only where it is reasonably clear that there are realistic and attainable alternatives.[149] The restrictions are indispensable if their absence would eliminate or significantly reduce the efficiencies that follow from the agreement or make it significantly less likely that they will materialize;

---

[145]   For example, see Commission decision *BT-MCI*, *supra* note 143, paragraph 55; Commission decision *Mérieux – Merck*, *supra* note 132, paragraphs 89–90.

[146]   Case C-238/05 *Asnef-Equifax v Ausbanc* [2006] ECR I-11125, [2007] 4 CMLR 224 paragraphs 66–71.

[147]   Article 101(3) Guidelines, *supra* note 107, paragraph 73. See also *Vis International – Multilateral interchange fee*, OJ 2002 L318/17, [2003] 4 CMLR 283 at paragraph 98 where it was found that restrictions must be indispensable for the benefits as such and not merely for the contractual system said to give rise to those benefits. See also Case 42/84 *Remia BV and others v Commission of the European Communities* [1985] ECR 2545 where it was found that the restriction must be objectively necessary and only impose such a degree of restraint in order to achieve the main purpose of the contract.

[148]   In Case 56/65 *Société Technique Minière v Maschinenbaum Ulm GmbH*, ECR [1966] 337, the Court held that an exclusivity clause was not necessarily a restriction when it was *necessary* to conclude the agreement that allows the party to enter the market. See also Case 258/78 *L.C. Nungesser KG and Kurt Eisele v Commission of the European Communities* [1982] ECR 2015 paragraphs 57–58, which held that an exclusivity clause in the circumstances was considered necessary given the license concerned a new technology previously not available in the relevant market and the licensee would not have been willing to accept the commercial risks associated with investing in the new technology absent the exclusivity.

[149]   Article 101(3) Guidelines, *supra* note 107, paragraphs 75–76. The parties must be able to show that alternatives are significantly less efficient, taking into account business realities and market conditions.

the assessment of the alternative solutions must take into account the actual and potential improvement in the field of competition by the elimination of a particular restriction or the application of a less restrictive alternative; and the more restrictive the restraint the stricter the test under the third condition.[150] The indispensability of a restriction may apply for a limited time period, for example during a start-up phase or even where an industry needs a transitional period to make changes needed to operate in a more competitive manner.[151] Hardcore restrictions in block exemptions are unlikely to be considered indispensable

iv. No Elimination of Competition

An agreement must not give the parties the possibility of eliminating (actual or potential) competition in respect of a substantial part of the relevant market.[152] The Commission is of the view that a restrictive agreement that maintains, creates, or strengthens a market position approaching that of a monopoly cannot normally be justified on the grounds that it also creates efficiency gains.[153] This is supported in the Guidelines, which state that the protection of rivalry and the competitive process is given priority over potentially pro-competitive efficiency gains that could result from restrictive agreements.[154] In other words, the

---

[150]   Ibid., paragraph 79.

[151]   Ibid., paragraph 81. See also DSD, OJ 2001 L319/1, [2002] 4 CMLR 405 where a grant of exclusivity, reduced from 15 years to 11 years to give the grantee sufficient time to achieve an economically satisfactory return on their investment, satisfied Article 101(3).

[152]   Case T-395/94 *Atlantic Container Line v Commission* [2002] ECR II-875, [2002] 4 CMLR 1008 paragraphs 330–332. The degree of market concentration and market power are factors to be taken into consideration if it affects the structure of competition of the relevant market. Even if the parties achieve dominant position, this may not be sufficient to meet the elimination of competition test. See joined Cases T-191/98, T-212/98 to T-214/98, *Atlantic Container Line AB and Others v Commission of the European Communities (Atlantic Container)* [2003] ECR II-3275, paragraph 939. See also the General Court's decision in Case T-17/93 *Matra Hachette v Commission* [1994] ECR II-595, paragraph 153 that the creation of dominant position is not prohibited under Article 101.

[153]   COMP/38689 CISAC, decision of 16 July 2008, [2009] 4 CMLR 577 at paragraph 252 where the Commission expressed concern at the long-entrenched monopolistic positions of the collecting societies which were a factor in eliminating competition in the relevant markets. See also Vertical Guidelines, *supra* note 109, paragraph 127.

[154]   Article 101(3) Guidelines, *supra* note 107, paragraph 105.

elimination test is not a balancing exercise but an assessment of the overall effect of whether a restrictive agreement eliminates competition, regardless of whether the other three criteria of Article 101(3) are met.[155] As such, the efficiencies and improvements through collaborative innovation between integrated drug discovery organization and industry will likely fail to qualify for exemption if the end result is the elimination of competition.

F. REMARKS: AN ARGUMENT FOR SECTOR-SPECIFIC CONSIDERATIONS

The potential of a new innovation is inherently uncertain and extra-ordinarily high at the inception of a collaboration agreement in drug discovery and development. Furthermore, the nature of early stage discovery, as a form of information that may have unknown applications to other diseases, gives rise to difficulties in defining the boundaries of the technology for the purposes of assessing the collaborative relationship between integrated drug discovery organizations and industry under competition law. Such inherent uncertainties combined with the significant financial investment typically associated with the drug discovery and development process inevitably leads to agreements that provide for a great deal of control and protection for the parties involved, which in turn invites and possibly increases the scrutiny of competition policy. Organizations involved in highly innovative fields, such as drug discovery and development, become successful by bringing a new product or process to the market. Instead of gradually acquiring market share as in most traditional industries, in highly innovative markets, the existing market leader is often replaced when a competitor successfully enters the market with a new or improved product. As such, competition in highly innovative industries displays features not typically found in traditional sectors of the economy. The question is whether the same principles and rules of competition law should apply in the same way to highly innovative industries, and, if so, what are the effects of competition on the rate of innovation? If the objective of competition policy is to enhance economic and public welfare, in the context of the pharmaceutical industry where the intensity of competition has an impact on the rate of innovation by way of adequate incentives, does the traditional

---

[155] M. Marquis, *O2 (Germany) v Commission and the Exotic Mysteries of Article 81(1) EC.* EUROPEAN LAW REVIEW, 32(1), 29–47 (2007) at 38–39. See also Anderman and Kallaugher., *supra* note 36 at 61.

approach of discouraging conduct that limits competitors and their ability to compete in the market achieve such an objective? Preserving the competitive process is only one aspect of EU competition law. Consumer welfare, market integration, and fostering innovation are among some of the other values that the Commission has prioritized.

As previously discussed, the pharmaceutical sector sits on the fault lines of a number of contentious policy objectives. When the interaction between these objectives gives rise to competing interests, the conflict can have serious impacts and consequences on the pharmaceutical sector and the public as a whole. Because there is no explicit balance mechanism, the interplay between competition law and patent policy will have to be built on interpretive work of the Commission and the EU courts on a case-by-case basis. A more nuanced framework that takes into account the nature of the pharmaceutical industry would help reduce potential conflicts. Arguably, the Commission has indirectly acknowledged that the unique nature of the pharmaceutical industry may justify the application of competition rules in a manner that differs from the way they are applied to other sectors in the *Lederle-Praxis Biologicals* case,[156] where the Commission refused to apply the general rule on compulsory licensing to the pharmaceutical sector because of this unique nature. Competition policy is susceptible to change to reflect the current values and aims of society, as political views and government changes occur over time. A legal framework that has, as its mandate to promote innovation and facilitate the dissemination of new technologies, must also protect the interests of parties contributing to the process since innovation is a cumulative process that typically requires input and investment by contributing parties.[157] As such, when assessing partnerships that involve collaborative R&D and subsequent licensing of successful results, due consideration should be given to the transactions that are essential to the innovation process.

---

[156] Commission Decision 94/770/EC, of 6 October 1994, relating to a proceeding pursuant to Article 85 of the EC Treaty (now Article 101 TFEU) and Article 53 of the EEA Agreement (IV/34.776 – *Pasteur Mérieux – Merck*), 1994, OJ L309/94, pp. 1–23.

[157] David J. Teece, *Profiting from Technological Innovation: Implications for Integration, Collaboration, Licensing and Public Policy*. RESEARCH POLICY, 15(6), 285–305 (1986) at 288–90.

PART II

Analysis and application of EU competition
law to the integrated drug discovery and
development model

4. Application of competition law to the integrated drug discovery and development model: research and development block exemption regulation

A. INTRODUCTION

As governments seek to reduce financial expenditures on public health due to austerity measures,[1] there is evidence that industry has sought to mitigate the decrease in funding by relying on commercial strategies to maximize the scope, extent, and duration of their patent rights to prolong revenue streams.[2] In view of the number of blockbuster drugs that will or have come off patent and the resulting decline of revenue,[3] pharmaceutical companies continue to employ various commercial strategies to

---

[1] See OECD Health Statistics 2013 at http://stats.oecd.org/index. aspx?DataSetCode=HEALTH_STAT. The OECD reported reductions in public spending on health in many OECD countries with a sharp decrease in public health spending in 2010 followed by a stagnation in 2011, which is expected to continue into the future due the financial crisis. While health spending grew 5% on average from 2000 to 2009, the collapse in government health spending has slowed growth down near zero (around 0.5%) in 2010 and 2011 (see http://www. oecd.org/els/health-systems/health-spending-continues-to-stagnate-says-oecd.htm).

[2] Nicoleta Tuominen, *Patenting Strategies of the EU Pharmaceutical Industry: Regular Business Practice or Abuse of Dominance*. WORLD COMPETITION, 35(1), 27–54 (2012).

[3] See for example Simon Bishop and Mike Walker, *The Economics of EC Competition Law: Concepts, Application, and Measurement* (Sweet & Maxwell 2010), who said: 'Beginning in 2010, the pharmaceutical industry faced one of the biggest waves of drug patent expirations in history, a phenomenon referred to as the "patent cliff". A significant number of top selling drugs in the history of the pharmaceutical industry will experience patent expirations over the next 5 years. … [i]n November 2011 alone, four major drugs – Lipitor (atorvastatin),

generate profit to fund further R&D. However, such behavior may attract greater scrutiny of the competition authority as commercial strategies test the limits of what may be tolerated. The Commission's sector inquiry in the pharmaceutical industry brought attention to the necessity of intellectual property rights and competition to promote innovation and ensure a competitive exploitation of pharmaceutical products,[4] suggesting an imbalance between the two may have a negative effect on innovation and the market. The economic reality of the current drug discovery and development process is such that pharmaceutical companies are faced with increasing financial pressures, leading to an increased need for sufficient incentives to justify investment into R&D,[5] which places further tension on the already fragile fault lines between intellectual property and competition policy.[6] In the drug discovery and development context, this tension takes on another dimension – incentive to innovate

---

Caduet (amlodipine/atorvastatin), Combivir (lami vudeine/zidovudine), and Solodyn (minocycline extended release tablet) – lost patent protection. Combined, these four drugs accounted for more than $7 billion in sales. In total, patents on drugs worth $12 billion expired by the end of 2011, and in 2012 that figure is expected to increase to more than $30 billion in annual sales. Furthermore, it is estimated that generic competition will have eroded $67 billion from the top drug companies' annual sales in the United States between 2007 and 2012 alone, as more than three dozen drugs lose patent protection during this time. That figure represents approximately 50% of the companies' combined U.S. sales in 2007. With patents on many so-called blockbuster drugs about to expire, an estimated $250 billion in sales is at risk between now and 2015'.

    [4]   European Commission Pharmaceutical Sector Inquiry, Final Report, July 8, 2009.

    [5]   As Korah said, '... most attempts to find a cure for particular problems by the pharmaceutical companies do not work. Of those that do, many never get far through their safety trials. So a small loss is made on most drugs. A few almost get to the market, but then some side effect appears and those cost the inventor a great deal. Only a few drugs are successful and the company must make a large profit on these to make up for the losses on the other[s], or R&D will not be worthwhile', Valentine Korah, *Merck v Primecrown – The Exhaustion of Patents by Sale in a Member State where a Monopoly Profit Could Not Be Earned.* EUROPEAN COMPETITION LAW REVIEW, 4, 265–273 (1997) at 272–273. See Alfonso Gambardella, Luigi Orsenigo, and Fabio Pammolli, *Global Competitiveness in Pharmaceuticals: A European Perspective.* Office for Official Publications of the European Communities (2001), who noted that companies are difficult to replace if they stop investing in R&D, so the fewer pharmaceutical companies engage in the translation of science to new medicines, the fewer new products will be developed in the future.

    [6]   In spite of increasing investments in R&D, companies appear to be having trouble refilling the product pipeline as the number of novel medicines

vs. access to medicine. The social welfare function of pharmaceutical products gives rise to very passionate reactions to the business practices of the pharmaceutical industry, which has a primary purpose to make profit. While other business sectors take advantage of patent strategies for commercial gain, the public tends to feel more personally affected when those same strategies are employed by the pharmaceutical sector. However, as one legal scholar warned:

> [The pharmaceutical industry] is an environment typified by imperfect competition, where the legislative and judicial organs of the Community must maintain a balance between realizing the Single Market while respecting the function and integrity of IP rights, as well as ensuring the social element of the pharmaceutical industry is not sacrificed on the altar of the Single Market. Unlike other sectors, the barriers to entry are such as to naturally exclude new entrants – for the pharmaceutical industry requires huge sums to be invested with no guarantee of any return and high risk of failure. There is no scope for pursuing the wrong economic policy in a market in which the chances of success are between 0.02 and 0.03% of a successful new discovery.[7]

Competitive concerns are especially important in technology-based industries where the key factor for growth and economic success is directly related to innovations driven by the R&D process. High-technology industries, such as the pharmaceutical industry,[8] are characterized by strong dependency on R&D, significant economies of scale, high entry barriers, reliance on strong intellectual property protection, and high levels of technical complexity.[9] According to one survey, the only industry in which patents are thought to play a highly important role

---

reaching the market has been decreasing. Combined with other factors, companies have increasingly become dependent on the revenues from their existing best-selling products, which they inevitably wish to maintain for as long as possible. As a result, there are some indications that industry has been employing a variety of strategies to extend the commercial life of their medicines, causing a delay for generics to enter the market. See, Communication from the Commission, *Executive Summary of the Pharmaceutical Sector Inquiry Report,* (COM 351, 2009).

[7] Russell G. Hunter, *The Pharmaceutical Sector in the European Union: Intellectual Property Rights, Parallel Trade and Community Competition Law,* Institute for European Law at Stockholm University (2001) at p. 16.

[8] OECD Directorate for Science, Technology and Industry Economic Analysis and Statistics Division, *Classification of manufacturing industries into categories based on R&D intensities* (OECD, 2011).

[9] OECD Directorate for Financial, Fiscal and Enterprise Affairs, *Merger Review in Emerging High Innovation Markets* (OECD 2003).

in bringing new products to market is the pharmaceutical industry.[10] In other words, innovation is a significant competitive feature and R&D is instrumental in discovering, developing, and commercializing new products.[11] As previously discussed, the risks and uncertainty associated with R&D in the drug discovery and development process is particularly high.[12] The obvious benefit to collaborative R&D is that costs can be minimized, efficiency increased, risks shared, and complementary assets pooled together to exploit economies of scale. However, R&D collaborations could reduce competition in the research market, especially if there are only a limited number of parties conducting research in the area, by limiting the number of competing technologies in development.[13] Although integrated drug discovery and development organizations have the freedom to contract and negotiate the terms of collaboration with industry partners, the next step is then to determine whether the agreement can be exempt under the R&D Regulation and/or TTBER.

---

[10]   See Michele Boldrin and David K. Levine, *Against Intellectual Monopoly* (Cambridge University Press 2008) at 112.

[11]   See Alan S. Gutterman, *Innovation and Competition Policy: A Comparative Study of the Regulation of Patent Licensing and Collaborative Research & Development in the United States and the European Community* (Kluwer Law International 1997) at 97 and Jonathan Faull and Ali Nikpay, *The EC Law of Competition* (Oxford University Press 1999) at 372.

[12]   See for example, Frederic M. Scherer, *Antitrust, Efficiency, and Progress.* NEW YORK UNIVERSITY LAW REVIEW, 62, 998 (1987), which found that approximately 60% of successful innovations in the chemical, drug, electronics, and machinery businesses are imitated within four years, at a cost of 65% of the original innovation.

[13]   Alexis Jaquemin, 'Goals and Means of European Antitrust Policy after 1992' in Harold Demsets and Alexis Jaquemin (eds), *Anti-trust Economics – New Challenges for Competition Policy* (Lund University 1994) at 34; Gene M. Grossman and Carl Shapiro, *Research Joint Ventures: An Antitrust Analysis.* JOURNAL OF LAW, ECONOMICS AND ORGANIZATION, 2(2), 315–337 (1986) at 324; Michael L. Katz, *An Analysis of Cooperative Research and Development.* RAND JOURNAL OF ECONOMICS, 527–543 (1986) at 529; Joseph Kattan, *Antitrust Analysis of Technology Joint Ventures: Allocative Efficiency and the Rewards of Innovation.* ANTITRUST LAW JOURNAL, 61(3), 937–973 (1993) at 944.

B. RESEARCH AND DEVELOPMENT BLOCK EXEMPTION REGULATION

Recognizing that collaborative R&D can have pro-competitive effects, the Commission adopted a block exemption regulation under Article 101(3) with respect to R&D agreements, referred to herein as the R&D Regulation. Where R&D agreements may be caught by Article 101(1), the R&D Regulation is intended to facilitate R&D while protecting competition by defining categories of R&D agreements that normally satisfy the conditions of Article 101(3) without the need to carry out an in-depth assessment because the positive effects of such agreements are presumed to outweigh any negative effects on competition.[14] The Guidelines on the applicability of Article 101 of the Treaty on the Functioning of the European Union to horizontal co-operation agreements (hereinafter referred to as the 'Horizontal Guidelines')[15] specifically recognize collaborations for R&D and commercialization of results as a form of horizontal agreement[16] and provides complementary guidance on the application of the R&D Regulation. The economics-based approach of the R&D Regulation, as exemplified to a large extent in the recitals, suggests a greater emphasis on assessing the impact of R&D agreements on the relevant market[17] and gives parties greater contractual freedom to create efficient agreements so long as the pro-competitive effects of the

---

[14] Commission Regulation No 1217/2010 on the application of Article 101(3) of the Treaty on the Functioning of the European Union to categories of research and development agreements, OJ 2010 L335/36 (the 'R&D Regulation'), recitals 2, 3, and 4.

[15] Communication from the Commission, *Guidelines on the applicability of Article 101 of the Treaty on the Functioning of the European Union to horizontal co-operation agreements* (OJ C11/01, 2011) ('Horizontal Guidelines').

[16] Ibid., at paragraph 105, which discuss the various forms and scope of R&D agreements. The Horizontal Guidelines expressly state their applicability to all forms of R&D agreements, including related agreements concerning the production or commercialization of the R&D results, provided that the R&D agreement is the most upstream indispensable building block of the co-operation.

[17] R&D Regulation, *supra* note 14, recital 6 which states that agreements on the joint execution of research work or the joint development of the results of the research, up to but *not* including the stage of industrial application, generally do not fall within the scope of Article 101(1). In other words, it is not necessary to exempt agreements that do not proceed to joint commercialization since is it unlikely to generate anticompetitive effects on the market. See Valentine Korah, *An Introductory Guide to EC Competition Law and Practice* (9th edn, Hart Publishing 2007) at 339.

agreement outweigh the anticompetitive effects. Because competition is one of the main drivers of innovation, an argument can be made that the interaction between competition and innovation policy has the ability to encourage the flow of knowledge and lead to greater competition, as in the case where undertakings collaborate to promote innovation through R&D.[18] This appears to be supported by the R&D Regulation which states:

> Cooperation in research and development and in the exploitation of the results is most likely to promote technical and economic progress if the parties contribute complementary skills, assets or activities to the co-operation. This also includes scenarios where one party merely finances the research and development activities of another party.[19]

In summary, the R&D Regulation sets out certain conditions that must be met and certain restrictions that must not be included for the agreements to benefit from automatic exemption. If the agreement does not meet these conditions, the agreement cannot benefit from the automatic protection of the R&D Regulation but can still be individually assessed as to whether it qualifies for exemption under Article 101(3). One of the noteworthy changes to the R&D Regulation that came into force on January 1, 2011 is the expansion of scope to include 'paid for research' as an exemptible form of R&D agreement where one party agrees to finance the R&D carried out by the other party.[20] Another significant change is the definition of 'joint' in the context of activities carried out under the R&D agreement, which includes 'allocated between the parties by way of specialization in the context of research and development or exploitation'.[21]

---

[18]   Rosa Greaves, 'EU Competition Law, and Research and Development Agreements' in Marilyn Pittard, Ann L. Monotti, and John Duns (eds), *Business Innovation and the Law: Perspectives from Intellectual Property, Labour, Competition and Corporate Law* (Edward Elgar Publishing, 2013) 299–311 at 299.

[19]   R&D Regulation, *supra* note 14, recital 8.

[20]   Ibid., Article 1(1)(p). In the integrated drug discovery model, the R&D activity is collaborative but allocated according to the respective competencies of the parties, and the financial contribution made by industry to the collaboration constitutes only a part of the total cost of the collaboration. As such, it is not clear whether the collaborative R&D under the integrated drug discovery model would satisfy the definition of 'paid for research' as it is not clear whether the R&D has to be carried out entirely by one party or if the financing party has to finance the entire R&D effort.

[21]   Ibid., Article 1(1)(m)(iii).

It would therefore appear that the collaboration between integrated drug discovery organizations and industry, particularly the collaborative R&D aspect of the agreement, could fall within at least one of the definitions of research and development agreement set out in the R&D Regulation, which is defined as an agreement 'entered into between two or more parties which relate[s] to the conditions under which those parties pursue joint research and development of contract products or contract technologies excluding joint exploitation of the results'.[22] Furthermore, the Horizontal Guidelines also recognize that most R&D agreements do not fall under Article 101(1), especially early stage R&D that is far removed from the exploitation of possible results.[23] Because the subject matter of the collaboration between integrated drug discovery organizations and industry are early stage discoveries with the intention of establishing proof of concept, the collaboration agreement may not even require exemption under the R&D Regulation. However, this will of course require a case-by-case assessment.[24]

Article 2(1) of the R&D Regulation exempts research and development agreements to the extent that they contain restrictions of competition falling within the scope of Article 101(1). Furthermore, the R&D Regulation is applicable to agreements 'containing provisions which relate to the assignment or licensing of intellectual property rights to one or more of the parties to carry out the joint research and development, paid-for research and development or joint exploitation, provided that those provisions do not constitute the primary object of such agreements,

---

[22]   Ibid., Article 1(1)(a)(iii).

[23]   Horizontal Guidelines, *supra* note 15, paragraph 129. See Vivien Rose and David Bailey, 'EU Competition Law and its Territorial Reach' in Vivien Rose and David Bailey (eds), *Bellamy & Child European Union Law of Competition* (7th edn, Oxford University Press 2013) at 94 where it was commented that the Commission has developed a 'hierarchy of acceptability' in regards to the types of R&D agreements that are presumed not to be restrictive.

[24]   R&D Regulation, *supra* note 14, recital 6 states that agreements on joint R&D that do not include the stage of industrial application generally do not fall within the scope of Article 101(1), but if the parties agree not to carry out other research and development in the same field, thereby foregoing the opportunity of gaining competitive advantages over other parties, such agreements may fall within the scope of Article 101(1) and the R&D Regulation. In the case of the collaboration agreements between industry and integrated drug discovery organizations, it is not uncommon for industry to expect an exclusive arrangement whereby the integrated drug discovery organization is not to engage in R&D on competing projects with other industry partners.

but are directly related to and necessary for their implementation'.[25] Applied to the collaboration agreement between integrated drug discovery organizations and industry, it is unclear whether the R&D Regulation would apply to the collaboration agreement as a whole, including the associated license agreement to commercialize the results generated from the collaboration project if successful, or to the collaboration agreement alone. An argument can be made that the licensing of successful project intellectual property in the associated licensing agreement constitutes licensing of intellectual property rights to industry to exploit the results of the collaboration and should therefore fall under the R&D Regulation. However, a stronger argument can be made that because the licensing of successful project intellectual property is made in a separate but associated agreement, the licensing arrangement is therefore a primary object of the agreement. As such, the associated license agreement falls outside the scope of the R&D Regulation. This is further supported by the fact that TTBER is intended to deal with block exemptions related to technology transfer and licensing. Furthermore, exploitation under the R&D Regulation requires contract products or contract technologies to be identified. Because of the nature of drug discovery and development, typically, no specific product or technology is identified at the outset of a basic discovery project. Only after collaborative R&D to achieve proof of concept, and if there are successful results, can the parties identify the potential of the discovery and negotiate exploitation options.

Although the R&D Regulation previously required joint exploitation of the results for the exemption to apply, the current R&D Regulation now allows parties to allocate the right of exploitation, such as where one party specializes in exploitation.[26] In the case of the integrated drug discovery and development model, given that industry is the only party in the collaboration that is active in the pharmaceutical market, the industry partner would likely qualify as a party that specializes in exploitation. Uncertainty arises from the definition of 'exploitation of the results', which includes licensing intellectual property rights required for the manufacture of the contract product or application of the contract technology.[27] One of the possible outcomes of the collaboration agreement does contemplate the licensing of successful resulting project intellectual property from the integrated drug discovery organization to industry for translation and commercialization. Does that mean integrated

---

[25] R&D Regulation, *supra* note 14, Article 2(2).
[26] Ibid., recital 11.
[27] Ibid., Article 1(g).

drug discovery organizations also engage in exploitation, as defined by the R&D Regulation, because they license the successful project results to the industry partner or does the definition only consider licensing to external third parties to constitute exploitation? Arguably, the R&D Regulation does not contemplate joint exploitation of the results to mean one party licensing and the other party commercializing.[28]

i. Competitors vs. Non-competitors

Article 3(2) of the R&D Regulation specifically states that the exemption applies to agreements involving research institutes, academic bodies or undertakings which supply research and development as a commercial service without normally being active in the exploitation of results. Similarly, the Horizontal Guidelines confirm the exemption of research institutes because the complementary nature of such collaborations do not normally give rise to restrictive effects on competition.[29] It would seem somewhat inconsistent with competition policy to essentially make all R&D agreements with research organizations immune from competition law simply because they are not normally active in the exploitation of their research, especially in today's context where research institutes and academic bodies are more and more active in licensing out the results of their research to third parties.[30] Asked in a different way, is it the intention of the competition authorities to exempt industry whenever they enter into an R&D agreement with research institutes and academic bodies that may grant them sole rights to the resulting technology without further investigation into the potential pro-competitive and anticompetitive effects of the collaboration, outside the

---

[28] Ibid., Article 1(m) defines activities that are considered joint under the R&D Regulation. Read in conjunction with Article 1(g) definition of exploitation and recital 6 on industrial application, it is not clear whether the collaboration agreement between industry and integrated drug discovery organizations falls within or outside the scope of the R&D Regulation.

[29] Horizontal Guidelines, *supra* note 15, paragraph 131.

[30] See for example, Robert M. Yeh, *The Public Paid for the Invention: Who Owns It?* BERKELEY TECHNOLOGY LAW JOURNAL, 27, 453 (2012); Hafiz A. ur Rehman, *Equitable Licensing and Publicly Funded Research: A Working Model for India?* SOUTHWESTERN JOURNAL OF INTERNATIONAL LAW, 16, 75–78 (2010) and Thomas P. Stossel, *Regulating Academic-Industrial Research Relationships: Solving Problems or Stifling Progress?* NEW ENGLAND JOURNAL OF MEDICINE, 353(10), 1060 (2005).

assessment of hardcore and excluded restrictions set out in the R&D Regulation?[31]

One possible interpretation could be that the exemption of research organizations simply confirms that Article 101 does not apply to R&D agreements between research institutes and industry because they are not considered competitors. Where the parties are not competitors, the exemption is available irrespective of market power for the duration of the R&D.[32] However, if research organizations are de-facto considered non-competitors, why is there a need for a specific exemption for academic bodies and research institutions if they are presumed not to be considered actual or potential competitors on any market? One possible conclusion is that academic bodies or undertakings can in some circumstances be considered competitors. Article 1(1)(r) defines a competing undertaking as an actual or potential competitor. Essentially, undertakings are treated as actual competitors if they are active on the same relevant market.[33] The key to defining the relevant market when assessing the effects of an R&D agreement is to identify those products, technologies, or R&D efforts that will act as the main competitive constraints on the parties.[34] Because integrated drug discovery organizations do not make or sell any pharmaceutical products, they cannot be considered actual competitors on the product market. Realistically, integrated drug discovery organizations are also highly unlikely to enter the product market and become potential competitors with their industry partners. Among many other requirements, integrated drug discovery organizations lack the skill, resources, mandate, and equipment to become players in the product market, and would therefore be unlikely (and unable) to make the necessary investment to enter the product market. However, integrated drug discovery organizations do offer R&D services to industry and license their research to third parties. As such, the relevant market for analysis is the technology market and the innovation market.

Before launching into an analysis of the technology and innovation markets, the Horizontal Guidelines appear to state definitively that integrated drug discovery organizations and industry are not competitors under the R&D Regulation. Paragraph 130 of the Horizontal Guidelines

---

[31]   R&D Regulation, *supra* note 14, recital 13 states that the exemption granted under the R&D Regulation shall be limited to R&D agreements that do not provide the undertakings with any possibilities of eliminating competition.
[32]   Ibid., Article 4(1).
[33]   Horizontal Guidelines, *supra* note 15, paragraph 10. See also R&D Regulation, *supra* note 14, Article 1(1)(s) for the definition of actual competitors.
[34]   Horizontal Guidelines, *supra* note 15, paragraph 112.

clearly states that collaborations between non-competitors generally do not give rise to restrictive effects on competition, as in the case where the parties are not able to carry out the necessary R&D independently, for instance due to limited technical capabilities of the parties requiring the bringing together of complementary skills and resources.[35] The reason integrated drug discovery organizations and industry collaborate under the integrated drug discovery and development model is because neither party alone has the skills and resources to translate and commercialize early stage discoveries. If the decisive question is whether each party independently has the necessary ability to carry out drug discovery and development independently,[36] then it is reasonably clear that integrated drug discovery organizations and industry are not considered actual or potential competitors. Although collaborative R&D between non-competitors generally does not give rise to anticompetitive effects, the Horizontal Guidelines do caution that such collaborations can give rise to foreclosure concerns[37] if one of the parties has significant market power and receives exclusive exploitation of results to a key technology.[38] In other words, competition in innovation of new products and technologies that may replace existing or create new ones will under certain circumstances be able to produce restrictions on competition. In order to assess the competitive effect of the collaboration between integrated drug discovery organizations and industry, the technology market and the innovation market needs to be defined.[39]

ii. Innovation Market

When the Commission examines an agreement, it tries to assess whether the agreement is likely to substantially restrict competition in innovation.[40] Competitive issues may arise relating to the intermediate market for R&D rather than the product or technology market, for example if the collaborating parties decide to suppress or delay R&D that may lead to a new product that would reduce sales of existing products. When two

---

[35] Ibid., paragraph 130.
[36] Ibid.
[37] Ibid., paragraphs 69–71 which discusses anticompetitive foreclosures.
[38] Ibid., paragraph 130.
[39] The relevant market seeks to restrict attention only to those products or services, which have a 'significant' impact on competition. See Simon Bishop and Mike Walker, *The Economics of EC Competition Law: Concepts, Application, and Measurement* (Sweet & Maxwell 2010) at 109–154.
[40] Horizontal Guidelines, *supra* note 15, paragraphs 119–122.

parties bring their expertise and resources together to develop a new innovation, competition to produce that innovation is arguably reduced[41] and the competitive consequence needs to be considered by evaluating the R&D for the new innovation and any competing R&D for developing substitutes.[42] In other words, the innovation market is the upstream market from the technology market and may be used to limit the ability of a party to exercise market power in R&D.[43] The innovation market concept attempts to capture the potential dynamic whereby collaboration between parties could lessen competition in a market that may exist in the future but does not currently exist,[44] but can only be challenged at the R&D stage as it would be too late to address at a later stage.[45] However, the absence of innovation is not easily observable nor is it readily

---

[41]   See Joseph A. Schumpeter, *Capitalism, Socialism and Democracy* (Harper Perennial, reprint of 1950 edition, 2008). Schumpeter believed that market structure determines the rate of innovation; he did not believe that more competition leads to more innovation. On the other hand, Kenneth Arrow concluded that greater competition leads to greater innovation because of the greater incentive given to the one who innovates successfully by way of higher profits. See Lawrence B. Landman, *The Economics of Future Goods Markets.* WORLD COMPETITION, LAW AND ECONOMICS REVIEW, 21(3), 63–90 (1997) at 69, with reference to Arrow's 'Economic Welfare and the Allocation of Resources to Invention' in *The Rate and Direction of Inventive Activity* (Princeton University Press 1962). To date, neither Arrow nor Schumpeter has been conclusively proven correct, the evidence is inconclusive and because the markets vary greatly, no generally accepted theory has emerged. See also OECD Working Papers, *Application of Competition Policy to High Technology Markets* (OECD 1997) at 7.

[42]   John T. Lang, *European Community Antitrust Law: Innovation Markets and High Technology Industries.* FORDHAM INTERNATIONAL JOURNAL, 20, 717 (1997). However, others have made the criticism that innovation is speculative and could include parties that are unidentifiable at the time an assessment is made. See Michael A. Carrier, *Two Puzzles Resolved: Of the Schumpeter–Arrow Stalemate and Pharmaceutical Innovation Markets.* IOWA LAW REVIEW, 93, 393–450 (2008).

[43]   Bishop and Walker, *supra* note 39.

[44]   Kristen Riemenschneider, *New Economy: Antitrust Review of Merger Analysis Using Innovation Markets*, Antitrust Modernization Commission Public Comment (2006) at 7.

[45]   The restriction of innovation would appear only as a 'non-event' as products that fail to enter the market because of a collaboration will be hard to detect, if at all. In other words, it will not be apparent after the fact what is missing from the marketplace. This is especially worrisome in the pharmaceutical industry where innovation is critical to public health. See Carrier, *supra* note 42.

apparent. The goal of innovation market analysis is to preserve as many different paths to innovation as possible.[46]

Unlike the United States where the innovation market is expressly defined,[47] the European practice of defining the innovation market is not formalized. The concept has mostly been debated and developed in relation to merger analysis and academic commentary. For example, in *Glaxo Wellcome/SmithKline Beecham*,[48] the Commission considered whether a sufficient level of competing R&D would remain after a merger. The Commission considered that both parties had products on the existing market and were developing products for these existing markets as well as for markets where neither party was active. Of particular concern to the Commission were areas of activity where Glaxo had a strong market position, which required the Commission to assess the impact of the merger on both existing markets and the innovation market.[49] Because there were a number of other third party companies engaged in R&D for the products at issue and at a similar stage of development, the Commission concluded that there was no risk of

---

[46] Ronald W. Davis, *Innovation Markets and Merger Enforcement: Current Practice in Perspective*. ANTITRUST LAW JOURNAL, 71(2), 677–703 (2003) at 680–681.

[47] US Department of Justice & Federal Trade Commission, *Antitrust Guidelines for the Licensing of Intellectual Property* (1995) at §3.2.3 which states: 'An innovation market consists of the research and development directed to particular new or improved goods or processes, and the close substitutes for that research and development. The close substitutes are research and development efforts, technologies, and goods that significantly constrain the exercise of market power with respect to the relevant research and development, for example by limiting the ability and incentive of a hypothetical monopolist to retard the pace of research and development. The Agencies will delineate an innovation market only when the capabilities to engage in the relevant research and development can be associated with specialized assets or characteristics of specific firms'. However, even in the US context where innovation market is defined, the concept has been the subject of much disagreement. For example, in the proposed merger between Genzyme and Novazyme, the Federal Trade Commission disagreed on whether to challenge the merger. The majority decision stated the dangers in presuming anticompetitive harm without economic foundation, whereas the minority decision cited the dangers of mergers creating monopoly. See the discussion in Benjamin R. Kern, *Innovation Markets, Future Markets, or Potential Competition: How Should Competition Authorities Account for Innovation Competition in Merger Reviews?* WORLD COMPETITION LAW AND ECONOMICS REVIEW, 37(2), 173–206 (2014).

[48] Case No COMP/M.1846 *Glaxo Wellcome/SmithKline Beecham* (2000).

[49] Ibid., at paragraph 71.

eliminating actual competition on the innovation market. Similarly, the merging of the parties' research pipelines was found not to be restrictive of potential competition in existing markets or on overall R&D despite Glaxo's position in the market because of the number of other similar products that were under development by third party competitors.[50] In the merger case of *Upjohn/Pharmacia*,[51] the Commission also considered the impact of combining the innovation efforts of two pharmaceutical companies in competition in terms of R&D. The Commission found that both parties had similar products under development, but because Pharmacia's R&D was at such an early stage, the therapeutic profile was not ascertainable.[52] Regardless, because the Commission found that any new product that resulted from the merger would face competition from several credible third party competitors, there were sufficient grounds to conclude that the merger would not create or increase a dominant position on R&D nor the market for future developments.[53] Furthermore, the Commission noted that because both Upjohn and Pharmacia were considered medium-sized companies with limited independent resources, the merger would enable the new merged entity to become a true competitor in the development of pharmaceutical products.[54] Scholars commented on the similarities between the Commission's analysis of R&D-related merger cases compared to the US definition of innovation market.[55]

Commentators have largely expressed disagreement over the role of innovation markets.[56] Some argue that the concept of innovation markets is risky because competition authorities are attempting to establish whether a collaborative effort will have the effect of lessening innovation based on: (i) an assumption of the presence of competition between

---

[50]   Ibid., at paragraph 188.
[51]   Case No IV/M.631 – *Upjohn /Pharmacia*, OJ C294/4 (1995).
[52]   Lang, *supra* note 42 at p. 748.
[53]   Ibid.
[54]   Ibid.
[55]   Ibid., at pp. 760–765.
[56]   Richard T. Rapp, *The Misapplication of the Innovation Market Approach to Merger Analysis.* ANTITRUST LAW JOURNAL, 64(1), 19–47 (1995) at 20; Daniel F. Spulber, *How Do Competitive Pressures Affect Incentives to Innovate When There Is a Market for Inventions?* JOURNAL OF POLITICAL ECONOMY, 121(6), 1007–1054 (2013); Riemenschneider, *supra* note 44 at 2; Lang, *supra* note 42 at 764; Marcus Glader, *Research and Development Cooperation in European Competition Law: A Legal and Economic Analysis.* CFE Working Paper Series (2000) at 40–45; Bishop and Walker, *supra* note 39.

undertakings on a particular technological development; and (ii) incomplete information on details of R&D pipelines that are typically kept secret.[57] Others argue that innovation is difficult to measure and because there is no clear theoretical or empirical link between current R&D efforts and future innovation, it is purely speculative to relate any change in an R&D market to potential changes in future competition.[58] Some have also argued that since there is no empirical evidence to suggest that an increase in concentration of R&D will always lead to less R&D, one cannot infer that concentration in R&D efforts will always affect future prices or the variety of future products.[59] On the other hand, scholars that are positive towards the innovation market concept argue that when analyzing the competitive effects, actual or potential competition in existing markets may fail to capture the consequences of alteration in innovative effort, particularly if the transaction concerns a distant future product market.[60] Innovation markets are future-oriented and attempt to

---

[57]   Riemenschneider, *supra* note 44, at 12. Innovation is 'intangible, uncertain, unmeasurable, and often even unobservable, except in retrospect', Rapp, ibid., at 27. See also Dennis W. Carlton and Robert H. Gertner, 'Intellectual Property, Antitrust and Strategic Behavior' in Adam B. Jaffe, Josh Lerner, and Scott Stern (eds), *Innovation Policy and the Economy* (MIT Press 2003), Volume 3, who stated 'because the results of R&D are so difficult to predict, the analyst may be unable to determine all, or even most, of the relevant firms who might produce competitive products in the future'.

[58]   Teresa L. Morales and Jose Rivas, *Merger Control in the Pharmaceutical Sector and the Innovation Market Assessment: European Analysis in Practice and Differences with the American Approach* (CEU Ediciones Serie Política de la Competencia Número 25, 2008) at 11 and see generally Rapp, *supra* note 56. Is R&D the appropriate proxy or measurement of innovation and even if the relevant R&D pipeline can be identified, does it necessarily provide guidance on how it will affect competition for a particular good or service in the future? See Lang, *supra* note 42.

[59]   Rapp, *supra* note 56. See also Carlton and Gertner, *supra* note 57 at 38, which argued that more R&D does not necessarily result in more innovation because R&D efforts can be duplicative, and a merger that reduces R&D expenditure and redundancy may be beneficial if it allows the R&D to be conducted more efficiently to produce the same or greater knowledge at lower costs. See also Jonathan B. Baker, *Fringe Firms and Incentives to Innovate.* ANTITRUST LAW JOURNAL, 63(2), 621–641 (1995), who stated that whether Schumpeter's concentration of efforts or Arrow's incentive to innovate under competitive conditions maximizes innovation depends on factors that go beyond blanket assertions typically associated with the concept of innovation markets.

[60]   Richard J. Gilbert and Steven C. Sunshine, *Incorporating Dynamic Efficiency in Merger Analysis: The Use of Innovation Markets.* ANTITRUST LAW JOURNAL, 63(2), 569–601 (1995).

realistically assess actual market behavior in the future before collaboration negatively impacts R&D efforts as it would be difficult to intervene ex-post.[61] Although the approach to appraise R&D to identify constraints on competition has been heavily debated, the concept has largely gained traction over the years and appears to be an established part of the analysis regarding competition law cases.[62]

iii. R&D Poles

To assess the effects of R&D collaborations on competition in innovation, the Horizontal Guidelines suggests identifying R&D poles.[63] As previously discussed, an agreement can affect innovation when the parties involved are only one of a few entities that conduct R&D in a particular area of technology.[64] Competition policy with respect to innovation is primarily concerned with the exercise of market power in such a way as to slow the pace and variety in the R&D of products and technologies.[65] As such, when an agreement involves collaborative R&D, an assessment should be made as to whether the agreement is likely to substantially restrict competition and/or slow down the rate in R&D, especially if the parties are dominant in the relevant research sector or have unique research capabilities.[66] There is a risk of inefficiencies if the parties together become so strong that they acquire strong market

---

[61]   Thomas N. Dahdouh and James F. Mongoven, *The Shape of Things to Come: Innovation Market Analysis in Merger Cases.* ANTITRUST LAW JOURNAL, 64(2), 405–441 (1996) at 405–406 and 411–412.

[62]   For example, see Case COMP/M.2547 – *Bayer/Aventis Crop Science*, 2002 at paragraph 19 where the Commission stated '[i]n the past the Commission has often seen reasons for concern in the grouping of companies with strengths in R&D and innovation. For the purpose of this decision, the Commission considers that the parties' R&D capabilities and incentives have to be taken into account as regards the potential elimination of future competition'.

[63]   Horizontal Guidelines, *supra* note 15, paragraph 120.

[64]   See for example, Kern, *supra* note 47, who discusses the effects of mergers on innovation, including a scenario where the number of relevant competitors with respect to innovation can be much lower than the number of competitors on the actual product market, therefore giving rise to concerns with respect to anticompetitive innovation effects.

[65]   OECD Working Papers, *Application of Competition Policy to High Technology Markets* (OECD 1997) at 8.

[66]   Kern, *supra* note 47.

power.[67] On the other hand, if no similar research will be conducted absent the agreement, it has been argued that antitrust ought to be lenient and permissive, even when such agreement includes ancillary restraints because the net effect is likely to be positive.[68]

According to the Horizontal Guidelines, innovation markets are only relevant to agreements that involve the development of new products or technologies that may replace existing ones or create a completely new market.[69] To assess the effects on competition in innovation, the Horizontal Guidelines use the specific example of the pharmaceutical industry where 'the process of innovation is structured in such a way that it is possible at an early stage to identify competing R&D poles' to determine if R&D collaborations affect the number of independent and credible competing R&D poles.[70] R&D poles are defined as 'R&D efforts directed towards a certain new product or technology, and the substitutes

---

[67]   Scherer, *supra* note 12 at 999. The term X-inefficiencies stems from Harvey Leibenstein, *Allocative Efficiency vs. 'X-Efficiency'*. AMERICAN ECONOMIC REVIEW, 392–415 (1966) at 392. Monopolists have fewer incentives to act at a competitive level. Also see Lawrence B. Landman, *Innovation Markets in Europe*. EUROPEAN COMPETITION LAW REVIEW, 19, 21–31 (1998) at 22.

[68]   Grossman and Shapiro, *supra* note 13 at 328. See also Douglas L. Wald and Deborah L. Feinstein, *Merger Enforcement in Innovation Markets: The Latest Chapter – Genzyme/Novazyme*. ANTITRUST SOURCE, 1–11 (2004) with respect to developing drugs that are challenging or difficult to reach the market, particularly when there is no existing treatment, and that competition authorities should give greater weight to the efficiencies created by way of a merger or collaborative efforts. The more important goal in these cases is to increase the likelihood that one product reaches the market instead of ensuring the presence of two competing products in the market.

[69]   Horizontal Guidelines, *supra* note 15, paragraph 119.

[70]   Ibid., paragraph 120. Unlike other high-technology-based sectors, the requirement of clinical trials in the pharmaceutical sector prevents new R&D projects from being hidden. Antitrust authorities can therefore easily identify overlaps in R&D pipelines in the industry at the clinical trial phase when the R&D project is far into the development process to define the innovation market. '[P]roper enforcement involving future goods can only happen when the good is far enough in the development process to allow it to be identified as a source of potential competition, along with its close substitutes', Ilene K. Gotts and Richard T. Rapp, *Antitrust Treatment of Mergers Involving Future Goods*. ANTITRUST, 19, 100 (2004) at 102. From the perspective of the integrated drug discovery organizations and industry, if the assessment of the innovation market only takes place at the clinical trial phase, given the nature of drug discovery and the novelty of the basic research projects that form the subject matter of the collaboration, there is a greater likelihood that both integrated drug discovery organization and industry will be considered one of few R&D poles, rendering

for that R&D, i.e. R&D aimed at developing substitutable products or technology for those developed by the co-operation and having comparable access to resources as well as a similar timing'.[71] The starting point of the analysis is the identification of the R&D of the parties, followed by an identification of any credible competing R&D poles to determine whether a sufficient number of independent R&D poles remain in place to maintain effective competition in innovation.[72] Whether or not the rate of innovation will be negatively affected is determined by whether there are a number of substitutable credible R&D poles that can pose a degree of competitive constraint that would offset any party who may have the market power to affect the rate of innovation.[73] Competing R&D poles are identified on the basis of the particular products that may result from the collaboration.[74] In order for the R&D poles to be considered credible and competing: (i) the research efforts of the R&D poles need to be directed towards substitutable R&D being conducted at around the same time; and (ii) the size, scope and nature of the competing poles have to be comparable in regards to access to resources.[75] However, the Commission does not require independent R&D poles in every field[76] so long as downstream product competition is maintained.[77] In other words, the

---

these types of collaborations anticompetitive. Although difficult to assess, a more realistic assessment of the R&D landscape is to consider pre-clinical collaborations.

[71]   Horizontal Guidelines, *supra* note 15. In other words, the agreement must affect innovation aiming at creating a new product in a transparent industry. Transparent industries are generally those that contain long R&D cycles closely linked to important IPRs, such as the pharmaceutical industry, enabling such industries to engage in behavior that may affect competition. See Marcus Glader, *Innovation Markets and Competition Analysis*: *EU Competition Law and US Antitrust Law. New Horizons in Competition Law and Economics* (Edward Elgar Publishing 2006) at 99.

[72]   Horizontal Guidelines, *supra* note 15.

[73]   Morales and Rivas, *supra* note 58 at 29.

[74]   Glader, *supra* note 71 at 230.

[75]   Horizontal Guidelines, *supra* note 15, paragraph 120.

[76]   Lang, *supra* note 42 at 761.

[77]   See for example, Case No IV/34.796, *Canon/Kodak*, OJ 1997, C330/10 where two parties with significant market power entered into a development and licensing agreement for a new technology. Because there was evidence that the agreement would not eliminate competition by making the developed technologies available to third parties through licensing, the Commission exempted the agreement from Article 101(1); See also Case No COMP/M.1846 – *Glaxo Wellcome/SmithKline Beecham* (2000) where the Commission found, in a merger case, that there was no risk of eliminating actual R&D competition as there were

Commission appears to be willing to enable collaborative research by permitting parties to negotiate R&D agreements in a manner that is most efficient to their circumstances, so long as the product market remains competitive.[78]

Depending on how substitutability is defined for the purposes of assessing pharmaceutical R&D, the innovative nature of drug discovery and development is such that a limited number of parties engage in R&D in a particular area of technology.[79] For example, pharmaceuticals developed to treat rare and neglected diseases that affect only a small percentage of the population are termed 'orphan drugs' because of the lack of motive within the industry to develop such drugs. By definition, few parties engage in R&D on orphan drugs and when such parties enter into collaboration agreements, what impact does such agreement have on the assessment of R&D poles and on the innovation market? With respect to research in relation to more 'mainstream' health concerns, if substitutability is defined, for example, by the broad class of technologies being developed to treat a particular disease, then the number of credible R&D poles will be far greater than if substitutability is defined by, for example, the particular metabolic pathway, the particular target, or the particular protein being developed in the collaboration agreement.[80] If the collaboration is for the development of a drug that *prevents* the onset of a particular disease, is the simultaneous R&D for the *treatment* of the same

---

a number of other companies engaged in R&D for similar products, at a similar stage of development even though one party has significant market power. Similarly, in another merger case, Case No IV/M.631 – *Upjohn/Pharmacia*, OJ C294/4 (1995), the Commission found that it was unlikely that a dominant position would be created or increased in either the R&D, or the market for future developments as a result of the merger because there was evidence of competition from several competing products under development by other competitors.

[78]   Glader, *supra* note 56 at 41.

[79]   See for example, Dror Ben-Asher, *In Need of Treatment? Merger Control, Pharmaceutical Innovation, and Consumer Welfare.* JOURNAL OF LEGAL MEDICINE, 21(3), 271–349 (2000), stating that identical research tracks in drug discovery and development are unlikely, even if several parties are developing similar drugs, because the R&D will likely involve different concepts, targets, ideas, and directions that affect the likelihood, and degree of success and manner of achieving the end result. See also Arti K. Rai, Jerome H. Reichman, Paul F. Uhlir, and Colin R. Crossman, *Pathways Across the Valley of Death: Novel Intellectual Property Strategies for Accelerated Drug Discovery.* YALE JOURNAL OF HEALTH POLICY, LAW AND ETHICS, 8(1), 53–89 (2008).

[80]   Research paths in the pharmaceutical industry generally are not duplicative. Ben-Asher, ibid., and Rai et al., ibid.

disease considered a close substitute and therefore a credible R&D pole? Even if there are parallel R&D streams directed towards the same disease, it may be hard to predetermine the characteristics and effects of a future drug since its application could vary from proof of concept to pre-clinical to clinical stages of the drug discovery process. Does substitutability include players in the 'me-too drugs'[81] market where companies pursue cheaper and less risky independent parallel research based on clinical pathways discovered by third parties instead of pursuing R&D relating to drugs with a novel mechanism of action? To what extent is competition in innovation measured quantitatively (i.e. by the number of relevant R&D projects) or qualitatively (i.e. by the similarity of the R&D projects) and if such determination can be made, how many competing R&D projects are required for the innovation market to be competitive in the pharmaceutical context? Although the various block exemption guidelines and regulations make reference to or use examples involving the pharmaceutical industry as it relates to innovation markets,[82] none of the guidelines or regulations consider the actual nature and peculiarities of the industry to provide a clear answer as to how the concept of R&D poles help define and assess innovation markets.

Others argue that assessing innovation and determining competing R&D poles in the drug discovery and development process is not speculative because parties engaged in R&D efforts directed towards a certain product or technology (and its substitutes) can be identified by way of patent applications, industry publications, and through the regulatory authorities by way of the clinical testing process.[83] This implies

---

[81]   Me-too drugs are defined as chemically similar compounds or compounds with the same mechanism of action as an existing approved pharmaceutical product. Because of the cost in time and resources required for a drug to get FDA approval, investing in the development of a drug treatment similar to one with prior approval is cheaper and less risky than novel drugs, and will likely result in several similar drugs arriving on the market within a short period of time.
[82]   Horizontal Guidelines, *supra* note 15, paragraphs 120 and 121. Also, the principles of competition in innovation are illustrated by way of Examples 2 and 4 in the Horizontal Guidelines. The principles of TTBER are illustrated by way of Examples 1–3 in Communication from the Commission, *Guidelines on the application of Article 101 of the Treaty on the Functioning of the European Union to technology transfer agreements*, Official Journal C89, 28.03.2014, 3-50, using a biotechnology company as an example.
[83]   See for example, Susan DeSanti and William Cohen, 'Competition to Innovate: Strategies for Proper Antitrust Assessments' in Rochelle C. Dreyfuss,

that the assessment of innovation markets and R&D poles should apply to collaborations at later stages of development and not to collaborations involving early stage R&D and proof of concept. These scholars assert that if the goal of assessing innovation markets is to preserve R&D competition when it is most in danger of being suppressed, this occurs in the stages of regulatory approval closest to the marketplace.[84]

With respect to taking into consideration the nature of the R&D poles,[85] the difference in financial and human resources between 'big pharma'[86] and smaller pharmaceutical companies are significant. Research organizations such as integrated drug discovery organizations also differ vastly in regards to access to resources, equipment, and intellectual capital. In general, larger organizations are more likely to have the resources, economies of scale, expertise, and access to funding to endure the lengthy and arduous discovery, development, and commercialization process.[87] Applied to the integrated drug discovery and development collaboration agreements, it is uncertain whether integrated drug discovery organizations and industry will be considered credible R&D poles. On the one hand, because of the nature of the collaboration and the unique research capabilities and access to specialized resources, integrated drug discovery organizations and industry may be considered credible R&D poles. However, absent collaboration, the parties would not be able to proceed from basic discovery through to development and commercialization. On the other hand, because of the

---

Diane L. Zimmerman and Harry First (eds), *Expanding the Boundaries of Intellectual Property: Innovation Policy for the Knowledge Society* (Oxford University Press 2001) at 327; and Rebecca Henderson and Iain Cockburn, *Scale, Scope and Spillovers: The Determinants of Research Productivity in Drug Discovery.* RAND JOURNAL OF ECONOMICS, 27(1), 32–59 (1996).

[84] Carrier, *supra* note 42. Collaborations on early stage discoveries have not matured to the point where the concerns relating to restricting R&D and innovation can be reliably assessed.

[85] Horizontal Guidelines, *supra* note 15, paragraph 120.

[86] Big pharma is a term that denotes the largest players in the pharmaceutical industry and is often used to refer to companies having a revenue in excess of US$3 billion and/or R&D expenditure in excess of US$500 million.

[87] See for example Patricia M. Danzon, *Economics of the Pharmaceutical Industry.* NBER REPORTER, 14–17 (2006); Walter W. Powell, 'Networks of Learning in Biotechnology: Opportunities and Constraints Associated with Relational Contracting in a Knowledge-Intensive Field' in Rochelle C. Dreyfuss, Diane L. Zimmerman and Harry First (eds), *Expanding the Boundaries of Intellectual Property: Innovation Policy for the Knowledge Society* (Oxford University Press 2001) at 251–266.

early stage nature of the collaboration, it may be too premature to assess the impact of the collaboration on competing R&D and innovation efforts.

iv.   Relevant Market: Technology Market

Market definition is the starting point and central tool of assessing effects-based competition concerns that arise from the infringement of Article 101. According to the Commission Notice on the definition of relevant market,[88] market definition establishes a framework into which the objectives pursued by competition policy can be fitted.[89] The practical purpose of defining the relevant market is to determine the competitive constraints that undertakings may face by identifying the actual competitors that are capable of exerting competitive pressure on the market.[90] How the relevant market is defined will have a significant impact on the subsequent competition law assessment.[91] Defining the

---

[88]   Commission Notice on the definition of relevant market for the purposes of Community competition law [1997] OJ C372/5 (hereinafter referred to as the 'Relevant Market Notice').

[89]   Ibid., at paragraph 2: 'Market definition is a tool to identify and define the boundaries of competition between firms. It serves to establish the framework within which competition policy is applied by the Commission. The main purpose of market definition is to identify in a systematic way the competitive constraints that the undertakings involved face. The objective of defining a market in both its product and geographic dimension is to identify those actual competitors of the undertakings involved that are capable of constraining those undertakings' behaviour and of preventing them from behaving independently of effective competitive pressure. It is from this perspective that the market definition makes it possible *inter alia* to calculate market shares that would convey meaningful information regarding market power for the purposes of assessing dominance or for the purposes of applying Article 85'.

[90]   Ibid., paragraph 9. In other words, in order to define the relevant market for the purposes of competition law, the Commission needs to assess which products/services are regarded by consumers as interchangeable in a defined geographic area, and therefore which belong in the same relevant market. According to paragraph 8 of the Relevant Market Notice, *supra* note 88, 'the relevant geographic market comprises the area in which the undertakings concerned are involved in the supply and demand of products or services, in which the conditions of competition are sufficiently homogeneous and which can be distinguished from neighbouring areas because the conditions of competition are appreciably different in those areas'.

[91]   Richard Whish and David Bailey, *Competition Law* (Oxford University Press 2012) at 770, which stated 'much is at stake in the art or science of market definition'.

relevant market is a quantitative and qualitative exercise conducted via a systematic investigation of the competitive landscape and its relevant players,[92] assuming there is data readily available to assist in making such an assessment. The Commission recognizes that the dynamics of markets characterized by high rates of innovation and importance in R&D need to be considered when defining the market and assessing competitive effects.[93]

One of the main components of defining the relevant technology market is by reference to technologies that are substitutable or can be used by the consumer as substitutes.[94] As stated by the court in *Europemballage Corporation and Continental Can Company Inc. v Commission*:

> ... the definition of the relevant market is of essential significance, for the possibilities of competition can only be judged in relation to those character-istics of the products in question by virtue of which those products are particularly apt to satisfy an inelastic need and are only to a limited extent interchangeable with other products...[95]

---

[92] The Commission has used many tools and information already collected by interested parties to conduct an evidence-based effects analysis to determine relevant market, including the use of end-consumer surveys (Case COMP/M.4439 *Ryanair/Aer Lingus*), price correlation analysis to examine the extent to which the prices of two products move together over time (Case COMP/M.5153 *Arsenal/DSP*, Case COMP/M.4799 OMV/MOL), critical loss analysis to estim-ate how much the hypothetical monopolist's sales would have to fall in order to make a price increase unprofitable (Case COMP/M.4734 *INEOS/Kerling*), analy-ses of past shocks in the market to observe whether these can teach us something about competitive dynamics in that market (Case COMP/M.5335 *Lufthansa/SN Airholding*), and demand estimation (Case COMP/M.5658 *Unilever/Sara Lee*, Case COMP/M.5644 Kraft/Cadbury).

[93] See Case COMP/M.6203 *Western Digital/Viviti Technologies*; COMP/M.5984 *Intel/McAfee*; COMP/M.5529 *Oracle/Sun*; COMP/M.5421 *Panasonic/Sanyo*. See also OECD Roundtable on Market Definition DAF/COMP/WD (2012).

[94] Horizontal Guidelines, *supra* note 15, paragraph 117 provides very little guidance on how to assess substitutability by referring to substitutes which customers could switch to in response to a small but non-transitory increase in relative prices. Relevant Market Notice, *supra* note 88, paragraph 7 provides further assistance on the assessment of substitutability by assessing the product or technology's characteristic, prices, and their intended use.

[95] *Europemballage Corporation and Continental Can Company Inc. v Commission of the European Communities* C-6/72 [1973] ECR 215.

The concept of interchangeability and substitutability is particularly difficult to apply in the context of the pharmaceutical industry. It is often the case where there may be several drugs available to treat a particular ailment. However, each of these products may be delivered differently (e.g. intravenously, orally, or by way of a suppository), or be designed to treat the disease at different stages (e.g. preventative, early onset, or late stage treatment); or each of the drugs may interact with different target sites to produce the intended pharmaceutical effect (e.g. ibuprofen and acetylsalicylic acid are both over-the-counter pain relievers that seek to suppress the production of prostaglandins, but the mechanism of acetyl-salicylic acid is to *deactivate* the enzyme cyclooxygenase required to produce prostaglandins whereas ibuprofen *inhibits* the production of cyclooxygenase). Although a group of pharmaceutical products may have an effect on the 'same disease' (defined broadly) and therefore can be theoretically considered 'substitutable' on one level, the differences between the classification, metabolic pathway, and mechanism of action of these same drugs may render them not 'substitutable' on a different level.[96] This is exemplified in the case of *AstraZeneca v Commission*,[97] where the ECJ upheld the relevant market definition put forward by the Commission and accepted by the European Union General Court, holding that the definition of the relevant market is determined first by the category of pathology and then the phase of treatment that is required. Although the drugs in question were both for the treatment of 'acid related gastric conditions', the court found differentiated therapeutic uses between the drugs and that the older histamine receptor antagonists ('H2 blockers') failed to exercise significant competitive constraints over the new proton pump inhibitors (PPI). The drugs were therefore found to be in separate markets even though H2 blockers were the leading treatment for hyperacidity prior to the introduction of PPI treatment into the market.[98] AstraZeneca argued that the relevant market should be defined and based on the product's therapeutic indications (ATC classification 3), as in prior case law, as opposed to the drug's mode of action (ATC classification 4), which was the approach adopted by the Commission when assessing the impact on competition.[99] In the pharmaceutical

---

[96]   See for example, *AstraZeneca v European Commission*, Case C–457/10 P, judgment of 6 December 2012.
[97]   Ibid.
[98]   Ibid.
[99]   See *Teva/Ratiopharm* Case No. COMP/M.5865 Commission decision of 3 August 2010. However, in *Teva/Ratiopharm* the Commission adopted a more narrow market definition based on ATC4 because the case involved generics,

context where the substitutability of prescription medicines depends not only on their physical, technical or chemical properties but also on their functional substitutability as viewed by medical practitioners,[100] and where prior case law has found that technical superiority of a product in a given pharmaceutical category does not shield it from competitive constraints from other similar products,[101] it is not clear to players involved in the drug discovery and development process what technologies will be considered substitutes. AstraZeneca argued that its product was in competition with other medicines to treat hyperacidity. Although the sales of PPIs increased gradually, the courts attributed the delay to the caution displayed by doctors towards a new medicine whose properties were not yet entirely known, rather than because of a competitive constraint exercised by H2 blockers over PPIs.[102] Arguably,

---

which tend to be close substitutes of the original product. See for example, Case COMP/M.5253 *Sanofi-Aventis/Zentiva*, Commission decision of 4 February 2009 and Case COMP/M.5295 *Teva/Barr*, decision of 19 December 2008. The *Teva/Ratiopharm* decision provides some general insight into the Commission's approach to market definition in pharmaceutical markets, suggesting that the Commission is prepared to move away from the broad ATC3 intended use classification to adopt a more nuanced approach that takes into account a range of factors including molecule class, pharmaceutical formulation, and mode of action. See David W. Hull, *The Application of EU Competition Law in the Pharmaceutical Sector*. JOURNAL OF EUROPEAN COMPETITION LAW & PRACTICE, 2(5), 480–488 (2011). However, this could potentially result in a greater number of companies being found to hold a dominant position in relation to single pharmaceutical products that have been found to form separate markets even though the product has the same therapeutic indication as existing products on the market.

[100]   Commission Decision 97/469/EC of 17 July 1996 in a proceeding pursuant to Regulation No 4064/89 Case IV/M.737 – *Ciba-Geigy/Sandoz* OJ 1997 L 201, p. 1, recital 21.

[101]   Commission Decisions of 27 May 2005 Case COMP/M.3751 – *Novartis/ Hexal* and Case COMP/M.1878 – *Pfizer/Warner-Lambert* of 22 May 2000.

[102]   This raises a significant concern of legal uncertainty. When a new product is introduced into the market, it is hard to determine whether an existing product is retaining market share because of the quality of the product (positive evidence of competitive constraint) or because doctors are initially reluctant to prescribe new products due to unfamiliarity with the product's properties (not evidence of competitive constraint, according to the *AstraZeneca* case). Furthermore, given that the reluctance from doctors to prescribe PPIs was largely dependent on the possible serious side effects associated with them, the continued use and preference for H2 blockers because of their less risky side effects should therefore constitute a competitive restraint on PPIs. If side effects are a significant consideration when deciding on substitutability, the courts should not

this case illustrates how the success of a pharmaceutical product can be used against a company in an ex-post manner because competitors had the ability to compile a body of data for the courts to apply hindsight and find a trend of asymmetrical substitution that characterized the growth in sales of PPIs and the corresponding decrease in sales of H2 blockers to conclude that H2 blockers did not exercise a significant competitive constraint on PPIs.[103] The ECJ agreed that:

> had [the General Court] misconstrued the relevance of the gradual nature of the increase in the use of PPIs at the expense of H2 blockers and the development of the competitive relationship between those two products during the period at issue, namely ... between 1993 and 2000, that error would be such as to call into question that assessment in its entirety and the conclusions which the General Court drew from it.

However, in this case, the ECJ found that the General Court was entitled to conclude that there was no causal link between the gradual increase in sales of PPIs and any competitive restraint exercised by H2 blockers. The *AstraZeneca* decision is significant as it validates the recent trend of the Commission to adopt a more narrow approach to defining the market in both competition and merger cases involving the pharmaceutical industry.

v.   Market Share

For the purposes of analyzing the collaboration between integrated drug discovery organizations and industry, because the parties are not considered competitive undertakings, there is no need to calculate the market share of the parties because the thresholds do not apply to agreements between non-competitors. As set out in Article 4 of the R&D Regulation and confirmed in the Horizontal Guidelines, agreements between non-competitors qualify for exemption irrespective of the market shares of the parties.[104] However, it is worth noting that the literature is generally critical of the difficulty in determining market share, especially in the

---

have ignored this factor when deciding whether products fall in the same relevant market. See Hull, *supra* note 99.

[103]   The specific facts of the *AstraZeneca* case, which included AstraZeneca submitting misleading facts to the patent office and adopting strategies that made it difficult for generic companies to enter the market, viewed in the context of the Commission's pharmaceutical sector inquiry final report also played a significant role in the final outcome of the case.

[104]   R&D Regulation, *supra* note 14, Article 4(1) and Horizontal Guidelines, *supra* note 15, paragraph 126.

context of high technology sectors such as the pharmaceutical industry, as it is very difficult to calculate the exact market share of the new product and to define the correct market.[105] Even when the correct market can be established, the threshold is often exceeded because a new innovation worth commercializing typically means the product enjoys certain advantages over existing products.[106]

vi. Restrictions

The R&D block exemption sets out a list of hardcore restrictions, and a list of excluded restrictions.[107] Hardcore restrictions are restrictions the Commission considers to infringe Article 101(1). The inclusion of a hardcore restriction in the agreement disqualifies the agreement as a whole from exemption under the R&D Regulation and is subject to individual assessment under Article 101(3).[108] However, hardcore clauses will in most cases render an exemption impossible because they are regarded as a good indication of restrictions that are not indispensable to a collaboration agreement.[109] Most of the hardcore restrictions relate to the manufacture and distribution of products, which have no applicability to the collaboration agreement between integrated drug discovery organizations and industry. The only hardcore prohibition that may have some relevance to the integrated drug discovery and development platform is the restriction on the parties to carry out independent R&D activities alone or in collaboration with third parties. The application of this restriction will be contemplated in Chapter 6 when the clauses of the

---

[105]   Glader, *supra* note 56 at 31.
[106]   Gutterman, *supra* note 11 at 394.
[107]   R&D Regulation, *supra* note 14, Articles 5 and 6.
[108]   Ibid.
[109]   Ibid. Article 5 sets out the hardcore restrictions, which effectively disqualifies the entire agreement from the exemption provided for in Article 2 should the agreement include any of the listed hardcore restrictions. See also Horizontal Guidelines, *supra* note 15, paragraph 142 which states '[r]estrictions that go beyond what is necessary to achieve the efficiency gains generated by an R&D agreement do not fulfil the criteria of Article 101(3). In particular, the restrictions listed in Article 5 of the R&D Block Exemption Regulation may mean it is less likely that the criteria of Article s(3) will be found to be met, following an individual assessment. It will therefore generally be necessary for the parties to an R&D agreement to show that such restrictions are indispensable to the co-operation.

collaboration agreements will be analyzed in view of the R&D Regulation. Excluded restrictions are also restrictions the Commission considers to fall within the scope of Article 101(1) but will not disqualify the entire agreement from exemption. Outside the hardcore and excluded restrictions, other clauses of the agreement will be assessed to determine whether a less restrictive form could be sufficient to achieve the same benefits from it.

C.   REMARKS: THE NEED FOR COLLABORATIVE R&D

The pharmaceutical industry is arguably quite different compared to most other industry sectors. Pharmaceutical companies face a significantly higher risk of failure. A product may never reach the market despite the considerable upfront investment in time and money required for the development process. If a new drug candidate is ultimately successful and does make it to market, it is usually made commercially available when much of the patent life has already expired. Within this shortened exclusivity period, industry needs to fully recoup its investment, not only in respect of the successful innovation, but also for the many failed projects. The word 'commercialization' is usually associated with the concept of profit. However, in the drug discovery and development context, commercialization is a much more complex word that incorporates the concept of making basic drug discovery research available to the public. The reality is that drug discovery and development requires the involvement of both academia and industry. As a 'quid pro quo' for making life-saving products available to the benefit of public health, efficient and effective translation of publically funded research through university–industry collaborations is a necessity.

Innovation is one of the fundamental sources of competitiveness in the pharmaceutical industry, but it is also a factor that may delay the launch of products and consequently negatively affect consumer welfare.[110] In most cases, at the time collaborations between integrated drug discovery organizations and industry are created, the technology that forms the subject of the collaboration is at an early stage, with no foreseeable exploitation potential. As discussed in this chapter, most agreements

---

[110]   See Giulio Bottazzi, Giovanni Dosi, Marco Lippi, Fabio Pammolli, and Massimo Riccaboni, *Innovation and Corporate Growth in the Evolution of the Drug Industry.* INTERNATIONAL JOURNAL OF ORGANIZATION, 19(7), 1161–1187 (2001) at p. 1162. See also OECD, *supra* note 1.

relating to collaborative R&D at an early stage far removed from the potential of exploiting the results do not fall under Article 101(1) or qualify for exemption under the R&D Regulation. Moreover, because both integrated drug discovery organizations and industry are not able to carry out the necessary R&D independently to translate discoveries into commercializable products, as non-competitors, the collaboration is unlikely to give rise to anticompetitive effects. However, R&D collaborations between non-competitors can still give rise to foreclosure effects with respect to the innovation market. The relationship between competition policy and innovation markets is based on several assumptions that are debatable. Specifically, the potential anticompetitive effects on the markets for future products that may result from collaboration on the innovation markets is based on the assumption that concentration of R&D efforts will lead to less R&D and a slower rate of innovation. Although there may be support for the general conclusion that a concentration of R&D efforts in a particular field may be a contributing factor to a reduced rate of technological progress in that field, in reality it is very difficult to assess for a certain industry where the critical concentration ratio lies. The second general assumption is that less R&D will lead to a negative outcome. This ignores the possibility of concentration and cooperation leading to efficiencies by avoiding duplication in R&D efforts, resources, and time. It is difficult to establish a balance between quantifiable efficiencies in R&D and future potential competition disadvantages that may only appear later after the collaborative R&D has borne fruit and new products are marketed.

Compared to other established industries where development time and cost are generally much lower and where business infrastructure costs can be amortized and used for the commercialization of other products, it is difficult to see how competition policy can achieve its purpose across all industries when the specific dynamics of the pharmaceutical industry are so different from traditional industries. As stated by Alexis Jaquemin:

> Partners who have achieved inventions want to control the processes and products, which embody the results of their collaboration, in order to recuperate jointly and as quickly as possible, their R&D investment. If the firms are prevented from such a joint exploitation and if the benefits of cooperative R&D are expected to be very quickly dissipated through intense market competition, the parties may be tempted to avoid R&D cooperation and to maintain wasteful competition in the pre-innovation market or to use their cooperation to limit unduly their R&D. If this is true, a regulation of R&D cooperation excluding any cooperation at the level of final markets could discourage or destabilize many valuable agreements. However, allowing an extension of cooperation in R&D to manufacturing and distribution

encourages collusive behaviour that impedes competition. This is the dilemma faced by the European Antitrust Authorities.[111]

To date, there has been no judgment by the European Court of Justice on the R&D Regulation. The absence of authoritative guidance on its interpretation gives rise to uncertainty for those wishing to enter into a collaborative R&D agreement, especially when it incorporates a technology transfer component of the results because the onus is on the parties to work out for themselves whether their agreement comes within the terms of the various block exemptions.

---

[111]   Jaquemin, *supra* note 13 at 42.

5. Application of competition law to the integrated drug discovery and development model: technology transfer block exemption regulation

A. INTRODUCTION

As stated by the World Intellectual Property Organization and the Commission, the underlying principle of licensing technology is that it contributes to economic development and facilitates a more efficient exploitation of intellectual property by providing a means to disseminate innovative creations.[1] In theory, licensing can therefore be said to encourage the production and introduction of new products into the market, which in turn can stimulate further innovation and generate competition. To facilitate the licensing of technology for the purpose of maximizing the benefit of disseminating knowledge, the Commission introduced the technology transfer block exemption (TTBER), which sets out the basis for providing safe harbor to a category of agreements relating to the licensing of intellectual property while attempting to provide flexibility to respect contractual freedom instead of imposing

---

[1] According to the World Intellectual Property Organization: 'In a globalized economy, technology licensing and transfer of technology are important factors in strategic alliances and international joint ventures in order to maintain a competitive edge in a market economy. Thus, policy tools to facilitate licensing and technology transfer at the international level have often been considered in the context of creating an appropriate climate for investment and economic development' (see http://www.toolipvaluation.com/patent-transfer/). See also European Commission, *Antitrust: Commission Consults on Proposal for Revised Competition Regime for Technology Transfer Agreements* (IP/13/120 2013) where the Commission states: 'Licensing is vital for economic development and consumer welfare as it helps to disseminate innovation and allows companies to integrate and use complementary technologies'.

strict compliance of rigid rules.[2] The guidelines on the application of TTBER (the 'TTBER Guidelines')[3] provide directions to undertakings to engage in a self-assessment of the application and compliance of their agreement with TTBER. Because the former ways of determining competitive effects tended to be formalistic and imposed too great a restraint without regard to economic consequences,[4] the overall objective of TTBER is to promote dynamic competition through innovation by being more flexible and economically oriented towards technology transfer agreements.[5]

On May 1, 2014, a revised version of TTBER and the TTBER Guidelines came into force. Before the expiration of the prior version of TTBER, various drafts and public consultations[6] indicated the Commission's increasing concern with the effects of technology licensing and use

---

[2]   Commission Regulation No 316/2014 on the application of Article 101(3) of the Treaty on the Functioning of the European Union to categories of technology transfer agreements, OJ 2014 L93/17 ('TTBER'), see recitals. See also Maurits Dolmans and Ana Piilola, *The New Technology Transfer Block Exemption*. WORLD COMPETITION, 27(3), 351–363 (2004) at 360 and European Commission, *Commission Evaluation Report on the Transfer of Technology Block Exemption Regulation* No. 240/96 (COM 786 Final, 2001) at paragraph 76 commenting on TTBER's flexibility to allow parties to design their licensing agreements in accordance with their commercial needs instead of straitjacketing them to comply with the regulation, which may have a discouraging effect on the dissemination of technology.

[3]   Communication from the Commission, *Guidelines on the application of Article 101 of the Treaty on the Functioning of the European Union to technology transfer agreements*, Official Journal C89, 28.03.2014, 3–50 (hereinafter referred to as 'TTBER Guidelines').

[4]   Valentine Korah, *Intellectual Property Rights and the EC Competition Rules* (Hart Publishing 2006) at 250. See also Richard Whish and David Bailey, *Competition Law* (Oxford University Press 2012).

[5]   Dolmans and Piilola, *supra* note 2 at 351.

[6]   Draft Commission Regulation (EU) on the application of Article 101(3) of the Treaty on the Functioning of the European Union to categories of technology transfer agreements (accessible at http://ec.europa.eu/competition/consultations/2013_technology_transfer/regulation_en.pdf); Draft Guidelines on the application of Article 101 of the Treaty on the Functioning of the European Union to technology transfer agreements (accessible at http://ec.europa.eu/competition/consultations/2013_technology_transfer/guidelines_en.pdf). See also Overview of Submissions Received from Stakeholders in the Public Consultation on the Draft Proposal for a Revised Block Exemption Regulation for Technology Transfer Agreements and for Revised Guidelines (accessible at http://ec.europa.eu/competition/consultations/2013_technology_transfer/summary_public_consultation_en.pdf).

of intellectual property in markets that are highly dependent on innovation.[7] As a result, the 2014 TTBER and TTBER Guidelines included a number of substantive changes including, *inter alia*: (i) a clarification of the scope of TTBER with respect to other block exemptions such as the R&D Regulation; (ii) additional guidance on the method of calculating market shares; (iii) revisions to the catalogue of 'hard-core' and excluded restrictions; and (iv) additional guidance on the compatibility of technology pools with competition policy.

The TTBER Guidelines specifically recognize that intellectual property law and competition law share the same basic objective of promoting consumer welfare and an efficient allocation of resources:

> Intellectual property rights promote dynamic competition by encouraging undertakings to invest in developing new or improved products and processes. So does competition by putting pressure on undertakings to innovate. Therefore both intellectual property rights and competition are necessary to promote innovation and ensure a competitive exploitation thereof.[8]

---

[7] Joaquín Almunia, Vice President of the European Commission responsible for Competition Policy, *Industrial and Competition Policy: Quo Vadis Europa?*, Address at the New Frontiers of Antitrust 3rd International Concurrences Conference (Feb. 10, 2012) (SPEECH/12/83) (accessible at http://europa.eu/rapid/press-release_SPEECH-12-83_en.pdf) where the vice president recognized that monopolies and tight oligopolies tend to resist change in favor of preserving their business model. As such, keeping markets open to new entrants is key to promoting innovation. It is therefore a priority of competition policy to control the use of patents rights to ensure that new businesses are given a fair chance to have effective access to technologies to develop freely to their utmost potential. Similarly, see Alexander Italianer, Director General of the European Commission Directorate-General for Competition, Prepared Remarks on: Level-Playing Field and Innovation in Technology Markets, Address at the Conference on Antitrust in Technology (Jan. 28, 2013) (accessible at http://ec.europa.eu/competition/speeches/text/sp2013_01_en.pdf) where the Director General spoke on the balance between enforcement of competition policy and maintaining incentives to innovate in high tech markets, which requires careful and cautious analysis of the facts and the market developments. The Commission needs to intervene to ensure that markets remain open enough for innovation to be able to flourish. Entrenched market positions can be used anticompetitively to exclude existing competitors or prevent potential ones from entering the market, for example, when companies invest substantially to develop a technology and are resistant to change.

[8] TTBER Guidelines, *supra* note 3 at paragraph 7. See also TTBER, *supra* note 78 at recital 4 which states; 'Technology transfer agreements concern the licensing of technology. Such agreements will usually improve economic efficiency and be pro-competitive as they can reduce duplication of research and

The overall philosophy expressed in TTBER and the TTBER Guidelines is that most license agreements do not restrict competition and actually create pro-competitive economic efficiencies by reducing duplication, incentivizing innovation, and facilitating commercialization.[9] Recognizing the Commission's position that the great majority of license agreements are compatible with Article 101, it can be argued that the Commission is generally supportive of technology transfer agreements, even if they include some restrictions.[10] TTBER tolerates certain restrictions in order to promote licensing and dynamic competition, even if they may result in short-term loss of static competition. TTBER expressly adopts an economic approach when assessing the impact of agreements on competition,[11] which may suggest an attempt by the Commission to allow companies a certain amount of flexibility to draw up license agreements according to their commercial needs, while protecting competition and encouraging innovation.

TTBER can be summarized as comprising of three main elements:

---

development, strengthen the incentive for the initial research and development, spur incremental innovation, facilitate diffusion and generate product market competition. The assumption in the TTBER Guidelines that a competitive market structure is likely to give rise to incentives to innovate appears to be more in line with the findings of Arrow as opposed to the claims made by Schumpeter that a concentrated market or monopoly leads to more innovation (see Chapter 3, this volume). This implies that the Commission believes intervention by competition law in favor of protecting market rivalry should therefore pressure firms to innovate as oppose to discourage innovation by stifling investments in the development and commercialization of new technology

[9]   See TTBER, *supra* note 2, recitals and TTBER Guidelines, *supra* note 3 at paragraphs 5, 9, and 17 and paragraph 42 which states that many license agreements fall outside Article 101(1), either because they do not restrict competition at all or because the restriction of competition is not appreciable.

[10]   See TTBER, *supra* note 2 at recital 5, which states: 'The likelihood that such efficiency-enhancing and pro-competitive effects will outweigh any anti-competitive effects due to restrictions contained in technology transfer agreements depends on the degree of market power of the undertakings concerned and, therefore, on the extent to which those undertakings face competition from undertakings owning substitute technologies or undertakings producing substitute products'.

[11]   Recital 4 of the 2004 version of TTBER specifically sets out the economics-based approach of TTBER to assess the impact of agreements on the relevant market as opposed to the previous approach of listing exempted clauses. TTBER places a greater emphasis on an analysis of market power possessed by the parties and their ability to produce anticompetitive effects through commercial arrangements.

1.   Creating a safe harbor for technology transfer agreements between two undertakings, provided their combined market share does not exceed 20% in the case of agreements between competitors, and in the case of agreements between non-competitors, the market share of each of the parties shall not exceed 30%;[12]

2.   Setting out a list of hardcore restrictions that are not to be included in a technology transfer agreement. Agreements containing hard-core restrictions fall outside the scope of the block exemption in their entirety and typically do not qualify for exemption under Article 101(3);[13] and

3.   Setting out a limited list of excluded restrictions that are subject to individual assessment.[14] Their inclusion in an agreement does not exclude the application of the block exemption to the rest of the agreement.

Agreements that fulfill the conditions of TTBER are block exempted from the prohibition contained in Article 101(1). Agreements that fall outside the scope of TTBER are *not* automatically deemed to violate Article 101(1) but are subject to individual assessment of its likely effect on the relevant market to determine if the agreement qualifies for exemption under Article 101(3).[15] Article 101(3) exemption will be further considered in the context of the analysis of the actual agreements received from the four integrated drug discovery organizations in the following chapter.[16]

---

[12]   TTBER, *supra* note 2 at Article 3.

[13]   Ibid., at Article 4. See also TTBER Guidelines, *supra* note 3 at paragraph 18 which states: 'Hardcore restrictions are unlikely to fulfil the conditions of Article 101(3). Such agreements generally fail (at least) one of the first two conditions of Article 101(3). In general they do not create objective economic benefit of benefits for consumers'.

[14]   TTBER, *supra* note 2, at Article 5. See also TTBER Guidelines, *supra* note 3 at paragraph 41.

[15]   TTBER Guidelines, *supra* note 3 at paragraphs 43, 79, and 156 which collectively set out the need to examine whether an individual agreement is caught by Article 101(1) and whether the conditions of Article 101(3) are satisfied if the agreement falls outside the scope of the block exemption.

[16]   How the Commission analyzes licensing agreements with respect to assessing the beneficial effects of licensing agreements under Article 101(1) compared to 101(3) is important because the standards are different in terms of analytical steps as well as burden of proof. Under Article 101(1), it is up to the Commission or complainant to prove that there is a restriction of competition, whereas under Article 101(3), the burden of proof is shifted over to the

In this chapter, the applicability of TTBER and the TTBER Guidelines to the integrated drug discovery and development model will be analyzed.[17] This evaluation will form the basis of the analysis in the following chapter of the specific clauses of the licensing agreements associated with the collaboration agreements collected from CD3, CDRD, LRD, and MRCT with respect to various types of licensing restraints included in such agreements.[18] Licensing restraints, which have often been viewed in the literature as a means for the licensor to appropriate a reward for the patent, are actually more complex and are often used to resolve transactional costs and manage third party opportunistic behavior. Furthermore, individual contractual restrictions on their own may not be sufficiently restrictive to attract the criticism of the Commission, but it is the cumulative effect of the clauses that make up the agreement as a whole which may give rise to an anticompetitive effect.[19]

---

contracting parties. See Council Regulation (EC) No 1/2003 of 16 December 2002 on the implementation of the rules on competition laid down in Articles 81 and 82 of the Treaty [now 101 and 102 TFEU] (Regulation 1/2003), OJ [2003] L 1/1, Article 2.

[17]   The licensing of technology can take many different forms, from simple license agreements involving mature and defined technologies to complex collaborative agreements involving the further development of the technology or its realization 'from scratch'. See for example Ashish Arora, Andrea Fosfuri and Alfonso Gambardella, *Markets for Technology and their Implications for Corporate Strategy*. INDUSTRIAL AND CORPORATE CHANGE, 10(2), 419–451 (2001) at 422.

[18]   Because the collaboration agreements collected from the integrated drug discovery organizations do not include any hardcore restrictions, the analysis will only focus on excluded restrictions and various types of restraints that are commonly included in license agreement. An introduction to and general discussion of hardcore restrictions will be included in the chapter but will not be included in the analysis sections of the chapter.

[19]   TTBER Guidelines, *supra* note 3 at paragraph 148 which expressly recognizes that the hardcore restrictions and excluded restrictions do not take into account any cumulative effects of restrictions, for example where potential licensees may be denied access to the necessary technology due to the cumulative effect of license agreements prohibiting licensors from licensing other licensees. See also TTBER Guidelines at paragraph 168.

B. TTBER AND THE COLLABORATIVE DRUG DISCOVERY AND DEVELOPMENT PROCESS

The Commission expressly recognizes in the TTBER Guidelines that the creation and exploitation of intellectual property rights often entails substantial investment and that it is often a risky endeavor:

> In order not to reduce dynamic competition and to maintain the incentive to innovate, the innovator must not be unduly restricted in the exploitation of intellectual property rights that turn out to be valuable. For these reasons the innovator should be free to seek appropriate remuneration for successful projects that is sufficient to maintain investment incentives, taking failed projects into account. Technology licensing may also require the licensee to make significant sunk investments (that is to say, that upon leaving that particular field of activity the investment cannot be used by the licensee for other activities or sold other than at a significant loss) in the licensed technology and production assets necessary to exploit it. Article 101 cannot be applied without considering such ex ante investments made by the parties and the risks relating thereto. The risk facing the parties and the sunk investment that must be committed may thus lead to the agreement falling outside Article 101(1) or fulfilling the conditions of Article 101(3), as the case may be, for the period of time required to recoup the investment.[20]

A question to consider is whether the application of TTBER, particularly to integrated drug discovery and development, is truly in line with economic theory and considerations.[21] It is also particularly noteworthy

---

[20]   TTBER Guidelines, *supra* note 3 at paragraph 8.

[21]   The reference to sunk investments seem to recognize licensing efficiency and transactional hazards in licensing as a relevant consideration. However, the TTBER Guidelines fail to explicitly explain how to balance *ex ante* incentives and market rivalry. The ambiguity is further exacerbated by stating that innovators should be free to seek 'appropriate remuneration' without any further explanation as to what constitutes appropriate remuneration 'sufficient to maintain investment incentives'. If TTBER is adopting an economic approach, does 'appropriate remuneration' mean the same thing as the social value of the invention in the economic literature, which generally accepts that an inventor should be entitled to the value that the technology creates for society. See for example, Stephen M. Maurer and Suzanne Scotchmer, *Profit Neutrality in Licensing: The Boundary between Antitrust Law and Patent Law*. AMERICAN LAW AND ECONOMICS REVIEW, 8(3), 476–522 (2006). Commentators have questioned whether the application of the TTBER achieves the objective of recognizing the need to protect ex ante incentives. See for example Valentine Korah, *Draft Block Exemption for Technology Transfer*. EUROPEAN COMPETITION LAW REVIEW, 25(5), 247–262 (2004) and Robert C. Lind and Paul

that the TTBER Guidelines demand a flexible and reasonable application of TTBER in light of the specific circumstances and facts of the agreement.[22] Having recognized the need to consider the risk and ex-ante investments in technology licensing, as well as the need to adopt a flexible approach to assessing licensing agreements, an argument can be made that the TTBER Guidelines indirectly consider sector or market-specific dynamics.[23] However, TTBER and the TTBER Guidelines do not appear to provide any particular guidance on the boundaries of the allowable flexibility, which leaves room for discretion and interpretation and creates legal uncertainty in direct contradiction to the mandate of TTBER.[24] In other words, the framework for analysis makes it difficult for parties to a licensing agreement to prove the beneficial effects or defend the necessity of certain clauses in order to protect against ex-ante risks associated with R&D.

Muysert, *The European Commission's Draft Technology Transfer Block Exemption Regulation: A Significant Departure from Accepted Competition Policy Principles.* EUROPEAN COMPETITON LAW REVIEW, 25(4), 181–189 (2004) at 185.

[22]   TTBER Guidelines, *supra* note 3 at paragraph 9 which states 'the existing analytical framework is sufficiently flexible to take due account of the dynamic aspects of technology licensing'. See also TTBER Guidelines at paragraph 3 which states that each case 'must be assessed on its own facts and the guidelines must be applied reasonably and flexibly' in light of the circumstances specific to each case, thereby specifically excluding mechanical application of the TTBER Guidelines.

[23]   Although sector specific regulation does exist for certain industries, there is literature that questions the need for sector specific rules. See for example Marek Szydlo, *Sector-Specific Regulation and Competition Law: Between Convergence and Divergence.* EUROPEAN PUBLIC LAW, 15(2), 257–275 (2009).

[24]   TTBER, *supra* note 2, recital 4. See also TTBER Guidelines, *supra* note 3 at paragraph 15 which explicitly states that the pro-competitive effects of licensing agreements must be balanced against the negative effects in the context of Article 101(3), placing the burden of proof on the parties of the license agreement to establish how the beneficial effects of the agreement outweigh the anticompetitive effects. The burden of proving a restraint or agreement has positive effects on dynamic competition has been criticized in the literature as being unduly difficult and may increase legal uncertainty. See for example Korah, *supra* note 21 at 248.

C. INTERFACE BETWEEN TTBER AND THE R&D REGULATION

In determining the applicability of TTBER to the collaboration agreements between industry and integrated drug discovery organizations, it will become apparent that the agreements do not fit comfortably within the general framework and analysis of TTBER for the following reasons. Firstly, the collaboration agreements between industry and integrated drug discovery organizations contemplate a collaborative R&D component as well as general conditions for licensing the resulting R&D. The collaboration agreement also sets out conditions on subsequent exploitation by industry, which is to be reflected in a separate but associated license agreement setting out the negotiated terms for licensing the resulting R&D between the parties should the collaboration agreement lead to successful results for further development and commercialization.[25] As stated in the preamble of TTBER:

> [TTBER] should only apply to agreements where the licensor permits the licensee and/or one or more of its sub-contractors to exploit the licensed technology rights, possibly after further research and development by the licensee and/or one its sub-contractors, for the purpose of producing goods or services. It should not apply to licensing in the context of research and development agreements which are covered by the Commission Regulation (EU) No 1217/2010 …[26]

The question is whether the 'hybrid' collaboration agreement can be subject to *both* TTBER and the R&D Regulation.[27]

The TTBER Guidelines discuss the relationship between TTBER and other block exemption regulations, including but not limited to the R&D Regulation.[28] However, the TTBER Guidelines are not particularly clear as to whether TTBER applies to the licensing of the resulting R&D *between the same parties*, within the same agreement that sets out the

---

[25] TTBER, *supra* note 2, Article 1(c) sets out four requirements that must be met for the applicability of TTBER. First, there must be (a) a transfer of technology (b) between two parties relating to (c) valid intellectual property rights or know-how (d) for the production of contract products.

[26] TTBER, *supra* note 2, recital 7.

[27] Ibid., Article 9, which contemplates the possibility of its applicability to licensing arrangements in research and development agreements that fall outside the scope of the R&D Regulation.

[28] See TTBER Guidelines, *supra* note 3 at paragraphs 69–78 and specifically paragraphs 73–74 as they relate to R&D agreements.

conditions of collaborative R&D or in a separate but associated license agreement.[29] The TTBER Guidelines specifically recognize that the parties may set out the conditions of licensing the resulting technology from the R&D within the R&D agreement to *third parties*, and the licensing to any such third parties falls within the purview of TTBER. The TTBER Guidelines further state that:

> [The R&D Regulation] covers agreements whereby two or more undertakings agree to jointly carry out research and development and to jointly exploit the results thereof … The Regulation also covers paid-for research and development agreements whereby two or more undertakings agree that the research and development is carried out by one party and financed by another party, with or without joint exploitation of the results thereof.[30]

One possible interpretation of the TTBER Guidelines, as applied to the collaboration agreements, is that the licensing of the resulting technology *between the parties of the R&D agreement* may be covered by the R&D Regulation instead of TTBER.[31] However, such an interpretation would seem to contradict Article 2(2) of the R&D Regulation, which is quite clear that the R&D Regulation applies only to R&D agreements that 'contain provisions relating to the licensing of intellectual property rights necessary to carry out joint research and development, paid-for research

---

[29] Ibid., at paragraph 74 which reads, 'It follows that [R&D Regulation] covers licensing between the parties and by the parties to a joint entity in the context of a research and development agreement. … In the context of such agreements the parties can also determine the conditions for licensing the fruits of the research and development agreement to third parties. However, since third party licensees are not party to the research and development agreement, the individual license agreement concluded with third parties is not covered by [R&D Regulation]. That license agreement is covered by the block exemption in the TTBER if the conditions of it are fulfilled'.

[30] Ibid., at paragraph 73.

[31] Commission Regulation No 1217/2010 on the application of Article 101(3) of the Treaty on the Functioning of the European Union to categories of research and development agreements, OJ 2010 L335/36 (the 'R&D Regulation'), Article 1(1)(g) which defines exploitation as including the licensing of intellectual property rights. Given that Article 1(1)(a) of the R&D Regulation defines research and development agreements as the 'joint exploitation of the results of research and development of contract products or contract technologies jointly carried out pursuant to a prior agreement between the same parties', licensing of the resulting intellectual property, whether in the collaboration agreement or in a separate but associated license agreement between industry and integrated drug discovery organization seems to fall within the scope of the R&D Regulation.

and development, or joint exploitation'.[32] In the context of the collaboration between industry and integrated drug discovery organizations, the agreement relates to joint R&D with general conditions of exploitation, including the possibility of licensing the resulting intellectual property to the industry partner or to third parties for commercialization. Because the exploitation is not defined as joint according to R&D Regulation, the more logical interpretation would be that both TTBER and R&D Regulation are applicable to the licensing and R&D aspects of the collaboration agreement, respectively. Support for the possibility that two block exemption regulations can apply to different aspects of the same agreement may be found in the TTBER Guidelines with respect to the interface between TTBER and the Commission Regulation on Vertical Agreements.[33]

Assuming that TTBER is applicable to the licensing component of the collaboration agreements (as well as the separate but associated licensing agreement), the second consideration on the applicability of TTBER is whether the collaboration agreement falls within the scope of TTBER. TTBER and the TTBER Guidelines apply to agreements between two parties where there is a direct link between the licensed technology and the production of a contract product created with the licensed technology.[34] In other words, to qualify for the block exemption, the

---

[32]   The collaboration agreement between industry and integrated drug discovery organization includes provisions relating to the licensing of intellectual property rights necessary to carry out joint research and development, but the exploitation options set out in the same agreement are not defined as joint according to the R&D Regulation. According to Articles 1(1)(m) and (1)(1)(g) of the R&D Regulation, *supra* note 31, joint exploitation includes allocating exploitation activities between the parties by way of specialization, whereby research is conducted by one party and production by another. In the context of the collaboration agreement, R&D is conducted jointly but explicit exploitation of the results is left outside the agreement.

[33]   TTBER Guidelines, *supra* note 3 at paragraphs 77 and 78 which describes the application of TTBER to an agreement wherein the licensor grants a license to a licensee to sell products incorporating the licensed technology and the application of the regulation on vertical agreements to the same agreement which may also set obligations on the licensee as to the way in which the licensee must sell the products incorporating the licensed technology. These two paragraphs suggest how both regulations can apply to the same agreement while respecting the intention and objectives of each of the individual regulations.

[34]   TTBER, *supra* note 2, Article 2 and TTBER Guidelines, *supra* note 3 at paragraph 58 which states it is a condition for the application of TTBER that the agreement must concern 'the production of contract products'. Contract products are defined in Article 1(1)(g) of TTBER as goods produced with the licensed

agreement must enable the licensee to exploit the licensed technology for the production of goods or services.[35] There is no requirement for the licensed technology to be ready for immediate commercialization since TTBER applies to agreements where licensees are required to carry out further *development work*; however, TTBER does not apply to agreements where licensees need to carry out further *research and development*.[36] For greater clarity, paragraph 45 of the TTBER Guidelines reads as follows:

> TTBER also applies to agreements whereby the licensee must carry out development work before obtaining a product or a process that is ready for commercial exploitation, *provided* that a contract product has been identified. Even if such further work and investment is required, the object of the agreement is the production of an identified contract product. On the other hand, the TTBER and the guidelines do not cover agreements whereby a technology is licensed for the purpose of enabling the licensee to carry out further research and development in various fields. For instance, the TTBER and the guidelines do not cover the licensing of a technological research tool used in the process of further research activity. The framework of the TTBER and the guidelines is based on the premise that there is a *direct link between the licensed technology and an identified contract product*. In cases where no such link exists the main object of the agreement is research and development

technology. As such, in the context of the collaboration agreements between industry and the integrated drug development organization where the successful collaborative technology is licensed to the industry partner for use in the production of new pharmaceuticals, it would appear that such agreements would fall within the purview of TTBER. As will be discussed later in this chapter, not all of the collaboration agreements contemplate a license of the successful collaborative IP to the industry partner as the only option to commercialize the jointly developed IP. The question becomes whether TTBER and the TTBER Guidelines apply to the collaboration agreement if the agreement contemplates three possible routes of commercialization, two of which involves licensing the IP to a third party. Because TTBER only applies to license agreements between two parties, to what extent does TTBER apply to an agreement that contemplates multi-party licensing as a possible commercialization option? The answer appears to lie in paragraph 40 of the TTBER Guidelines, which states that: 'Licence agreements concluded between more than two undertakings often give rise to the same issues as licence agreements of the same nature concluded between two undertakings. In its individual assessment of licence agreements which are of the same nature as those covered by the block exemption but which are concluded between more than two undertakings, the Commission will apply by analogy the principles set out in the TTBER'.

[35]   See TTBER, *supra* note 2, recital 7 and paragraph 58 of the TTBER Guidelines, *supra* note 3.
[36]   TTBER Guidelines, *supra* note 3 at paragraph 65.

as opposed to bringing a particular product to the market; in that case the analytical framework of the TTBER and the guidelines may not be appropriate. For the same reasons the TTBER and the guidelines do not cover research and development sub-contracting whereby the licensee undertakes to carry out research and development in the field of the licensed technology and to hand back the improved technology package to the licensor. The main object of such agreements is the provision of research and development services aimed at improving the technology as opposed to the production of goods and services on the basis of the licensed technology.[37]

In the context of the collaboration agreements between industry and integrated drug discovery organizations, a specific contract product has not necessarily been identified at the outset. One of the main purposes of the collaboration agreement is to take early stage discoveries through to proof of concept. The collaboration agreement reflects the desire of the parties to enter into a collaborative relationship concerning, for example, the discovery and validation of novel targets or development of projects in a particular therapeutic area without a specific contract product in mind. If the resulting technology from the collaborative R&D ultimately has proven viability, the collaboration agreement contemplates various commercialization and exploitation strategies. Furthermore, any successful technology resulting from the collaborative R&D that is licensed to industry still requires clinical trials to be conducted prior to the production of products incorporating the licensed technology. The TTBER Guidelines make it clear that further work and investment on the licensed technology with the object of producing the 'identified contract product' constitutes development work, which would presumably include clinical trials in the drug discovery and development context. The type of technology licensing contemplated in TTBER and the TTBER Guidelines seems to only anticipate the licensing of a developed technology where a contract product can be easily identified. In the case of the integrated drug discovery and development model, at the time the collaboration is created, typically, the initial discovery has not yet matured to the point where a specific product can be identified. At best, the parties may only be able to contemplate a class of products within an identified therapeutic area, the discovery may be used if the collaboration ultimately provides successful proof of concept. For example, if the subject of the collaboration agreement is the identification of targets and leads having indications for cystic fibrosis but evolves during the R&D process into a product to treat another type of inflammatory respiratory disease, does

---

[37] Ibid. (emphasis added).

TTBER still apply to the collaboration agreement if the 'identified contract product' is no longer the same product as originally contemplated (i.e. treatment for cystic fibrosis) but remains in the same classification of disease it was intended to treat (i.e. inflammatory respiratory disease)? Furthermore, there is always the possibility that through the development process, another application may be discovered for a target or lead in a completely different therapeutic area.[38] TTBER and the TTBER Guidelines specifically state that it should not be restrictive or interpreted as creating obstacles to an agreement, particularly when taking into account the specific dynamics of the agreement. Given the unpredictable nature of the drug discovery and development, the ultimate discovery of a product in the therapeutic area identified at the inception of the agreement should be viewed by TTBER as akin to identifying a contract product itself. As such, TTBER would therefore apply and make block exemption available to the licensing of the resulting technology from successful collaborative R&D for the production of a pharmaceutical product in an identified therapeutic area.

D. ARTICLE 101(1) RESTRICTION AND ARTICLE 101(3) EXEMPTION

Agreements that fall within the purview of TTBER are limited in scope to agreements infringing Article 101(1) but are exempted even if they infringe Article 101(1), provided such agreements meet all the conditions for exemption under TTBER.[39] Agreements that do not qualify for exemption under TTBER can still be deemed non-restrictive when analyzed within the ordinary framework provided under Article 101.

---

[38] For example, at the time sildenafil citrate was being developed at the Pfizer European Research Centre, scientists were interested in discovering potential new approaches to the treatment of cardiovascular diseases, including angina and hypertension. During clinical trials, the drug had very little demonstrated effect on angina but did have positive indications for inducing penile erections. As a result, Pfizer decided to market sildenafil citrate for the treatment of erectile dysfunction. Branded as Viagra, sildenafil citrate was approved by the FDA in 1998 as the first oral treatment for the treatment of erectile dysfunction in the United States. See Mitradev M. Boolell, M.J. Allen, S.A Ballard, S. Gepi-Attee, G.J. Muirhead, A.M. Naylor, I.H Osterloh, and C. Gingell, *Sildenafil: An Orally Active Type 5 Cyclic GMP-specific Phosphodiesterase Inhibitor for the Treatment of Penile Erectile Dysfunction.* INTERNATIONAL JOURNAL OF IMPOTENCE RESEARCH, 8(2), 47–52 (1996).
[39] TTBER, *supra* note 2, Article 2.

E. COMPETITORS vs. NON-COMPETITORS

Whether the parties to the collaboration agreement are considered competitors or non-competitors according to TTBER has a bearing on the application of TTBER since each are treated differently. In general, license agreements between non-competitors raise fewer competition concerns and are therefore subject to more lenient rules than agreements between competitors.[40] According to TTBER and the TTBER Guidelines, the assessment of whether an actual or potential competitive relationship exists between the parties should be made in the absence of the agreement and at a time prior to the parties entering into the agreement.[41] Competitors are defined as undertakings that compete on the relevant technology market or the relevant product market.[42] In other words, the application of TTBER requires an assessment of the competitive relationship between the parties (actual or potential) with respect to the relevant market (technology or product market). Case law suggests that in order to assess the competitive relationship between the parties, the relevant

---

[40] Cooperation between competitors is generally perceived as more suspicious from a competition perspective. See paragraph 27 of the TTBER Guidelines, *supra* note 3. See also Article 4(1) of TTBER, *supra* note 2, which sets out the list of hardcore restrictions applicable to competitors compared to Article 4(2) of TTBER, which sets out the list of hardcore restrictions applicable to non-competitors. The difference in treatment between competitors and non-competitors was seen as a key indication of the economic approach to the analysis in competition law. See for example Steven D. Anderman and John Kallaugher, *Technology Transfer and the New EU Competition Rules: Intellectual Property Licensing after Modernisation.* OXFORD UNIVERSITY PRESS ON DEMAND (2006) at 40.

[41] See Article 4(3) of TTBER, *supra* note 2 and paragraphs 28 and 38 of the TTBER Guidelines, *supra* note 3. It would otherwise be unfair to assess the competitive relationship ex post as the parties would likely be active in the same product or technology market after investments have been made by both parties to the licensing agreement. See for example Erik Vollebregt, *The Changes in the New Technology Transfer Block Exemption Compared to the Draft.* EUROPEAN COMPETITION LAW REVIEW, 25(10), 660 (2004) at 664 and Korah, *supra* note 24.

[42] The definition of competing undertakings can be found in Article 1(1)(n) of TTBER, *supra* note 2. Read in conjunction with the definition of relevant market in Article 1(1)(m), it is sufficient that the parties are competitors in either the product or technology market to be defined as competitors for the stricter rules in TTBER to apply. Specifically, Article 1(1)(n)(i) defines competing undertakings on the relevant technology market, whereas Article 1(1)(n)(ii) defines competing undertakings on the relevant product market.

product market and relevant technology market should be defined to assess what impact licensing may have on such markets.[43]

Applying these concepts to the integrated drug discovery and development model, in the absence of the collaboration agreement, one can assert with a reasonable certainty that industry and integrated drug discovery organizations cannot be considered actual or potential competitors on the product market for reasons previously discussed. Assessing the actual and potential competitive relationship between industry and integrated drug discovery organizations with respect to the *relevant technology market* is not such an easy endeavor. The TTBER Guidelines define technology as an input that can be integrated into a product or production process.[44] Because technology is essentially an input that can be incorporated into a product or process of manufacture, the licensing of such input can therefore affect competition on the technology market.[45] It is therefore necessary to assess the technology market when considering agreements that involve the development and licensing of such 'inputs' when defining the relevant market.[46] The TTBER Guidelines define the relevant technology market as including:

> the licensed technology and its substitutes, that is to say, other technologies which are *regarded by the licensees* as interchangeable with or substitutable for the licensed technology, by reason of the technologies' characteristics, their royalties and their intended use ... [s]tarting from the technology which

---

[43]   See for example, Commission Decision COMP/M.5675 *Syngenta/ Monsanto* where the Commission analyzed the merger of two vertically integrated sunflower breeders by examining both: (i) the upstream market for the trading (namely the exchange and licensing) of varieties (parental lines and hybrids); and (ii) the downstream market for the commercialization of hybrids. In COMP/M.5406, *IPIC/MAN Ferrostaal AG*, the Commission defined the market for the production of high-grade melamine as also an upstream technology market for the supply of melamine production technology. See also COMP/ M.269, *Shell/Montecatini*.

[44]   TTBER Guidelines, *supra* note 3 at paragraph 20.

[45]   Ibid.

[46]   Communication from the Commission, *Guidelines on the applicability of Article 101 of the Treaty on the Functioning of the European Union to horizontal co-operation agreements* (OJ C11/01, 2011) ('Horizontal Guidelines') at paragraph 43 which states: 'The starting point for the analysis of market power is the position of the parties on the markets affected by the co-operation. To carry out this analysis the relevant market(s) have to be defined by using the methodology of the Commission's Market Definition Notice. Where specific types of markets, such as purchasing or technology markets, are concerned these guidelines will provide additional guidance'.

is marketed by the licensor, one needs to identify those other technologies to which licensees could switch in response to a small but permanent increase in relative prices, that is to say, the royalties. [Emphasis added.][47]

Based on the definition, it can be argued that any restriction relating to the licensing of technology can potentially affect competition because of the limits that may be imposed on the use of the technology being offered on the market.[48]

Applied to the collaboration agreements between integrated drug discovery organizations and industry, assessing interchangeability or substitutability of the licensed technology in the context of drug discovery and development can be quite difficult. One of the primary objects of the collaboration between industry and the integrated drug discovery organizations is to determine the potential of early stage research by way of cooperation and concentration of efforts. Given that TTBER seems to apply to the transfer of technology component of the collaboration agreement, it would therefore be logical that the relevant technology market should be assessed at the time the collaboration yields proof of concept of a discovery and leads to a licensable technology.[49] If the relevant technology market should properly be defined at the time the collaboration is successful and therefore assessed at the time the licensing provisions of the collaboration agreement is triggered, determining whether there is an interchangeable or substitutable technology will depend on how equivalence is assessed, assuming there is an equivalent, given the potential novelty of the developed technology. As discussed in Chapter 3, equivalence is not easy to establish and depends on the particular circumstances. In different contexts, equivalence can be measured differently. For example, for the purpose of FDA approved generic drugs, generics are considered to be therapeutic equivalents and thus substitutable (can be expected to have the same clinical effect and safety

---

[47] TTBER Guidelines, *supra* note 3 at paragraph 22 and Article 1(k) of TTBER, *supra* note 2 which defines relevant technology market as including 'technologies which are regarded by the licensees as interchangeable with or substitutable for the licensed technology, by reason of the technologies' characteristics, their royalties and their intended use'.

[48] TTBER Guidelines, *supra* note 3 at paragraph 20.

[49] If the relevant market is defined at the time the collaboration agreement is created, because the prospects of the discovery that forms the subject of the collaboration is unknown at the time of the agreement, it would be difficult to evaluate or compare the early stage discovery in a meaningful way with any other technology to assess interchangeability or substitutability.

profile) if, among other factors, bioequivalence is established,[50] whereas for the purposes of pharmacokinetic studies, pharmaceutical equivalence (which does not necessarily imply therapeutic equivalence)[51] needs to be established for the purpose of determining the best formulation of a drug. From the perspective of TTBER, should equivalence be determined on a

---

[50] According to the Food and Drug Administration's Approved Drug Products with Therapeutic Equivalence Evaluations, otherwise known as the Orange Book, the FDA classifies as therapeutically equivalent those products that meet the following general criteria: (1) they are approved as safe and effective; (2) they are pharmaceutical equivalents in that they (a) contain identical amounts of the same active drug ingredient in the same dosage form and route of administration, and (b) meet compendial or other applicable standards of strength, quality, purity, and identity; (3) they are bioequivalent in that (a) they do not present a known or potential bioequivalence problem, and they meet an acceptable *in vitro* standard, or (b) if they do present such a known or potential problem, they are shown to meet an appropriate bioequivalence standard; (4) they are adequately labeled; (5) they are manufactured in compliance with Current Good Manufacturing Practice regulations. *The concept of therapeutic equivalence, as used to develop the List, applies only to drug products containing the same active ingredient(s) and does not encompass a comparison of different therapeutic agents used for the same condition (e.g., ibuprofen vs. naproxen for the treatment of pain).* Any drug product in the List repackaged and/or distributed by other than the application holder is considered to be therapeutically equivalent to the application holder's drug product even if the application holder's drug product is single source or coded as non-equivalent (e.g., BN). Also, distributors or re-packagers of an application holder's drug product are considered to have the same code as the application holder. Therapeutic equivalence determinations are not made for unapproved, off-label indications. The FDA considers drug products to be therapeutically equivalent if they meet the criteria outlined above, even though they may differ in certain other characteristics such as shape, scoring configuration, release mechanisms, packaging, excipients (including colors, flavors, preservatives), expiration date/time and minor aspects of labeling (e.g., the presence of specific pharmacokinetic information) and storage conditions. When such differences are important in the care of a particular patient, it may be appropriate for the prescribing physician to require that a particular brand be dispensed as a medical necessity. With this limitation, however, the FDA believes that products classified as therapeutically equivalent can be substituted with the full expectation that the substituted product will produce the same clinical effect and safety profile as the prescribed product (see http://www.fda.gov/drugs/developmentapprovalprocess/ucm079068. htm).

[51] Differences in the excipients and/or the manufacturing process, among other variables, can lead to differences in product performance and can therefore affect the resulting therapeutic effect. As such, pharmaceutical equivalence does not necessarily equate to therapeutic equivalence.

pharmaceutical basis (i.e. same active ingredients) or therapeutic basis (i.e. expected to have the same clinical effect)? What about pharmaceutical alternatives (i.e. products that contain the same therapeutic moiety) or bioequivalents (i.e. products that display comparable bioavailability)? The methodology for defining technology markets as described in the TTBER Guidelines, does not appear to offer any further assistance:

> Starting from the technology which is marketed by the licensor, it is necessary to identify those other technologies to which licensees could switch in response to a small but permanent increase in relative prices, that is to say, the royalties. An alternative approach is to look at the market for products incorporating the licensed technology rights.[52]

Perhaps an alternative perspective that may shed some light on assessing the substitutability of the resulting technology is to consider the dynamics that gave rise to collaboration itself. The mere fact that industry and integrated drug discovery organizations agree to collaborate on a particular project may suggest that the parties have strong reasons to believe in the potential of the technology that may arise from the collaboration. Industry will have likely conducted extensive strategic planning and research before deciding on which projects to collaborate on with integrated drug discovery organizations to avoid investing resources in an area that they will not be able to obtain patent rights should the collaborative R&D be successful. Similarly, the integrated drug discovery organizations, the project managers and the principal investigators associated with a particular discovery will likely have assessed the novelty and therapeutic potential of the project through their network of researchers. Assuming the decision to collaborate on a particular project reflects both parties' due diligence on the state of the art, perhaps the investment in the collaboration is a reliable indication that any resulting technology will likely be novel and innovative (i.e. the likelihood of there being substitutable technologies is minimal) and the parties do not anticipate there being other existing products on the market that incorporate the licensed technology.[53]

---

[52] TTBER Guidelines, *supra* note 3 at paragraph 22.

[53] TTBER Guidelines, *supra* note 3 at paragraph 22 which state: 'The methodology for defining technology markets follows the same principles as the definition of product markets. Starting from the technology which is marketed by the licensor, one needs to identify those other technologies to which licensees could switch in response to a small but permanent increase in relative prices, i.e. the royalties. An alternative approach is to look at the market for products incorporating the licensed technology'. The nature of drug discovery and

Regardless of any inferences that may be drawn from the circumstances giving rise to a collaboration, absent a clear methodology that is applicable to the drug discovery and development process to define the technology market, legal uncertainty arises if there is no meaningful way to clearly assess whether the parties are considered actual or potential competitors in the relevant technology market pursuant to TTBER and the TTBER Guidelines. Therefore, an argument can be made that the current competition law framework does not seem to provide an applicable methodology to help industry and integrated drug discovery organizations determine whether they are considered competitors (actual or potential) on the relevant technology market with respect to collaborative drug discovery and development. Despite the inability to clearly define the relevant technology market, the TTBER Guidelines do indirectly speak to the distinction between competitors and non-competitors on the technology market in a manner that may provide enough guidance to enable a determination of the competitive relationship between industry and integrated drug discovery organizations. If both parties are active in the same technology market, they are considered *actual* competitors for the purpose of TTBER.[54] If both parties, in the absence of the agreement, are likely to make the necessary additional investment to enter the relevant technology market and own substitutable technologies, then they are considered *potential* competitors.[55] However, according to the TTBER Guidelines, potential competition is only considered for the relevant product market and not taken into account on the relevant technology market for the application of TTBER.[56] As such, the assessment of the competitive relationship between the parties need only focus

---

development is such that the industry and integrated drug discovery organization would not invest the time and resources into developing the technology if there was a substitutable or equivalent technology.

[54]   See TTBER Guidelines, *supra* note 3 at paragraph 35.

[55]   Ibid., at paragraph 36.

[56]   Ibid. Paragraph 36 states: 'The parties are considered to be potential competitors on the technology market if they own substitutable technologies and the licensee is not licensing out his own technology, provided that it would be likely to do so in the event of a small but permanent increase in technology prices. In the case of technology markets, it is generally more difficult to assess whether the parties are potential competitors. This is why, for the application of the TTBER, potential competition on the technology market is not taken into account (see [paragraph] 83) and the parties are treated as non-competitors'. Paragraph 83 of the TTBER Guidelines states: 'Potential competition on the technology market is not taken into account for the application of the market share threshold or the hardcore list relating to agreements between competitors.

on demonstrating whether or not industry and integrated drug discovery organizations are *actual* competitors on the relevant technology market.

Parties are considered actual competitors in the relevant technology market if they both license out competing technology rights.[57] Applied to the collaboration between industry and integrated drug discovery organizations, two possible scenarios can arise when determining the competitive relationship between the parties. The collaborative relationship is typically created because both parties have identified a project that may provide the foundations for a new or improved pharmaceutical product, and the endeavor to achieve proof of concept of such project requires the skills of both undertakings. In one scenario, the collaboration exists because neither party has any existing competing technology rights, thereby inducing both parties to pool their respective resources to develop the project. In this case, an argument can be made that industry and integrated drug discovery organizations cannot be considered actual competitors on the technology market if neither party has an existing technology and neither party can develop the project technology alone without the assistance of the other. Arguably, either party could acquire the requisite skills and resources and make the investment to take projects through proof of concept without the other party, but, for a number of reasons, it would not be likely[58] nor would it make economic sense to do so. In a second and more likely scenario, the industry partner will likely have existing technologies developed independently or with other third parties prior to entering into a collaborative agreement with integrated drug discovery organizations. Whether industry is licensing out such existing technologies to third parties will depend on the particular circumstances. In such case, industry and integrated drug discovery organizations may be considered actual competitors.[59]

The analysis in Chapter 6 will proceed on the assumption that integrated drug discovery organizations and industry are considered actual competitors on the technology market. The purpose of such an

---

Outside the safe harbour of the TTBER potential competition on the technology market is taken into account but does not lead to the application of the hardcore list relating to agreements between competitors'. As such, potential competition in the relevant technology market may be relevant for analysis under Article 101 but not under TTBER.

[57]   Article 1(n)(i) of TTBER, *supra* note 2.

[58]   TTBER Guidelines, *supra* note 3 at paragraph 34, which states that 'a realistic competitive constraint entry has to be likely to occur within a short period ... normally a period of one to two years is appropriate'.

[59]   Ibid., at paragraph 35.

assumption is to determine how the stricter standards of competition law impacts collaborative drug discovery and development. The self-assessment nature of TTBER may lead parties to an erroneous conclusion that they are non-competitors when the stricter standards of competitors should have applied. However, mechanical application of the stricter rules designed to prevent anticompetitive conduct between competitors in the product market to agreements where the parties are only considered competitors in the technology market may only result in undesirable over-inclusive treatment of licensing restrictions whose effects do not operate in the market where the parties are deemed competitors.[60]

F. MARKET SHARE

Market shares are assigned to the various sources of competition once the relevant market has been defined as a measure of the market strength of the parties.[61] In other words, TTBER attempts to assess individual clauses in their legal and economic context in order to assess the possible anticompetitive effects on the market.[62] Intervention should therefore

---

[60]   See for example, Frank Fine, *The EU's New Antitrust Rules for Technology Licensing: A Turbulent Harbour for Licensors.* EUROPEAN LAW REVIEW, 29(6), 766–787 (2004) at 776.

[61]   TTBER Guidelines, *supra* note 3 at paragraph 25. TTBER provides a general exemption for technology transfer agreements involving patents, know-how, and other forms of intellectual property depending on the parties' competitive relationship and market share in the relevant product or technology market. Paragraph 79 of the TTBER Guidelines further state: 'According to Article 3 of the TTBER the block exemption of restrictive agreements is subject to market share thresholds confining the scope of the block exemption to agreements that although they may be restrictive of competition can generally be presumed to fulfill the conditions of Article 101(3).

[62]   Although scholars have generally been supportive of the use of market share thresholds, there are arguments against their use, claiming that they lead to less legal certainty because of the difficulties of defining relevant markets and the burden of acquiring the relevant information, and because the volatility of market shares can render the thresholds too low. The application of market share is too complicated for parties to undertake on a self-assessment basis and therefore increases legal uncertainty. See for example the joint comments by the American Bar Association's Section of Antitrust Law, Section of International Law and Section of Intellectual Property Law on Commission Regulation on the Application of Article 81(3) of the EC Treaty to Categories of Technology Transfer Agreements and Commission Notice on Guidelines on the Application of Article 81 to Technology Transfer Agreements (February 2012) (accessible at http://

only occur in cases where the parties to the agreement have market power or achieve such a position through the license.[63] According to TTBER, if the parties to the agreement are competing undertakings, the TTBER exemption shall apply if the combined market share of the parties does not exceed 20% of the relevant (technology and product) market.[64] If the parties are not competing undertakings, the TTBER exemption shall apply if the market share of each of the parties does not exceed 30% of the relevant (technology and product) market.[65] As discussed above, the stricter market share threshold of 20% still applies where the parties are competing in the technology market but not in the product market. Therefore, agreements between competitors on the technology market will be subject to harsher treatment even if there is no market power on the product market, leading to an inaccurate assessment from an economic perspective. TTBER further defines market share of a party on the relevant technology market on the basis of total licensing income from royalties[66] or in terms of the presence of the licensed technology on the relevant product market.[67] With respect to the proposed methodology for calculating market shares of the parties in the relevant technology market on the basis of total licensing income, the TTBER Guidelines recognize the potential difficulty in doing so because of the possible lack of information on royalties.[68] In addition, without an

---

ec.europa.eu/competition/consultations/2012_technology_transfer/americanbar association_en.pdf) and Pat Treacy and Thomas Heide, *The New EC Technology Transfer Block Exemption.* EUROPEAN INTELLECTUAL PROPERTY REVIEW, 26, 414–420 (2004) at 419.

[63]   Market shares do not *per se* constitute proof of market power but are seen as an important indicator that requires further investigation based on the facts. See recital 13 of TTBER, *supra* note 2.

[64]   TTBER, *supra* note 2 at Article 3(1).

[65]   Ibid., Article 3(2)

[66]   TTBER Guidelines, *supra* note 3 at paragraph 23 which states: 'In the case of technology markets, one way to proceed is to calculate market shares on the basis of each technology's share of total licensing income from royalties, representing a technology's share of the market where competing technologies are licensed'.

[67]   TTBER, *supra* note 2, Article 3(3) defines a licensor's market share on the relevant technology market as the combined market share on the relevant product market of the contract products produced by the licensor and its licensee.

[68]   TTBER Guidelines, *supra* note 3 at paragraph 25 which states that calculating market shares on the basis of licensing income from royalties 'may often be a mere theoretical and not a practical way to proceed because of lack of clear information on royalties etc.'. See also Treacy and Heide, *supra* note 62 at 419.

applicable methodology to define the relevant technology market in the drug discovery and development context, any assessment of market shares based on a 'best effort' attempt to define the technology market is likely to generate unreliable results relating to market shares. It is difficult to estimate the use of new technology and thereby define relevant markets.[69]

The TTBER Guidelines offer an alternate method in situations where information on royalties is not available by assessing market shares on the basis of sales of products incorporating the licensed technology on downstream product markets.[70] Generally, the nature of market conditions in the pharmaceutical industry is such that markets tend to be concentrated and market share ceilings tend to be low when the cost of R&D is high,[71] which means the parties to the collaboration agreement may easily exceed the threshold set out in TTBER within a relatively short period of time after commercialization.[72] More specifically, if the collaboration leads to commercialization of the resulting technology, the parties will likely be accredited with no market share initially (because they have yet to generate any sales) but may exceed the market share thresholds fairly shortly after commercialization because markets tend to be concentrated in the pharmaceutical industry. In other words, the collaboration agreement will likely qualify for the block exemption at the outset with respect to the market share assessment. However, if the parties decide to commercialize (i.e. industry will likely assume the risk of development only if there is a high probability of financial return on the investment), when sales begin, the technology may very quickly accumulate market share and exceed the market share threshold, taking the collaboration agreement outside the exemption offered by TTBER

---

[69]   Korah, *supra* note 24 at 253. It may also be difficult to access information on the market shares of the contracting parties because such information may be confidential, especially for the industry partner in the context of the collaborative drug discovery and development process.

[70]   TTBER Guidelines, *supra* note 3 at paragraph 22 which states: 'An alternative approach, which is the one used in Article 3(3) of the TTBER is to calculate market shares on the technology market on the basis of sales of products incorporating the licensed technology on downstream product markets'.

[71]   Valentine Korah, *Intellectual Property Rights and the EC Competition Rules* (Hart Publishing 2006) at 331.

[72]   New technologies and products are dynamic, leading to sharp fluctuations in market shares. See for example Cyril Ritter, *The New Technology Transfer Block Exemption under EC Competition Law*. LEGAL ISSUES OF ECONOMIC INTEGRATION, 31(3), 161 (2004) at 175.

and subjecting it to individual scrutiny under Article 101(3).[73] Parties may even become dominant because of the accumulation of market shares in a market where potentially no or very few competitors exist. The TTBER Guidelines do caution that market shares, as a measure of the relative strength of available technologies, may need to be treated with caution in such circumstances.[74] Although the TTBER Guidelines state that the Commission will in individual cases '… have regard to the number of independently controlled technologies available in addition to the technologies controlled by the parties to the agreement that may be substitutable for the licensed technology at a comparable cost to the user',[75] in order to continue to qualify for exemption, the TTBER Guidelines require there to be four or more independently controlled technologies.[76] Given the nature of the drug discovery and development process, there may not be four or more independently controlled technologies that may be substitutable for the newly developed licensed technology in order for the agreement to continue to qualify for exemption.[77] Is it the intention of competition policy to treat parties who successfully engage in drug discovery and development like a monopolist because their market share accumulates in a market where no other competitors exist at the time their newly developed technology enters the market? The nature of drug discovery and development process is such that the uncertainty of R&D makes it difficult for parties to foresee any forthcoming market entries. These dynamics give rise to uncertainty and introduce another level of complexity associated with drafting a collaboration agreement in view of the likely Article 101 scrutiny. Assessing market share is particularly difficult for innovative technologies because

---

[73] TTBER Guidelines, *supra* note 3 at paragraph 79. Outside the safe harbor created by the market share thresholds, individual assessment is required. The fact that market shares exceed the thresholds does not give rise to any presumption either that the agreement is caught by Article 101(1) or that the agreement does not fulfill the conditions of Article 101(3). In the absence of hardcore restrictions, market analysis is required. Since market power may emerge with time, this individual assessment is inevitable, thereby guaranteeing an increase in transactional costs at some point in the future.

[74] TTBER Guidelines, *supra* note 3 at paragraph 162 states that outside the safe harbor of TTBER 'particularly in the case of technology markets, market shares may not always be a good indicator of the relative strength of the technology in question and the market share figures may differ considerably depending on the different calculation methods'.

[75] Paragraph 24 of the 2004 TTBER Guidelines.

[76] TTBER Guidelines, *supra* note 3 at paragraph 157.

[77] Ibid.

of the new markets they may create,[78] as well as the difficulty in defining the relevant market upon which the assessment of market power is based.

G. INNOVATION MARKET

The concept of innovation market relates to competitive issues that affect the intermediate market for R&D rather than the product or technology market. In other words, the innovation market is the upstream market from the technology market and is most relevant in situations where the subject R&D is expected to result in new innovation. The TTBER Guidelines state that:

> ... innovation is a source of potential competition which must be taken into account when assessing the impact of the agreement on product markets and technology markets. In a limited number of cases, however, it may be useful and necessary to also define innovation markets. This is particularly the case where the agreement affects innovation aiming at creating new products and where it is possible at an early stage to identify research and development poles. In such cases it can be analyzed whether after the agreement there will be a sufficient number of competing research and development poles left for effective competition in innovation to be maintained.[79]

TTBER and the TTBER Guidelines do not explicitly define innovation markets[80] but the above quoted paragraph of the TTBER Guidelines does suggest that innovation markets relate to the ability of undertakings to slow the rate of innovation in the absence of sufficient competing R&D poles.

---

[78]   Ibid. at paragraph 90, which states that where a new technology has not yet generated any sales, it will be considered to have a zero market share, with the market share accumulating as sales commence.

[79]   Ibid., at paragraph 26 where reference is made to the Horizontal Guidelines which state: '... research and development agreement[s] may bring together different research capabilities that allow the parties to produce better products more cheaply and shorten the time for those products to reach the market. A production agreement may allow the parties to achieve economies of scale or scope that they could not achieve individually'.

[80]   Unlike in the United States where the innovation market is defined in the 1995 Antitrust Guidelines for the Licensing of Intellectual Property § 3.2.3 as consisting of '... the research and development directed to particular new or improved goods or processes, and the close substitutes for that research and development (see http://www.justice.gov/atr/public/guidelines/0558.htm).

As previously discussed, one of the key reasons for the creation of collaborations between industry and integrated drug discovery organizations in the pharmaceutical sector is to bring together research capabilities and complementary skills to increase efficiencies in pharmaceutical R&D and bring better products to market more effectively and efficiently.[81] A necessary consequence of co-operation and the combining of resources is the reduction in the number of individual efforts conducting R&D in a particular area, some of which may be duplicative research efforts. In the pharmaceutical context, the question of whether there will be a sufficient number of remaining credible competing R&D poles aimed at developing substitutable products or technology is not easy to assess. As discussed in Chapter 4, the credibility of an R&D pole largely depends on its substitutability for the R&D efforts of the collaborating parties.[82] Understandably, TTBER (and the R&D Regulation) needs to define the outer limits of the types of agreements that are contemplated within its scope, but, without clear directions on how to measure and evaluate competition in innovation, the inclusion of the requirement to define innovation markets 'in a limited number of cases' creates uncertainty. Without specific guidance or indication of how many R&D competitors need to be identified,[83] the parties can derive no comfort, even with the professional assistance of legal advisors as to whether their agreement will qualify for exemption. As set out in the TTBER Guidelines, the licensing of technology for the production of a 'new' product

---

[81] Incidentally, as stated in paragraph 50 of the Horizontal Guidelines, *supra* note 46, the block exemption regulations are based on a similar premise where 'the combination of complementary skills or assets can be the source of substantial efficiencies in research and development …'.

[82] Horizontal Guidelines, *supra* note 46 at paragraph 120 which states: 'In order to assess the credibility of competing poles, the following aspects have to be taken into account: the nature, scope and size of any other R&D efforts, their access to financial and human resources, know-how/patents, or other specialised assets as well as their timing and their capability to exploit possible results. An R&D pole is not a credible competitor if it cannot be regarded as a close substitute for the parties' R&D effort from the viewpoint of, for instance, access to resources or timing'.

[83] TTBER Guidelines, *supra* note 3 at paragraph 157 mentions that 'Article 101 is unlikely to be infringed where there are four or more independently controlled technologies in addition to the technologies controlled by the parties to the agreement that may be substitutable for the licensed technology at a comparable cost to the user'. However, this paragraph relates to competition on the technology market and not to competition on the innovation market. The conspicuous absence of guidance on the assessment of innovation markets highlights the legal uncertainty.

may have an effect on the innovation market in addition to the product and technology market.[84] The question is how can this potential effect on the innovation market be realistically assessed? At the time of entering the agreement, the success or failure of the R&D is unknown and unpredictable; even if the R&D is successful, the clinical impact of the research results on the treatment of the disease is unknown until after clinical trials, the result of which will have significant consequences for the product and technology market. As such, it is virtually impossible to assess the impact of the agreement on innovation until the technology is ready for commercialization, which is an ex-post analysis with consequences to the parties which cannot be managed, anticipated, or avoided ex ante.

H. HARDCORE RESTRICTIONS

The agreement may not contain any 'hardcore restrictions', which will result in the whole agreement falling outside the scope of TTBER,[85] but different restrictions apply to agreements between non-competitors compared to agreements between competitors.[86] These restrictions of competition by object have such a high potential for negative effects on competition that it is unnecessary, to demonstrate any effects on the market.[87] When a license agreement contains a hardcore restriction, it follows from TTBER that the agreement as a whole falls outside the scope of the block exemption and cannot be severed from the rest of the agreement. Hardcore restrictions will only in very exceptional circumstances fulfil the four conditions of Article 101(3).[88]

---

[84]   TTBER Guidelines, *supra* note 3 at paragraph 26 which states that according to TTBER Guidelines, competition on existing product and technology markets 'may be affected by agreements that delay the introduction of improved products or new products that over time will replace existing products. In such cases innovation is a source of potential competition which must be taken into account when assessing the impact of the agreement on product markets and technology markets'.

[85]   TTBER Guidelines, *supra* note 3 at paragraph 14.

[86]   TTBER, *supra* note 2, Article 4(1) sets out the hardcore restrictions applicable to agreements between competitors and Article 4(2) sets out the hardcore restrictions applicable to agreements between non-competitors.

[87]   TTBER Guidelines, *supra* note 3 at paragraph 149. See also Case C-49/92 P, *Anic Partecipazioni* [1999] ECR I-4125.

[88]   TTBER Guidelines, *supra* note 3 at paragraphs 14, 18, and 95.

I. CONTRACTUAL RESTRICTIONS

The TTBER Guidelines specifically recognize that licensees often face substantial risk with respect to incurring upfront and sunk expenses and investments to start up or develop a product.[89] As such, it is essential to ensure the collaboration agreement and the associated licensing agreement are enforceable and in compliance with competition policy. However, the clauses that concern key business issues, such as exclusivity, non-compete obligations, field-of-use restrictions, territorial and customer restrictions, and the ownership of intellectual property rights, are precisely the ones that attract scrutiny and are therefore potentially the most vulnerable to challenge. The invalidity of a specific clause could undermine the success of the collaboration and therefore needs to be drafted with a view to ensuring compliance with competition policy. TTBER sets out 'excluded restrictions', which will not be exempted but will not affect the validity of the remaining provisions of the agreement.[90] If the agreement between industry and integrated drug discovery organizations contains broad restrictions relating to ongoing or future use and applications of the collaborative research results, such clauses will likely negatively affect the potential benefit of the technology from a research and commercial perspective. The assessment is based on the totality of the agreement – the cumulative effect of all the contractual restrictions found in the agreement and not an individual assessment of each restriction. In the following section, competitive concerns associated with various contractual restrictions typically found in license agreements will be discussed.

i. Exclusivity

Given the high cost of the drug development process, industry partners will normally seek an exclusive license.[91] Exclusivity is often one of the

---

[89]   TTBER Guidelines, *supra* note 3 at paragraph 126. With respect to agreements between non-competitors, the risks facing new licensee are likely to be substantial, in particular since the promotional expenses and investment in assets required to produce on the basis of a particular technology are often sunk, i.e. they cannot be recovered if the licensee exits the market.

[90]   TTBER, *supra* note 3, Article 5.

[91]   In the pharmaceutical context, one of the obligations of the industry licensee is the investment in performing clinical trials in order to commercialize the technology. From a business perspective, no potential licensee would agree to undertake such a substantial investment in the development process and accept

most important provisions of collaborative drug discovery and development because, in many cases, one of the primary incentives to enter into the collaboration is to give the industry party a competitive edge over other competitors active in the same market. However, from a competition law perspective, and having regard to the mission of integrated drug discovery organizations to respect research freedom and academic integrity, consideration needs to be given to the impact of granting an exclusive license to an industry partner, especially since such discoveries are derived in large part from public funds. By definition, exclusive licenses limit the dissemination of the licensed technology solely to the efforts of the licensee (who may or may not be effective in exploiting the technology) without the ability to grant further licenses to others. The TTBER Guidelines state that exclusive licensing between non-competitors will likely satisfy the conditions of Article 101(3), especially when an exclusive license is necessary to induce the licensee to invest in the commercialization of the licensed technology, particularly if the licensee is required to make a significant investment to develop the licensed technology.[92] However, the Commission will intervene if the licensee is dominant and obtains an exclusive license to one or more competing technologies and effectively forecloses third party licencees.[93] As such, to ensure compliance with TTBER, exclusive licenses between non-competitors should only grant a defined set of rights limited to those required by the licensee to meet its commercial needs and enable the development of a particular product based on the licensed technology (for example, in certain markets or for a particular use, during the term of the agreement) without affecting the ability of others to conduct ongoing academic research relating to a broader application of the licensed technology.

On the other hand, non-exclusive licenses would enable the integrated drug discovery organization to retain the right to grant more than one license to enable additional third parties to exploit the technology to facilitate product optimization. In between exclusive and non-exclusive licenses are arrangements such as 'co-exclusive' licenses (where a small number of licensees conduct R&D in parallel and compete in product

---

the risk of facing competition from other licensees when the technology reaches the market.

[92]   TTBER Guidelines, *supra* note 3 at paragraph 194.

[93]   Ibid., at paragraph 195 which states that agreements where dominant licensees obtain an exclusive license to one or more competing technologies are unlikely to fulfill the conditions of Article 101(3).

development and market penetration)[94] and hybrid licenses (where some rights are granted on an exclusive basis and others on a non-exclusive basis to allow for flexibility in accommodating both business and academic interests). There are multiple variants of hybrid license agreement. For example, a licensor may grant an exclusive license to a licensee to develop a product, based on the licensed technology, for a particular use, and in the same agreement grant a non-exclusive license for the development of products based on the same technology but outside the field of use to which the licensee has an exclusive right. A further example of a hybrid license is a convertible license, which enables the licensor to convert aspects of an exclusive license to a co-exclusive or non-exclusive license under certain triggering circumstances, such as if the exclusive licensee fails to meet certain performance milestones or fails to market the product within a mutually agreed upon timeframe, allowing competitors access to the market. A 'non-exclusive exclusive' license enables the licensee to earn certain exclusive aspects if the licensee complies with all the terms and conditions of the license agreement.

There is great flexibility in creating license arrangements with respect to defining the duration and conditions of exclusivity within the permissible parameters of TTBER and competition policy. This enables the creation of agreements that afford industry the competitive advantage they desire while respecting core academic values and mandate of integrated drug discovery organizations relating to the promotion and dissemination of publically funded research.

ii. Improvements and Grant Backs

A standard improvement clause usually stipulates that for the duration of the agreement, if the licensor develops or discovers any improvement to the licensed technology, the licensor shall provide full details of the improvement to the licensee and the licensee will usually demand a right

---

[94] Co-exclusive licenses are usually implemented where there is a substantial need for a particular product, for example in the case of certain vaccines. However, the involvement of multiple parties in such a competitive setting usually requires highly incentivized motivation given the risks and cost involved and increases the speed of development in comparison to exclusive licenses where failed product development will require the termination of the license, identification of a new licensee, and the negotiation of a new license to recommence product development.

of first refusal to obtain rights to the improvements.[95] Similarly, a standard grant back clause typically requires the licensee to grant rights in any of its improvements and know-how to the licensed technology back to the licensor so that the licensor can maintain control over the technology.[96] From a competition law perspective, the granting of rights in improvements is not likely to be seen as a neutral transaction,[97] especially in the context of collaborative drug discovery and development. By definition, the collaboration entails the translation and development of early stage discoveries to achieve proof of concept, and, if successful, there will likely be continual research and development to discover improvements after a first application of the original technology reaches the market. Without a grant back clause, ongoing innovation and development to realize the full potential of promising new technologies may be discouraged because licensees will likely be unwilling to disclose or engage in discovering improvements, absent some incentive.[98] Improvement clauses therefore provide incentive to licensees to grant back rights that allow the licensor to conduct ongoing R&D with the assurance that the licensee will have priority access to the improvement. It is the management of these obligations concerning improvements that one party owes to the other that may trigger competition law concerns. According to TTBER, an obligation on a licensee to grant back improvements to a licensor on an exclusive basis is excluded from the benefit of the block exemption. However, TTBER distinguishes between 'severable' and 'non-severable' improvements and only excludes exclusive grant backs relating to severable improvements from the safe harbor.

---

[95] See generally, William Cornish, David Llewelyn, and Tanya Aplin, *Intellectual Property: Patents, Copyrights, Trademarks and Allied Rights* (Sweet & Maxwell 2013) at Chapter 7 'Property Rights and Exploitation'.

[96] Ibid., see also Donald M. Cameron and Rowena Borenstein, *Key Aspects of IP License Agreements*. (Ogilvy Renault 2003) (accessible at http://www.jurisdiction.com/lic101.pdf).

[97] Competition law is concerned with the manner in which improvements derived from novel technologies are managed between licensor and licensee and whether any such arrangements between the parties affect the innovation and/or technology market.

[98] Products that incorporate new and improved technologies could potentially outcompete the licensee's products made with the original licensed technology and therefore reduce profits.

iii. Field of Use Restrictions

Field of use restrictions confines licensees to the development of a
defined product or series of products based on the licensed technology.
The TTBER Guidelines specifically recognize that it would be a disincentive if licensors were not able to set parameters on the use of the
licensed technology and prevent licensees from operating in fields where
the value and potential of the licensed technology is yet to be determined.[99] Otherwise, licensors would likely demand higher upfront royalties as compensation for possible future applications and/or foregone
opportunities,[100] which may in turn discourage the licensee from obtaining the license to exploit the technology. Field of use restrictions
therefore enable the licensor to carve out a particular application of the
technology, which can then be granted to the licensee with the security of
exclusivity, while permitting third parties to undertake product development for applications outside the field of exclusivity.

Field-of-use restrictions between non-competitors generally fall outside
of the Article 101(1) prohibition either because they do not restrict
competition or because they are justified by their pro-competitive effects.
If the licensor could not reserve certain fields, this could undermine its
incentive to grant a license at all. If a restriction is combined with an
exclusivity provision in a reciprocal license between actual or potential
competitors, this is treated as an impermissible hardcore restriction
because the exclusivity restriction prevents anyone other than the licensee
from exploiting the field of use. In other words, the competitors are
agreeing not to exploit the technology in the field licensed to the other,
which amounts to a market-sharing agreement.

iv. Territory Restrictions

A licensee may be limited to a specific territory such that it may not
manufacture or sell products produced by the licensed technology in
territories other than the geographic area agreed to in the agreement.
Territorial restraints allow the parties to exercise their rights to the
licensed technology in the exclusive territory without competition from

---

[99] TTBER Guidelines, *supra* note 3 at paragraph 212.
[100] A licensee may not have the resources, ability, or willingness to realize
the full potential of a licensed technology by developing products beyond the
scope of its core business.

third parties, including the contracting party in some cases.[101] From a competition law perspective, anticompetitive effects may arise if there is a lack of competitive pressure resulting from territorial restrictions.[102] In other words, territorial exclusivity eliminates competition that existed between licensees before the license. This could be exacerbated by cross-licensing arrangements where collusion may arise[103] or could give rise to pro-competitive effects if cross-licensing eliminates the transactional costs of securing rights to essential intellectual property. On the pro-competitive side, in order to induce investment into a technology, limiting the number of competitors in the market of a particular territory may lead to more efficient production.[104]

---

[101]   For example, the licensee can prevent the licensor from competing with it in its exclusive territory and the licensor can prevent the licensee from competing with it in its exclusive territory. In circumstances where the licensee does participate in or incur costs associated with R&D, the licensee may undercut the licensor if the parties are allowed to compete in the same territory. For general discussion, see Alan S. Gutterman, *Innovation and Competition Policy: A Comparative Study of the Regulation of Patent Licensing and Collaborative Research & Development in the United States and the European Community* (Kluwer Law International 1997) at Chapter 6 and Richard E. Caves, Harold Crookell, and Peter Killing, *The Imperfect Market for Technology Licenses*. OXFORD BULLETIN OF ECONOMICS AND STATISTICS, 45(3), 249–257 (1983). In the case of the collaboration between integrated drug discovery organizations and industry, because both parties have invested in the R&D process and only the industry partner will be active on the product market, such concerns do not arise.

[102]   See for example, Patrick Rey and Joseph Stiglitz, *The Role of Exclusive Territories in Producers' Competition*. THE RAND JOURNAL OF ECONOMICS, 26(3), 431–451 (1995). Without competitive pressure, parties may behave in a manner that is not beneficial to the public. However, competitive pressure exerted by other licensees in neighboring territories or competitors with rival technologies in the same territory should not be ignored.

[103]   Paul Demaret, *Patents, Territorial Restrictions and EEC Law – a Legal and Economic Analysis* (Max-Planck-Institut for Foreign and International Patent, Copyright and Competition Law, 1978) at 45.

[104]   Robert D. Anderson and Nancy T. Gallini (eds), *Competition Policy and Intellectual Property Rights in the Knowledge-Based Economy* (University of Calgary Press 2002); Donald F. Turner, *Basic Principles in Formulating Antitrust and Misuse Constraints on the Exploitation of Intellectual Property Rights*. ANTITRUST LAW JOURNAL, 53(3) 485–502 (1984) at 496; Valentine Korah, *The Rise and Fall of Provisional Validity: The Need for a Rule of Reason in EEC Antitrust*. NORTH WESTERN JOURNAL OF INTERNATIONAL LAW AND BUSINESS, 3, 320 (1981); John W. Schlicher, *Some Thoughts on the Law and Economics of Licensing Biotechnology Patent and Related Property Rights in the*

In the case of the associated license agreement between integrated drug discovery organizations and industry, only the industry partner will be active on the product market. Territorial restraints included in the agreement therefore do not serve the traditional purpose of preserving the licensor's market position or protecting the licensee from competitive pressures from third parties, including the licensor. Territorial restraints are therefore used to allow the industry partner to extract maximum profits and the full value of the licensed technology within the assigned territory.[105] The territorial exclusivity also gives industry the opportunity to recoup investments into developing the market in the territory and developing the technology into a commercializable product. The exclusivity also protects industry from opportunistic third parties attempting to misappropriate the investments into developing the technology. The inclusion of royalty rates ensures the integrated drug discovery organizations also reap some of the benefits enjoyed by the industry partner.

v. Restrictions on R&D

To prevent independent but related R&D activity that may be in direct competition with or have a negative impact on the collaboration, or to prohibit the parties from free-riding off the results of the collaboration, restrictions on R&D activity are often included in the collaboration agreement. Such restrictions can be pro-competitive to motivate the parties to use best efforts to jointly create new innovations without worrying that the collaborating partner could use the results of the collaboration to develop a competing technology with third parties during the course of the collaboration. However, if the restrictions are overly broad, they can stifle innovation. For example, if the restriction prohibits

---

United States. JOURNAL OF THE PATENT AND TRADEMARK OFFICE SOCIETY, 69, 263 (1987). However, some dispute that territorial restrictions should be justified on the basis of inducing investments or compensating for investments made by the licensee because there are other less restrictive methods of compensating the licensee, such as through negotiations with licensor on preferential royalty rates. See Malcolm E. Wheeler, *A Reexamination of Antitrust Laws and Exclusive Territorial Grants by Patentees.* UNIVERSITY OF PENN-SYLVANIA LAW REVIEW, 119(4), 642–666 (1971) at 657.

[105] Francisco Caballero-Sanz, Rafael Moner-Colonques, and Jose J. Sempere-Monerris, *Licensing Policies for a New Product.* ECONOMICS OF INNOVATON AND NEW TECHNOLOGY, 14(8), 697–713 (2005) and Richard J. Gilbert, *Converging Doctrines? U.S. and EU Antitrust Policy for the Licensing of Intellectual Property*, University of California, Berkeley, Competition Policy Working Paper (2004).

independent or collaborative R&D in fields that are *not* connected with the collaboration, such restriction is considered an impermissible restriction[106] as it would unnecessarily reduce innovation that would not have a negative impact on the collaboration. On the other hand, restrictions on R&D with third parties during the collaboration encourage the parties to commit to the collaborative effort. A best effort clause may obligate the parties to achieve the aims of the collaboration as much as possible. However, how far reaching such a clause can be to restrict the parties from engaging in related R&D is unclear.[107] From a competition law perspective, a best effort clause is seen as a softer version of a non-compete clause,[108] but applied to the collaboration agreement between integrated drug discovery organizations and industry, such a clause may effectively be seen as a less restrictive alternative to questionably permissible R&D restrictions. However, can the restriction be imposed for the entire term of the collaboration agreement if the collaboration has proceeded, for example, to the commercialization phase? The R&D regulation prohibits post-term restrictions on R&D, but, in the context of the collaboration between integrated drug discovery organizations and industry, does the term include the subsequent licensing and commercialization period? Based on the discussion in Chapter 4 and on the overlap between the R&D Regulation and TTBER, it would be arguable that the R&D restriction should only apply to the R&D phase of the collaboration and not for the entire duration of the collaboration, including the term of the associated license agreement. Otherwise, such a restriction may be treated similarly to the objections raised in regards to feed-back clauses, which are seen to reduce incentives to innovate and discourage R&D investment into follow-on innovation in the related field.[109] By extending the term to which the restriction on R&D in fields

---

[106]   This is a hardcore restriction under the R&D Regulation Article 5(a) which prohibits 'the restriction of the freedom of the parties to carry out research and development independently or in cooperation with third parties in a field unconnected with that to which the research and development agreement relates or, after the completion of the joint research and development or the paid-for research and development, in the field to which it relates or in a connected field.

[107]   A general statement that best effort obligations can substitute an R&D restriction or that it would be an acceptable less restrictive alternative is unknown.

[108]   Anderman et al., supra note 40; Valentine Korah, *Technology Transfer Agreements and the EC Competition Rules* (Clarendon Press 1996).

[109]   Turner, *supra* note 104 and Caves et al., *supra* note 101.

that are related to the collaboration applies, this delays and prevents third parties from investing in the development of second generation innovations.

J. REMARKS

The changes introduced to TTBER and the TTBER Guidelines in 2014 are likely to bring both benefits as well as uncertainty to parties that engage in technology licensing. Although TTBER attempts to expressly carve out from its application technology licensing in the context of R&D agreements, applied to the collaboration agreements between integrated drug discovery organizations and industry, it is still unclear whether the associated licensing agreement relating to the exploitation of the successful results from the collaborative R&D falls under the R&D Regulation or TTBER. Without a conclusive determination, integrated drug discovery organizations and industry must engage in self-assessment under both block exemptions, which puts additional unnecessary strain on the finite resources available to the parties to establish a collaboration. Secondly, the distinction between competitors and non-competitors on the technology market gives rise to further uncertainty and skewed assessments as different hardcore restrictions and market share thresholds apply, depending on whether parties are deemed to be competitors or non-competitors. An inaccurate characterization of the competitive relationship between the parties may result in the erroneous application of stricter or more relaxed rules under TTBER to license agreements that have identical effects on the market. Arguably, this uncertainty may have a limited consequential effect as licenses may still benefit from an exemption under an individual assessment. Nevertheless, this increases the risks and transaction costs for the parties to the agreement.

In the context of the integrated drug discovery and development model, innovation encompasses not only the end product that results from the collaboration but also includes the collaborative R&D process and the licensing of the resulting technology for further development into the commercializable product. The integrated drug discovery and development model is predicated on the fact that neither party alone has the expertise and resources to bridge the gap between basic research and commercialization. The collaboration agreement between integrated drug discovery organizations and industry facilitates the drug discovery and development process and resolves inefficiencies as well as transactional hazards typically associated with the process. However, the licensing component of the collaboration gives rise to a number of problems.

Firstly, as already discussed, there is the uncertainty of whether the R&D Regulation or TTBER applies. Secondly, contractual restraints in the agreements are necessary, not only as means to allow the parties to maximize profits but mainly to manage transactional hazards with unquantifiable costs. In other words, an argument can be made that the contractual restraints are justifiable because they are required to efficiently realize the pro-competitive purpose of licensing, which is the dissemination and commercialization of the licensed technology for the benefit of the public. If the concept of innovation includes licensing of technology for the purposes of commercialization, protection of innovation under competition policy must also permit contractual restrictions that facilitate efficiency enhancing licensing, even if they give rise to some anticompetitive effects. The legitimate business justifications for including particular contractual restrictions should be considered when considering and balancing the anticompetitive and pro-competitive effects of the agreements. Although an evaluation of contractual restrictions based on an assessment of efficiency does not directly quantify whether an agreement is, on balance, pro-competitive or anticompetitive, it does explain whether the contractual restriction achieves its stated purpose to resolve a particular transactional problem. A positive explanation establishes legitimacy of the inclusion of the contractual restriction for the purposes of promoting the pro-competitive result, which can then be used as a justification against the identified anticompetitive effects, if any are found.

The balancing of pro-competitive and anticompetitive effects is separate from the evaluation of whether specific clauses are acceptable. Balancing occurs under the assessment of whether the consumer receives a fair share of the benefits while the assessment of the indispensability of the restrictions rejects agreements where the same benefit could have been achieved by an alternative less restrictive restraint. In other words, Article 101(3) does not measure the overall beneficial effect of agreements but makes independent assessments based on the four cumulative factors under Article 101(3) that must all be satisfied.[110] As such,

---

[110]   Phedon Nicolaides, *The Balancing Myth: The Economics of Article 81(1) & (3)*. LEGAL ISSUES OF ECONOMIC INTEGRATION, 32(2), 123–145 (2006). In other words, if an agreement does not pass on benefits to consumers, it is rejected. If a less restrictive arrangement can achieve the same desired result, the agreement is rejected. If competition is eliminated, the agreement is rejected. Because the factors are cumulative, failure to meet one condition will result in the agreement not qualifying for exemption.

agreements that on the whole benefit consumers and facilitates innovation and commercialization may still fail to qualify for exemption if a contractual restraint is found to be too restrictive or if market rivalry is favored. It is interesting to note that an assessment by the Commission of less restrictive alternatives and elimination of competition is made with perfect hindsight and with the assumption that the Commission has an understanding of the context under which the agreement was made and the objective and rationale behind the restriction in question. As shown in the analysis of this chapter and in the next, the Commission has not demonstrated that it has given sufficient recognition to the particular dynamics that shape the agreements being assessed.

The assessment of contractual restraints and their overall effect on competition can only be fairly evaluated if the objective of the agreement is understood. In the context of the collaboration agreement and associated licensing agreement between integrated drug discovery organizations and industry, contractual restraints need to be viewed as means to induce joint investment and participation in collaborative R&D to achieve proof of concept in early stage discoveries in order to facilitate the drug discovery and development process. Contractual restraints in the associated licensing agreement may reduce transaction costs, resolve transactional hazards, strategically manage third party competition in light of the particular dynamics that plague the pharmaceutical industry, and disseminate technology in an efficient and cost effective manner by concentrating efforts and eliminating duplication costs. In other words, contractual restraints found in collaboration agreements and associated licensing agreements should be assessed on the basis that they serve a dual purpose of protecting the interests of the parties as well as managing transactional hazards.

PART III

Case study: agreements between industry and integrated drug discovery organizations

6. Analysis of collaboration agreements between integrated drug discovery organizations and industry

A. INTRODUCTION

In this chapter, various clauses found in collaboration agreements and associated licensing agreements between industry and integrated drug development organizations will be analyzed with reference to the provisions of the R&D Regulation, TTBER, and Article 101. More specifically, individual clauses contained in the agreements collected from CD3, CDRD, LRD, and MRCT with respect to various types of contractual restraints found in the collaboration agreements, and licensing restrictions found in the associated licensing agreements, will be analyzed. The purpose of this chapter is to explore and determine whether the existing competition law framework supports the type of collaboration contemplated under the integrated drug discovery and development model.

For reasons of confidentiality, the specific industry partner and the source of the particular collaboration and associated licensing agreement being analyzed will not be identified. To ensure the anonymity and confidentiality of the information provided by each of the integrated drug discovery organizations, the clauses of the individual agreements (set out in the boxes below) have been amalgamated and analyzed as a single collaboration agreement and a single associated license agreement without reference to a specific source.

B. ANALYSIS OF THE COLLABORATION AGREEMENT

The express object of the agreement is to enter into an exclusive strategic collaboration under which the integrated drug discovery organization will search for and propose to the industry partner potential research projects of interest (i.e. in the particular field which industry has expertise in) for industry to develop into novel therapeutic products. Only projects that are unencumbered by third party rights (i.e. the integrated drug discovery organization has the right to license exclusive commercial rights to the results of the research project to industry) and projects not currently being worked on by other pharmaceutical companies will form the subject matter of the collaboration agreement. Industry shall have the sole right to decide which projects to select. Once a project is agreed upon, the integrated drug discovery organization will conduct or manage the conduct of research in accordance with a mutually agreed research plan with the aim of establishing proof of concept. The research shall be partially funded by industry with the goal of commercializing the technology should the collaboration give rise to successful results from the selected research project. Development and commercialization options are set out within the agreement and will be chosen and negotiated accordingly. Within the framework of the collaboration, the parties are expected to share and exchange related and/or background intellectual property, know-how, and confidential information related to the project. However, each party shall remain the sole and exclusive owner of its background or related intellectual property.

The exemptions offered by the R&D Regulation only applies to collaborations below a certain level of market power[1] and outside such threshold levels, individual case-by-case assessment will need to be made under Article 101(3). As such, the following analysis will proceed on the presumption that the parties exceed the market share threshold to determine if the exemptions still apply under individual assessment, taking into account factors such as market structure on the relevant market.[2]

i. Ownership of Resulting Project Intellectual Property

> The integrated drug discovery organization shall own the entire rights, title and interest in and to all project intellectual property. It is anticipated that industry may make or generate intellectual property in the course of this agreement and/or participation in particular projects. In such an instance, the parties agree that, in order to maintain the integrity of all intellectual property, such intellectual

---

[1] Recital 4 of the Commission Regulation No 1217/2010 on the application of Article 101(3) of the Treaty on the Functioning of the European Union to categories of research and development agreements, OJ 2010 L335/36 (the 'R&D Regulation'), which sets out the presumption that the positive effects of research and development agreements will outweigh any negative effects on competition below a certain level of market power.

[2] Ibid., at recitals 5 and 16.

> property shall be owned by the integrated drug discovery organization, except as the parties may otherwise agree with respect to industry's participation in any specific project. Industry *assigns* and agrees to assign to the integrated drug discovery organization its interest in the resulting project's intellectual property (excluding any such IP made or generated by industry pursuant to work under a project for which the Parties have agreed in writing that industry shall retain ownership).

R&D Regulation requires that parties should have full access to the final results of the collaboration for the purpose of further research and development and exploitation.[3] Only where one party specializes in exploitation may access to the results for the purpose of exploitation be limited.[4] However, the party that owns the intellectual property is the integrated drug discovery organization and not the industry partner that specializes in commercialization. Without further examination on how the issues of access will be dealt with given the ownership position, arguably, the exclusive ownership of the entire rights, title and interest in and to all project's intellectual property by the integrated drug discovery organization could limit industry's access to the results beyond the allowable scope provided in the R&D Regulation. The issue of access will be discussed below in how the parties deal with intellectual property arising from declined projects and successful projects.

Some of the collaboration agreements set out a different ownership structure:

> Industry and the integrated drug discovery organization will become the joint owners of all rights, titles and interest in and to the intellectual property resulting from the project and project results. All patent applications and patents relating thereto shall be made in the name of both parties.

This ownership clause appears to better reflect the intentions of the R&D Regulation whereby joint ownership usually suggests full and equal access to the resulting project's intellectual property.

---

[3]   Ibid., at recital 11 and Article 2(2).
[4]   Ibid., at recital 11.

ii. Background Intellectual Property

One of the conditions for exemption under the R&D Regulation requires the fair management of intellectual property rights, including access to any pre-existing know-how that is necessary for carrying out the R&D project.[5]

> In the event that industry owns or controls any proprietary information and/or patent rights or other intellectual property that is known to the parties to be useful or needed for the selected project, industry will grant to the integrated drug discovery organization *limited, non-exclusive royalty free license rights* of such applicable information and intellectual property solely as necessary for the conduct of the selected project. For clarity, the foregoing licenses grant to the integrated drug discovery organization no interest or rights under any such information or intellectual property of industry for any purpose, except the limited right to conduct the applicable selected project.
>
> Further, In the event that the parties agree that industry shall conduct certain aspects of a particular selected project, and there exists integrated drug discovery organization background IP rights that would be useful or needed for industry to conduct such aspects of the selected project, then the integrated drug discovery organization will grant to industry the *limited, non-exclusive license rights (with no rights sub-license)* of such applicable background IP rights solely as needed for industry to conduct its aspects of the selected project.

Understandably, access to the extent required to conduct the collaboration is essential to ensuring the success of the project. However, it is equally understandable that limits should be placed on the scope of access granted to protect confidential intellectual property. However, neither the R&D Regulation nor the Horizontal Guidelines provide guidance on this matter. As such, it may be reasonable to conclude that contractual freedom will be respected in this regard to protect the interests of the parties.[6]

---

5   Ibid., at Article 3(3).
6   Iohann le Frapper, *Striking the Right Balance Between Co-operation and Competition: Several Antitrust Pitfalls in R&D Alliances and Other Strategic Partnerships.* INTERNATIONAL IN-HOUSE COUNSEL JOURNAL, 5(18), 1–18 (2012).

iii.   Continued R&D of Declined Projects

One of the conditions of exemption under the R&D Regulation is in regards to access to the final results of the R&D collaboration, including any resulting intellectual property rights and know-how for the purpose of further R&D and exploitation.[7] However, the R&D Regulation and Horizontal Guidelines are silent on whether restrictions may be placed on ongoing access if the collaboration does not lead to exploitation of the results, as defined within the scope of the collaboration. From the perspective of integrated drug discovery organizations, declined projects may still have generated useful results that may be applied in a different field or application, which may be explored with other industry partners.

> In the event that (i) information or intellectual property of industry is used pursuant to a license granted pursuant to the foregoing in the conduct of a particular selected project and is reasonably necessary for the continued development and/or commercialization of products within the scope of the selected project, and (ii) such particular selected project becomes a declined project, then industry agrees, if requested by the integrated drug discovery organization, to grant to the integrated drug discovery organization a *non-exclusive, royalty-bearing, sublicensable license* for such industry information and/or intellectual property as reasonably needed in such development and commercialization, on commercially reasonable terms to be negotiated and agreed to by the parties in good faith.

One of several options available to industry at the conclusion of the R&D is to decline the project, meaning industry may elect not to pursue and further develop or exploit the project results. According to this clause, industry will continue to have access to the resulting intellectual property, even if industry elects to decline pursuing the project, but is required to license any related intellectual property to the integrated drug discovery organization, if requested. Both parties have ongoing access and the integrated drug discovery organization has secured its ability to continue R&D of the declined project.

---

[7]   R&D Regulation, *supra* note 1, Article 3(2).

> All rights, titles and interest in and to the compounds not selected by the parties to be developed as part of the project will be with the integrated drug discovery organization. The integrated drug discovery organization will not exploit such compounds in the field of the collaboration without a prior written agreement of industry.

According to the above clause, by declining a project, industry elects to give up all rights to the project's intellectual property, including the final results of the collaboration. In other words, industry must relinquish its right to have ongoing access if it decides not to pursue a project. As such, regardless of the uncertainty of whether the condition of access in the R&D Regulation requires both parties to have ongoing access to the project results, the collaboration agreement requires industry to voluntarily forego its rights to ongoing access should it choose to decline a project. However, whatever competition concerns the clause may give rise to for restricting industry's access, ensuring that R&D efforts in declined projects are not wasted if industry is not interested in further development may factor into any independent assessment of the clause under Article 101(1) and/or Article 101(3) to balance against the potential restrictive effect.

The second part of this clause arguably borders on a hardcore restriction. The R&D Regulations prohibit restrictions imposed on the parties to carry out research and development in the field to which the project relates subsequent to the completion of the project.[8] The requirement of written consent from industry in order for the integrated drug discovery organization to commercialize the declined project's intellectual property in the field of collaboration could be construed as being tantamount to the prohibition set out in Article 5(a) of the R&D Regulations and could therefore disqualify the agreement as a whole from exemption.

> If rejected, the integrated drug discovery organization expressly preserves the right to further develop a select number of such rejected targets. If the results of the rejected target are derived from the integrated drug discovery organization's compound collection, industry shall *assign* its interest in the joint results to the integrated drug discovery organization for further development without further obligation to industry.

---

[8]   Ibid., Article 5(a).

If the results of the rejected target are derived from industry's compound collection, industry shall *license* its interests in the results to the integrated drug discovery organization *for the sole purpose* of enabling the integrated drug discovery organization to further develop the rejected target subject to industry retaining an option to negotiate an exclusive license to develop any successful results.

If industry elects not to seek an exclusive license to develop and commercialize the results, the integrated drug discovery organization shall have the option to negotiate a license to any industry background or related IP in order to allow the integrated drug discovery organization to develop and commercialize without any further obligation to industry.

This clause provides for ongoing access to industry should the results be derived from industry's compound collection, but no ongoing access if the results are derived from the integrated drug discovery organization's compound collection. As stated above, requiring industry to forego access if it elects to decline a project should not be in violation of the R&D Regulation as the intention of the clause is to preserve the ability to further develop rejected results and not to impose restrictions. Furthermore, even if it is scrutinized, the clause would likely be exempted under Article 101(3) for reasons discussed above.

iv. Commercialization Options

The R&D Regulation applies to agreements containing provisions that relate to the assignment or licensing of intellectual property rights to carry out joint research and development or joint exploitation, provided that those provisions do not constitute the primary object of such agreements.[9] In the present case, to the extent that the collaboration agreement includes licensing and commercialization clauses, they will be examined under the R&D Regulation. Because the parties enter into a subsequent but associated license agreement should the collaboration achieve proof of concept, such a license agreement shall be examined under TTBER.

---

9   Ibid., Article 2(2).

For each selected project, there are several potential commercialization paths for the IP rights resulting from the selected project. For each selected project, industry has an option right, exercisable during the decision period, to notify the integrated drug discovery organization of its decision regarding which of the following potential future commercialization paths industry would like to pursue with respect to the IP rights resulting from the selected project.

(a)   Industry seeks to establish further collaboration research on the selected project;
(b)   Industry seeks to negotiate and enter into a development and commercialization license with the integrated drug discovery organization under which industry would obtain the license right to further develop and commercialize the selected project IP rights; or
(c)   Industry seeks to work with the integrated drug discovery organization to form a new entity that would have the rights to further develop the selected project.

During the decision period applicable to the selected project, industry may elect to provide notice that it is not interested in participating in any further development or commercialization of the IP rights resulting from the selected project. If industry declines or does not notify the integrated drug discovery organization of a decision on any commercialization path prior to the expiration of the decision period, the selected project shall be deemed a declined project.

Further Collaboration

If industry elects to conduct further research on the selected project, the integrated drug discovery organization shall discuss with and seek to obtain the agreement of the other relevant members to extend the selected project and expand the research on it. If the project group agrees to extend and expand the research, then industry and the integrated drug discovery organization shall discuss in good faith the terms and conditions of the extended research. If the Parties do not come to an agreement within the time period, industry may notify the integrated drug discovery organization that it seeks to negotiate licensing terms. If industry does not provide notice within a prescribed period, then the selected project shall be deemed a declined project.

License

If industry provides the integrated drug discovery organization with a notice for license with respect to the selected project, the integrated drug discovery organization shall enter into an *exclusive negotiation* with industry regarding the terms for the grant of an *exclusive license* to industry of the integrated drug discovery organization's rights in and to the selected project's IP rights specific to the selected project, and, if necessary for the commercialization of the selected project's IP rights, at least a *non-exclusive license* to industry of the integrated drug discovery organization's rights in and to the applicable background IP rights related to the selected project. Such license terms shall be commercially reasonable for the rights to be licensed, *and typically will include* payment terms involving an upfront license fee, milestone payment, royalty payments, and other similar license considerations appropriate for the rights licensed and the market. If the integrated drug discovery organization and industry agree on mutually acceptable terms within the negotiation period, then the selected project shall thereafter be deemed a commercialized project. Otherwise, upon the end of the negotiation period, the selected project shall thereafter be deemed a declined project.

New Entity

If industry provides the integrated drug discovery organization with a notice to establish a new entity with respect to the selected project, the integrated drug discovery organization shall enter into an *exclusive negotiation* with industry regarding the terms for the formation of a new entity with respect to the IP rights resulting from the selected project. The specific details and conditions for the creation and terms of the new entity shall be negotiated in good faith by the parties, including the granting to the new entity of an *exclusive license (or an exclusive option to license) and/or assignment* of the integrated drug discovery organization's rights in and to the applicable IP rights related to the selected project (and provisions for the license (or option to license) to the new entity of any intellectual property rights controlled by industry that are necessary to the development or commercialization of the selected project IP rights) and that industry and the integrated drug discovery organization *may, but shall not be obliged to, own interests in the new entity*. If the integrated drug discovery organization and industry agree on mutually acceptable terms and conditions to establish the contemplated new entity, the selected project shall be deemed a commercialized project. Otherwise, the selected project shall thereafter be deemed a declined project.

Declined Projects

For the selected project that is deemed a declined project, industry's option right shall terminate and cease with respect to the selected project, and the integrated drug discovery organization thereafter shall have *exclusive rights* to: (a) further research, develop, and commercialize all IP rights resulting from the selected project (*alone or with other parties*), including products comprising, based on, or derived from same; and (b) seek, negotiate and enter into one or more license(s), partnership(s) or other similar transaction agreement(s) with one or more third parties to further research, develop, exploit, and/or commercialize all the selected project's IP rights (including products comprising, based on or derived from same), and/or to create a new company to further research, develop, and commercialize all such selected project IP rights (including products comprising, based on, or derived from same), all of the foregoing without any further obligation to industry.

By restricting the commercialization options to options that only contemplate the exclusive involvement of a particular industry partner and integrated drug discovery organization, an argument can be made that such options may have the effect of eliminating competition in the relevant technology market.[10] However, an argument can also be made

---

[10] Ibid., recital 13.

that the commercialization options merely offer a right of first refusal and that third parties have an opportunity to become involved with the commercialization of the resulting intellectual property.

Some of the collaboration agreements set out a different exploitation strategy:

It is the intention and primary aim of both parties to out-license the resulting project's IP, together with the background and related IP and third parties with the aim of developing and commercializing the selected compounds and other potential therapeutics in the field of collaboration.

The integrated drug discovery organization and industry shall co-operate to achieve exploitation of the resulting project IP and project results *in the field of collaboration*. Neither the integrated drug discovery organization nor industry shall have any right to exploit the resulting project's IP or project results without the express written permission of the other party, which shall not unreasonably be withheld. All agreements for exploitation with respect to the resulting project's IP or project results shall be made jointly in the name of and executed by both parties.

Neither party shall sell, assign or in any other way encumber its part of the background or related IP or resulting project's IP to any third party without the prior written consent of the other party.

Industry can at its own discretion exploit the background and/or related IP. However, industry shall inform the integrated drug discovery organization of any interest in the background and related IP immediately. Industry shall endeavor to exploit the background and related IP without causing interference to the exploitation of project results and the resulting project's IP. For example, industry shall not out-license background and/or related IP exclusively to third parties to the extent it would restrict commercialization of the resulting project's IP.

During the term of the agreement and two years thereafter, unless terminated earlier, in which case until such termination and three years thereafter, industry shall not initiate with a third party nor grant a third party rights to initiate the identification of modulators of the target without the written consent of the integrated drug discovery organization. Furthermore, in the case a third party demonstrates an interest in initiating a screening using small molecules that have been investigated as part of the collaboration, the parties shall consider and negotiate in good faith a joint collaboration with such a third party.

If the technology that results from a research collaboration could be used in different fields, some of which are not of interest to or within the industry partner's field of use, then a transfer of the full scope of intellectual property resulting from the collaboration to that industry partner will unlikely be considered indispensable in order to achieve the goal of getting new and technically improved products to the market. In order for the results of a research collaboration to reach the market, a full assignment of intellectual property rights to the industry partner may be desirable from the perspective of the industry partner but not a necessary condition in order to achieve the objective of competition law of 'promoting technical or economic progress' within the scope of the collaboration. A well-drafted exclusive license to the industry should normally be sufficient. By using a license rather than an assignment, other contractual clauses may be helpful in achieving a swift market introduction, and thus discouraging attenuation in the innovation process. One example is a clause, which provides for minimum royalty payments regardless of whether the licensed technology is actually marketed, possibly combined with a (realistic) timeline for market introduction, the continuation of the license being made dependent on the company succeeding in this market introduction. This would also avoid a conflict with Article 6(b) of the R&D Regulation, which forbids clauses that have as their object 'the obligation not to grant licenses to third parties to manufacture the contract products or to apply the contract technologies unless the agreement provides for the exploitation of the results of the joint research and development or paid-for research and development by at least one of the parties and such exploitation takes place in the internal market vis-à-vis third parties'.[11]

v. Research Restrictions

As set out in Article 5(a) of the R&D Regulation, restriction on the freedom of the parties to carry out R&D in a field unconnected with the subject matter of the collaboration agreement is strictly prohibited, as is any restriction on R&D in fields related to the collaboration agreement after the completion of the collaboration. This implies that competition law should tolerate restrictions on R&D in related fields during the term of the collaboration.

During the term of the agreement, the integrated drug discovery organization agrees not to undertake any research relating to any selected targets with other commercial third party without prior written consent. The integrated drug discovery organization further agrees to notify industry prior to entering into any discussion with a commercial third party regarding any rejected targets.

---

[11]   Ibid.

This clause appears to also satisfy the condition of Article 3(1) as both parties have full access to the final results even after termination of the collaboration. Although use is restricted to 'research purposes' only, the clause contemplates and allows for future exploitation and exploitation by third parties subject to consent by the integrated drug discovery organization. As previously discussed, case law seems to indicate the Commission's willingness to allow parties to negotiate terms in a manner that is most efficient to their circumstances, so long as the product market remains competitive.[12] The consent clause would appear to appease concerns of restrictive effects.

One common clause that is typically found in collaboration agreements between integrated drug discovery organizations and industry that may conflict with the restrictions of the R&D Regulation are the conditions or limitations (but not outright restriction) on the freedom of the parties to carry out R&D independently or in cooperation with third parties on subject matter that may have some tangential relation to the subject matter to which the collaboration agreement relates.[13] Typically, the Commission will tolerate restrictions on R&D activity that is related to the field in which the research collaboration is intended during the term of the agreement.[14] However, it is not unusual to have some kind of limitation or condition on the parties to carry out research in the same or connected field for the duration of the contract and for a period thereafter. However, any restriction of independent or collaborative R&D after the completion of the collaboration would disqualify the entire collaboration agreement from exemption.[15] Some scholars suggest that, in principle, short periods of post-term non-compete obligations could be allowed or at least justifiable under Article 101(3).[16] Public research

---

[12]   Marcus Glader, *Research and Development Cooperation in European Competition Law: A Legal and Economic Analysis*. CFE Working Paper Series (2000), at p. 41.

[13]   These types of clauses border on the type of hardcore restriction that is prohibited under Article 5(a) of the R&D Regulation, *supra* note 1.

[14]   See for example European Commission, *Commission approves the creation of Scandairy K/S, a joint venture between Arla ekonomisk förening and MD Foods amba* (Press Release IP/97/742, 1997) where a joint-venture between the dominant Danish and Swedish dairy co-operatives was restricted to new, 'functional' (i.e. having a physiological as well as a nutritional value) products and amended to further restrict the field by excluding co-operation with respect to conventional dairy products in order to qualify for exemption.

[15]   R&D Regulation, *supra* note 1, Article 5(1).

[16]   Jonathan Faull and Ali Nikpay, *The EC Law of Competition* (Oxford University Press 1999) at 388.

organizations such as integrated drug discovery organizations should not in any case accept any limitations on their own independent research directly or indirectly;[17] however, the problem could probably be solved if the collaboration agreement includes a clause whereby the integrated drug discovery organization grants the industry partner some kind of right of first refusal for a limited period of time to carry out a collaborative research project in the same or connected field after the original collaboration agreement.

> Industry shall during the term of the agreement and two years thereafter not collaborate with third parties regarding the discovery or development of small organic molecules investigated as part of the project. This includes that industry shall not transfer materials, know-how, or data to a third party for such purpose or that industry shall not grant rights to its background or related IP to a third party for such purposes.

These restrictions on research add an element of restricting the freedom of the parties to manufacture, sell, assign or license technologies or processes which compete with the contract products or contract technologies.[18]

> Industry and the integrated drug discovery organization retain a non-exclusive, non-transferable license to use the project results after termination of the project or this agreement free of charge for academic research purposes. Industry shall keep the integrated drug discovery organization fully informed of such academic research and shall not exploit or allow a third party to exploit any results obtained from such research without the prior written agreement of the integrated drug discovery organization, which consent shall not be unreasonably withheld.
>
> Industry grants the integrated drug discovery organization a free, sub-licensable exclusive license to use for any purpose the selected compounds outside the field of the collaboration.

---

[17] However, an indirect restriction of independent research sometimes follows from an obligation to assign or grant (non-)exclusive license to improvements to the technology that the research organization achieves on its own after the completion of the collaboration.

[18] R&D Regulation, *supra* note 1 at Article 5(b)(iv) which exempts such restrictions.

The R&D Regulation clearly warns that agreements restricting the parties from carrying out research and development in the same field shall fall within Article 101(1).[19] However, where academic bodies or research institutes are involved, the parties may agree to restrict the use of the results solely for the purpose of further research.[20]

The notification requirement regarding rejected targets flirts with Article 5(a) hardcore restriction on the freedom of the parties to carry out R&D with third parties in an unconnected field. Presumably, a rejected target would mean it is no longer connected to the project and the integrated drug discovery organization should be free to carry out R&D with third parties. However, a notification requirement is not the same as an outright restriction. This clause would likely be viewed with some suspicion but would not constitute a hardcore restriction.

vi. Conflict of Interest

How parties deal with conflict of interests could amount to a restriction on the parties' development of new technology known as restriction on own use.

> In the case that industry identifies a hit compound which was previously identified as an active compound in another collaboration between the integrated drug discovery organization and a third party outside the field of collaboration, the integrated drug discovery organization can decide to stop the continuation of the project plan for this specific compound. Upon such a situation, the integrated drug discovery organization will do its utmost best in order to allow the further collaboration between the integrated drug discovery organization and industry regarding the identified compound. If the project concerning this specific compound cannot be continued, all results regarding this compound shall be assigned to and owned by the integrated drug discovery organization.
>
> In the case industry that wishes to abandon its background or related intellectual property, it shall inform and consult with the integrated drug discovery

---

[19]   Ibid., recital 7 states that such circumstances, may restrict competition by forcing parties to forego the opportunity of gaining competitive advantages over the other party. Article 5(a) makes it a hardcore restriction to prohibit parties from carrying out research and development independently or in cooperation with third parties in an unconnected field during the research and development agreement or in the field after the completion of the research and development.

[20]   Ibid., recital 11. However, it is unclear whether the permissible restriction of the results solely for the purpose of further research extends to restricting the purpose of such further research to academic purposes only as opposed to research with an intent to commercialize should the results show potential.

> organization prior to such abandonment. Industry shall give the integrated drug discovery organization the opportunity to take over the background or related intellectual property should industry decide to abandon it.

In the above situation where the industry partner's ability to carry out further R&D on at least a component of the results derived from the collaborative R&D is restrained, even if the identified compound is an active compound outside the field of collaboration, this may give rise to significant anticompetitive concerns. Restricting industry's ability to translate and commercialize an identified hit compound hinders innovation and future competition in the technology, product, and innovation market.[21] However, assessing the effect of the restriction will largely depend on whether there are competing technologies available on the market. When there are few other competing technologies, the industry partner may be an important source of competition in the market and a restraint on industry to develop the results of the collaborative R&D may be unduly restrictive, especially if it has the necessary assets and capabilities to carry out the translation and commercialization of the technology.

The addition of a best effort obligation to continue the collaboration does soften the restriction. However, given the negative effect of potentially bringing a significant part of the collaboration to an abrupt end with all jointly developed intellectual property being assigned to the integrated drug discovery organization, it is unlikely that the inclusion of best efforts would offset the anticompetitive effect of terminating the innovation of a new product.

C. ANALYSIS OF ASSOCIATED LICENSE AGREEMENT

The stated intention of the agreement is to commercialize the jointly owned results generated from the collaboration between integrated drug discovery organization and industry. Given the position of industry, it is specifically recognized and agreed upon by the parties that in order for drug discovery and development to be carried out by industry, the

---

[21] Communication from the Commission, *Guidelines on the application of Article 101 of the Treaty on the Functioning of the European Union to technology transfer agreements*, Official Journal C89, 28.03.2014, 3-50 (hereinafter referred to as 'TTBER Guidelines') at paragraph 142.

integrated drug discovery organization must grant certain rights to industry to enable and facilitate commercialization of the project results.

The integrated drug discovery organization hereby grants to industry and industry hereby accepts (i) an *exclusive, even as to integrated drug discovery organization*, (ii) *worldwide*, (iii) *royalty-bearing right and license* (with the right to sublicense, and to further sublicense) under the integrated drug discovery organization's share in the resulting project's IP to utilize, incorporate or otherwise exploit the resulting project's intellectual property and to research, develop, manufacture, have manufactured, distribute, market, use, sell, offer to sell and/ or otherwise commercialize the products or compounds using the resulting project's intellectual property in the agreed upon territory (iv) *in the licensed field*.

The integrated drug discovery organization also hereby grants to industry a worldwide, perpetual, non-exclusive, sublicensable, irrevocable, royalty- and milestone-free license under the integrated drug discovery organization's background and related IP to the extent necessary to exploit the resulting project's IP and/or to research, develop, manufacture, have manufactured, use and commercialize products and compounds in the territory in the agreed upon field.

Because the grant is an exclusive license from the integrated drug discovery organization to industry of the resulting project's intellectual property for the purposes of commercialization without any cross-licensing obligations, the associated license agreement is considered a nonreciprocal agreement.[22] The analysis will proceed on the assumption that the parties are non-competitors on the product market[23] but actual competitors on the technology market under TTBER.[24] As previously discussed, but for the collaboration agreement, the parties would not be actual or potential competitors on the technology market because absent the collaboration agreement, the integrated drug discovery organization would not undertake R&D on a particular project. However, at the time of negotiating and concluding the associated license agreement, the integrated drug discovery organization has now acquired interest in the resulting technology and by granting a license to industry for such

---

[22]   Commission Regulation No 316/2014 on the application of Article 101(3) of the Treaty on the Functioning of the European Union to categories of technology transfer agreements, OJ 2014 L93/17 ('TTBER'), Article 1(1)(e).

[23]   As discussed in Chapter 5, the integrated drug discovery organization is neither an actual nor potential competitor on the product market as it is not active on the product market and is unlikely to enter the product market. See also paragraphs 36 and 38 of the TTBER Guidelines, *supra* note 21.

[24]   TTBER Guidelines, *supra* note 21 at paragraph 41.

resulting project's intellectual property, the integrated drug discovery organization may be seen as entering the technology market as a competitor pursuant to the definition set out in the TTBER Guidelines.[25]

i. Exclusive License

The TTBER Guidelines specifically and expressly state that non-reciprocal exclusive licenses involving research institutes that are not normally active on the product market and lack the resources to commercialize products incorporating the licensed technology are unlikely to be caught by Article 101(1).[26] Furthermore, exclusive licensing, if caught by Article 101(1), is likely to fulfill the conditions of Article 101(3) as exclusivity is generally necessary to induce the licensee to invest in the commercialization of the licensed technology, particularly when the investment is significant.[27] However, the Commission will intervene in exceptional circumstances like when the licensee owns substitutable technology or is a dominant licensee in the product market with an exclusive license to a competing technology, in which case, an exclusive license may be caught by Article 101(1) and unlikely to fulfill the conditions of Article 101(3).[28]

---

[25] Ibid. Paragraph 43 of the TTBER Guidelines contemplates the situation where parties can be seen as non-competitors on the relevant product market and the relevant technology market because the licensed technology is a drastic innovation, which creates a new market or excludes the existing technologies from the market. In the present case, the new pharmaceutical product that may result from the collaboration agreement may be deemed a drastic innovation. However, because this sort of assessment is not possible at the time the agreement is concluded, the parties will therefore be considered to be competitors. The classification of the relationship between the parties may change to that of non-competitors if at a later point in time, it becomes obvious the licensed technology is considered a drastic innovation.

[26] Ibid., at paragraph 193 which states: 'A special case exists where the licensor and the licensee only compete on the technology market and the licensor, for instance being a research institute or a small research based undertaking, lacks the production and distribution assets to effectively bring to market products incorporating the licensed technology. In such cases Article 101(1) is unlikely to be infringed'.

[27] Ibid., at paragraph 194 which states 'To intervene against the exclusivity once the licensee has made a commercial success of the licensed technology would deprive the licensee of the fruits of its success and would be detrimental to competition, the dissemination of technology and innovation'.

[28] Ibid., at paragraph 195 which states 'for Article 101(1) to apply, entry into the technology market must be difficult and the licensed technology must constitute a real source of competition on the market. In such circumstances an

In the present case, industry is likely to select projects that are within their particular field of expertise, meaning there is a likelihood that industry will already own technology the Commission may consider substitutable. Furthermore, as stated in the collaboration agreement, integrated drug discovery organizations will use best efforts to identify and propose projects not being worked on by other pharmaceutical companies in order to develop novel pharmaceuticals, meaning industry will have the potential of becoming a dominant player with an exclusive license to the technology. In either scenario, depending on the industry partner and the technology being developed, an exclusive license clause in the associated license agreement could give rise to intervention by the Commission, creating uncertainty for the parties.

An exclusive license in the present context also narrows the analysis to inter-technology competition between the parties and from third parties. The TTBER Guidelines explain the distinction between intra-technology competition (i.e. competition between undertakings using the same technology) compared to inter-technology competition (i.e. competition between undertakings using competing technologies).[29] Because industry is the sole and exclusive licensee of the resulting project intellectual property, no other third parties will have access to use the resulting project intellectual property, except sub-licensees of industry, which does not form a part of the present analysis. As such, at the time the agreement is concluded, there are no third party users of the same technology.

ii. Territorial Restraints

In general, territorial restraints are considered anticompetitive because territorial exclusivity prevents third parties from manufacturing or selling in the territory, thereby diminishing the intensity of competition and the possibility for third parties to use the licensor's technology. However, territorial restraints can be pro-competitive with respect to dissemination of the licensed technology. The rules on territorial protection in TTBER and the TTBER Guidelines are diffuse and depend on a number of factors and definitions. Firstly, a distinction is made between restrictions as to production within a given territory and sales of products incorporating the licensed technology in a given territory.[30] In the present context, industry has an exclusive worldwide right and sole responsibility

---

exclusive licence may foreclose third party licensees, raise the barriers to entry and allow the licensee to preserve its market power'.

[29]   Ibid., at paragraph 11.
[30]   Ibid., at paragraph 189.

and decision-making authority to manufacture and commercialize the products incorporating the licensed technology. As such, the term exclusive in the context of the associated license agreement means industry enjoys protection against both manufacturing as well as sales within the licensed territory, which in this case is worldwide.[31] In the case of *Nungesser v Commission*, the court introduced the term open license, defined as a duty on the licensor not to produce and sell into the licensee's assigned territory.[32] Given that the collaboration agreement between industry and integrated drug discovery organizations specifies that the grant is exclusive, even as to the licensor, the associated license agreement qualifies as an open exclusive license with respect to manufacturing and commercialization, including both active and passive sales. And of course, the distinction between competitors and non-competitors, as well as reciprocal and non-reciprocal agreements in Article 4(1) TTBER apply to territorial restraints.[33]

TTBER regulates non-reciprocal licenses between competitors, which attempts to prevent market sharing between competitors. Article 4(1)(c)(i) of TTBER allows restraints imposed on both parties not to produce products incorporating the licensed technology in one or more exclusive territories reserved for the other party. Article 4(1)(c)(ii) of TTBER permits active and/or passive sales by licensee and/or licensor into the exclusive territory. Given that it is assumed that integrated drug discovery organization and industry are only competitors on the technology market, one possible restraint on competition is the foreclosure of

---

[31] According to Article 1(1)(q) of TTBER, *supra* note 21, exclusive territory is defined as a given territory within which only one undertaking is allowed to produce the contract products. Paragraph 190 of the TTBER Guidelines, *supra* note 21, defines exclusive license as prohibiting the licensor from producing products incorporating the licensed technology rights and from licensing the licensed technology to third parties in a particular territory. In other words, according to TTBER, exclusivity refers only to manufacturing and does not prevent sales in the territory. This confusing use of the term has been discussed in the literature. See for example Valentine Korah, *Intellectual Property Rights and the EC Competition Rules* (Hart Publishing 2006) at 69.

[32] Case 258/78 *Nungesser v Commission*, [1982] ECR 2015, paragraphs 49–53.

[33] See Article 1(1)(d) and (e) of TTBER, *supra* note 22 for the definition of reciprocal and non-reciprocal agreements and paragraphs 27–39 of the TTBER Guidelines, *supra* note 21 for the distinction between competitors and non-competitors.

third party access to the integrated drug discovery organization's technology, which would have existed absent the associated license agreement. As discussed above, the collaboration agreement contemplates terminating the project plan for a specific compound in the event the compound was previously identified as an active compound in another collaboration between the integrated drug discovery organization and a third party outside the field of collaboration. However, the collaboration agreement states that best efforts will be used to allow the collaboration with industry to continue despite existing third party interests. Having regard to the foregoing, in addition to the representations and warranties included in the associated licensing agreement essentially assuring industry that the (worldwide, perpetual, non-exclusive, sublicensable, irrevocable, royalty-free and milestone-free) license from the integrated drug discovery organization to industry of its background and related intellectual property is unencumbered by third party rights, it can be argued that the scope of the grant in the license agreement goes too far and may negatively impact competition by diminishing the number of competitors that are allowed access to the integrated drug discovery organization's existing technology. In other words, inter-technology competition may be affected.[34] Arguably, such restraints may also reduce intra-technology competition by reducing access to the integrated drug discovery organization's existing technology worldwide, which may have the effect of facilitating collusion.[35] In other words, licenses between competitors (or potential competitors) in the technology market may potentially restrict both inter- and intra-technology competition by limiting third-party access to the licensor's technology.

Whether territorial restraints have the object or effect of restricting competition is assessed with respect to the market position of the parties. When the parties are only competitors (or potential competitors) on the technology market, the test set out in the TTBER Guidelines seems rather inadequate because the effects of such licenses are equivalent to a license between non-competitors.[36] In the absence of the agreement, the parties

---

[34]   For a definition and the distinction between inter-technology competition and intra-technology competition, see paragraph 27 of the TTBER Guidelines, *supra* note 21.

[35]   Ibid., at paragraph 173.

[36]   Ibid., at paragraph 193 which acknowledges that in situations where the licensor lacks the capacity to effectively exploit the technology in the licensee's territory, the agreement is unlikely to be caught by Article 101(1) and uses the example of agreements involving research institutes to illustrate the 'special case where the licensor and the licensee only compete on the technology market and

would not compete on the product market, hence the license can only restrain competition between licensees. However, these licenses are not completely excluded from the scope of Article 101(1). If a licensee with market power in the product market obtains an exclusive license to a competing technology, no third party will be able to challenge the licensee's market position. Such arrangements are likely to be caught by Article 101(1) even if the agreement involves parties that are only competitors on the technology market and are unlikely to fulfil the conditions of Article 101(3).[37] In the present case, because industry may be a dominant player in the relevant product market, the classification of whether the parties are actual or potential competitors on the technology market will make a significant difference with respect to the market share threshold (i.e. whether the parties can benefit from the 30% market share threshold or if they will be held to the 20% threshold). Depending on the market position of the industry partner and how narrowly the relevant market may be defined, the difference in market share threshold may make a difference in the outcome.

The main intention of Article 4(1)(c) of TTBER (and the associated provisions of the TTBER Guidelines) is to prevent or discourage negative effects on the product market. However, these provisions also capture agreements between competitors on the technology market because of TTBER's definition of competitors. This results in the over-inclusive effect of hardcore listing licenses between competitors in the technology market, even when such agreements do not give rise to the types of negative effects on the product market that Article 4(1)(c) is trying to target. Perhaps relief lies in an exemption under Article 101(3), as there may be an efficiency-based justification for granting territorial protection to the licensee if it can be established that the licensee is undertaking a

---

the licensor, for instance being a research institute or a small research based undertaking, lacks the production and distribution assets to effectively bring to market products incorporating the licensed technology. In such cases Article 101(1) is unlikely to be infringed'.

[37]   Ibid., at paragraph 195, which states: 'For Article 101(1) to apply, entry into the technology market must be difficult and the licensed technology must constitute a real source of competition on the market. In such circumstances an exclusive licence may foreclose third party licensees, raise the barriers to entry and allow the licensee to preserve its market power'. An agreement between competitors in the technology market can therefore fall under Article 101(1) despite paragraph 193 of the TTBER Guidelines if the licensee has a strong market position.

genuine risk with the transaction.[38] The focus on market shares makes the burden of proof to justify individual licensing restraints much more difficult for parties with market power because TTBER perceives anti-competitive effects as having a greater weight the more market power the parties to the agreement have.

Positive effects that may result from territorial restraints are the provision of incentives to create, invest in, and develop the licensed technology.[39] In the context of sales restrictions, the TTBER Guidelines state that in the case of non-reciprocal agreements between competitors, restrictions on active and/or passive sales into an exclusive territory will be caught by Article 101(1) when one or both of the parties have a significant degree of market power, but such restrictions may be indispensable for the dissemination of valuable technologies and may therefore fulfil the conditions of Article 101(3). This is particularly the case where the licensee has to make significant investments in order to efficiently exploit the licensed technology. The same rationale may be applied to allowing territorial protection on production as well. There is literature suggesting that the assessment under Article 101(3) should shift from the indispensability requirement and focus on the positive effects and consumer benefits related to efficient dissemination to justify territorial protection.[40] Such an approach would allow for an assessment that includes the distinction between incremental and radical improvements. Because radical improvements are likely to have greater positive effects, such consideration should be weighed against potential anticompetitive effects in conjunction with an assessment of whether the territorial restraint is indispensable for dissemination. If it can be demonstrated that

---

[38]   Ibid., at paragraph 199. See also paragraph 8 which specifically recognizes that transactional risk and sunk investments that must be committed in order to conclude a license agreement may lead to the agreement falling outside Article 101(1) or fulfilling the conditions of Article 101(3), as the case may be, for the period of time required to recoup the investment. Paragraph 10 confirms that license agreements that do restrict competition may often give rise to pro-competitive efficiencies, which are considered under Article 101(3) to assess the balance against the negative effects on competition.

[39]   Ibid., at paragraphs 107 and 108, which specifically recognizes that when restrictions give the parties an incentive to invest in and develop the licensed technology, the object of such agreement is therefore not necessarily to share markets.

[40]   See for example, Steven D. Anderman and John Kallaugher, *Technology Transfer and the New EU Competition Rules: Intellectual Property Licensing after Modernisation.* OXFORD UNIVERSITY PRESS ON DEMAND (2006) at 232.

a restriction is indispensable to dissemination but the improvement is only incremental, the benefit of such incremental improvement may not be sufficient to outweigh the anticompetitive effect, even if it meets the indispensability requirement. In other words, it has been suggested that more emphasis should be placed on the degree of benefit of the licensed technology.[41] However, an assessment of whether an improvement is radical or incremental can be highly subjective and difficult to conduct, thereby increasing risk and uncertainty.

From an economic perspective, territorial restraints in non-reciprocal licenses between competitors may be justifiable based on licensing efficiency to protect investments made by the licensee in the licensed technology in order to exploit the licensed technology.[42] Without such protection, the licensee could be deterred by the risks of not recouping investments incurred to develop the technology. From the licensor's perspective, territorial restraints may be justifiable based on the value of patent reward to induce licensing in order to disseminate the technology and recover the costs of R&D. Although royalty obligations absent territorial protection may be a less restrictive means to achieving the same goal, the obligation of royalties without a corresponding incentive may discourage licensing. Justifications of territorial restraints are quali-fied by the presence of market power,[43] thereby connecting the concept of market power with the determination of indispensability once again. TTBER attempts to establish a balance between significant investments, as an indication of transactional risk incurred, and the market power of the party taking the risk when assessing the indispensability requirement. However, if the balancing does not take the nature of the technology into consideration,[44] the outcome may have detrimental effects on the entire industry. Furthermore, TTBER provides no guidance on how to objec-tively or fairly measure or quantify the particular benefits of a license or the positive effects on welfare, creating great legal uncertainty on how the Commission will assess and conduct the balancing act. Market power implies larger market coverage and higher benefits since the technology is disseminated more efficiently in the market. In other words, licensing

---

[41] Regardless of the value associated with the technology, the public can derive a benefit from both incremental and radical improvements, and if concluding a licensing agreement is the only way the technology can be disseminated, an assessment based on the indispensability requirement would be appropriate.

[42] TTBER Guidelines, *supra* note 21 at paragraph 202.

[43] Ibid., at paragraph 199.

[44] Anderman and Kallaugher *supra* note 40.

through a licensee with market power may be a good business partner to cooperate with from an efficiency perspective. Additionally, since the presence of market power may also increase positive welfare effects, these should be balanced in the Commission's assessment.

Interestingly, there is no case law regarding territorial exclusivity in the context of patent licenses or technology transfer agreements but there are decisions relating to the licensing of other intellectual property rights, which may nevertheless shed some light on how the courts view territorial restrictions. In *Coditel v Ciné-Vog Films*,[45] the copyright holder of a motion picture assigned its copyright to a party in Belgium. The copyright holder had previously licensed the copyright to a television company in Germany. The German transmission was picked up by a Belgian television company, which re-transmitted the motion picture in Belgium. As such, the exclusive rights of the Belgian assignee to exhibit the film were allegedly infringed upon by the Belgian television company. The assignment did not explicitly provide for absolute territorial protection. However, the remedy the assignee sought from the courts essentially amounted to absolute territorial protection by preventing all third parties from transmitting the motion picture. The national court decided that a copyright holder has a right to remuneration for each 'performance' of the motion picture and unauthorized transmissions of the work could undermine the value of exhibiting the film by the copyright holder and its assignee.[46] The ECJ was then asked to determine whether the exclusive assignment that has the effect of territorial exclusivity was contrary to Article 101(1). The court opined that exclusivity amounting to absolute territorial protection does not *necessarily* fall within the scope of Article 101(1) as there may be legitimate interests to protect, given the nature of the cinematographic industry, in order for the creation and subsequent transmission of the work.[47] In other words, the court confirmed that territorial restrictions can be justified on the basis of protecting ex-ante investments in creating the work. Furthermore, the court considered the nature of the industry involved. In assessing whether the restrictions were indeed justifiable, the ECJ articulated a proportionality test when assessing the indispensability requirement by weighing

---

45   Case 262/81 *Coditel v Ciné-Vog Films* [1982] ECR 3381.
46   Case 62/79 SA *Compagnie générale pour la diffusion de la télévision, Coditel, and others v Ciné Vog Films and others*, ECR [1980] 881 at paragraph 12 which states 'the right of a copyright owner and his assigns to require fees for any showing of a film is part of the essential function of copyright in this type of literary and artistic work'.
47   *Supra* note 45 at 3391 and 3395.

the degree of restriction that is necessary to achieve the beneficial purpose of protecting the initial investments, having regard to the nature of the cinematographic industry.[48] At some point, a restraint goes beyond what is necessary to protect legitimate interests and falls within Article 101(1). Applying the reasoning of the ECJ in *Coditel* to the integrated drug discovery and development model, the proportionality test calls for a balancing of pro-competitive and anticompetitive effects, having regard to the *nature of the industry* and *investment in creating the work*. However, the findings are fact-specific without providing guidance on what constitutes a 'necessary degree of restriction' and what degree of exclusivity will be tolerated before it crosses the line from justifiable to prohibited.

In *Nungesser v Commission*,[49] the court was asked to consider an absolute territorial restriction in an exclusive plant breeders' right license. The Court stated that:

> [I]n the case of a licence of breeders' rights over hybrid maize seeds newly developed in one Member State, an undertaking established in another Member State which was not certain that it would not encounter competition from other licensees for the territory granted to it, or from the owner of the right himself, might be deterred from accepting the risk of cultivating and marketing that product; such a result would be damaging to the dissemination of a new technology and would prejudice competition in the community between the new product and similar existing products.[50]

Of particular relevance in the context of collaborative drug discovery and development is the focus on the risk and costs incurred by the licensee to sell a new product for the first time in the assigned territory. The court recognized that in certain circumstances, such as agreements concerning

---

[48] Hedvig Schmidt and Steven D. Anderman, *EU Competition Law and Intellectual Property Rights: The Regulation of Innovation* (Oxford University Press 2011) at 245 where the test applied in *Coditel II* is described as an indispensability test whereas the Commission refers to the test in subsequent decisions as a proportionality test. See Commission Decision 89/536/EEC of 15 September 1989 *Film purchases by German television stations (ARD)* OJ [1989] L 284/36, recital 44. The test has also been referred to as a balancing test by others. See Renato Nazzini, *Article 81 EC between Time Present and Time Past: A Normative Critique of 'Restriction of Competition' in EU Law.* COMMON MARKET LAW REVIEW, 43(2), 497–536 (2006) at 514 and Mario Siragusa, 'Technology Transfers under EEC Law: A Private View' in Barry E. Hawk (ed.). FORDHAM CORPORATE LAW INSTITUTE 95 (1982) 95 at 140.

[49] *Supra* note 32.

[50] Ibid., at paragraph 57.

the license of new technology, the absence of a restraint to protect the revenue stream of the licensee as a means to recoup investments incurred may discourage the licensee from agreeing to conclude the license at all.[51] Permitting a territorial restriction in such circumstances will have the effect of protecting the licensee of a novel product from competition by third parties, suggesting a recognition of concerns associated with opportunistic behavior such as third parties free-riding on the benefits derived from the investments made by the licensee.[52] However, the court only referred to risks associated with introducing a new product in a new market while under competition from third parties without specific reference to free-riding concerns as a possible justification for territorial restriction.[53] Because risk is a much broader concept than free-riding, the decision of *Nungesser* does not help delineate the specific circumstances that justify leniency under competition law. *Nungesser* could be interpreted as permitting territorial restraints, which could have far-reaching effects (i.e. higher profits than otherwise possible), in order to compensate the licensee for risky investments. Nevertheless, the decision does demonstrate the court's willingness to adopt an economic approach to its analysis and application of Article 101(1) by considering the economic and legal context of the agreement. Ultimately, the court found that absolute territorial protection could not be justified under Article 101(3) because the protection afforded to the licensee went beyond what is indispensable for the production and distribution or promotion of the

---

[51]   Commission Decision 85/410/EEC, *Velcro/Aplix (Velcro)*, OJ 1985 L 233/22; Hedvig Schmidt and Steven D. Anderman, *EU Competition Law and Intellectual Property Rights: The Regulation of Innovation* (Oxford University Press 2011) at 93.

[52]   Valentine Korah, *Exclusive Licenses of Patent and Plant Breeders Rights under EEC Law after Maize Seed.* THE ANTITRUST BULLETIN 28, 699 (1983) at 723; Oliver E. Williamson, 'Antitrust Lenses and the Uses of Transaction Cost Economics Reasoning' in Thomas M. Jorde and David J. Teece (eds), *Antitrust, Innovation and Competitiveness* (Oxford University Press 1992), 137–164; Anderman and Kallaugher *supra* note 40; Korah (2006), *supra* note 31.

[53]   Arguably, citing risky investments as a concern may be another way of expressing the problem of free-riding, but risky investments could also be related to the uncertainty of demand/success, which is an 'ordinary' business risk associated with economic activity that should not be sufficient to take the restriction outside of Article 101(1). On the other hand, free-riding merits special protection because no other less restrictive alternative can be used to eliminate that risk.

licensed technology.[54] Commentators have criticized the decision for failing to explain why the court thought that the risk undertaken by the licensee did not need protection to the degree of absolute territorial protection if the court accepted that the licensee's investments needed to be protected.[55] Arguably, the *Coditel* decision, which was delivered two months prior to *Nungesser,* is inconsistent with the *Nungesser* decision because absolute territorial protection was permitted under Article 101 in *Coditel* to protect the licensee's commercialization investments.

Pronuptia de Paris GmbH v Pronuptia de Paris Irmgard Schillgallis[56] is another case where investments by a party in the licensed technology can be protected by justifying restraints as falling outside Article 101(1). The restrictions purportedly served to prevent know-how acquired and developed by the franchisor from being misappropriated and used by others such as the franchisee in competition with the franchisor's own brand.[57] The court found that the cumulative effect of the restrictions contained in the franchisee agreement resulted in absolute territorial protection, which has been found in prior case law to limit competition for the purposes of Article 101(1).[58] The court also recognized the principle set out in prior case law that a prospective franchisee may not take the risk and invest in the franchise unless there was a degree of protection against competition from the franchisor and other franchisees. However, such a consideration should be part of an examination of the

---

[54] *Supra* note 32 at paragraph 77 where the court stated: 'As it is a question of seeds intended to be used by a large number of farmers for the production of maize, which is an important product for human and animal foodstuffs, absolute territorial protection manifestly goes beyond what is indispensable for the improvement of production or distribution or the promotion of technical progress, as is demonstrated in particular in the present case by the prohibition, agreed to by both parties to the agreement, of any parallel imports of INRA maize seeds into Germany even if those seeds were bred by INRA itself and marketed in France'. The court's attitude towards territorial protection as being in breach of Article 101(1) but not exemptible under Article 101(3) was consistent with its decisions in joined Cases 56 and 58–64, *Établissements Consten S.à.R.L. and Grundig-Verkaufs-GmbH v Commission of the European Economic Community*, ECR [1966] 429 and case 28/77 *Tepea BV v Commission of the European Communities*, ECR [1978] 1391.
[55] Valentine Korah, *Exclusive Licenses of Patent and Plant Breeders Rights under EEC Law after Maize Seed.* THE ANTITRUST BULLETIN 28, 699 (1983) at 740.
[56] Case 161/84 *Pronuptia de Paris GmbH v Pronuptia de Paris Irmgard Schillgallis*, [1986] ECR 353.
[57] Ibid., at paragraph 16.
[58] Ibid., at paragraph 24.

agreement under Article 101(3) and not form the basis of an exclusion from Article 101(1).[59] Following *Nungesser*, if the franchise was for a new or unknown business with an unknown brand, the territorial restraints may have a legitimate purpose (i.e. the franchisee would otherwise not accept the franchise), thereby justifying the exclusion of the agreement from Article 101(1). In other words, with respect to protecting investments made by the licensee in the further development or commercialization of the licensed intellectual property right, the court is more restrictive but supports that a licensee can be given limited territorial protection without necessarily breaching Article 101(1).

iii.   Royalty-bearing License

Remuneration in the form of granting a royalty-bearing right and license has several essential functions, the most important in the drug discovery and development context being an incentive mechanism for recovering the costs incurred for R&D.[60] Without royalties as a form of reward, third parties would be able to appropriate the value of new technologies, for example by reverse engineering, without incurring the substantial R&D costs. However, from a competition law standpoint, the remuneration mechanism may be used in a way to achieve a collusive outcome by manipulating the marginal costs of the licenses.[61] As such, in order to avoid anticompetitive concerns, consideration for licensing agreements must protect competition without creating obstacles for the licensing

---

[59]   Ibid.

[60]   See for example, Stephen M. Maurer and Suzanne Scotchmer, *Profit Neutrality in Licensing: The Boundary between Antitrust Law and Patent Law*. AMERICAN LAW AND ECONOMICS REVIEW, 8(3), 476–522 (2006); Louis Kaplow, *The Patent-Antitrust Intersection: A Reappraisal*. HARVARD LAW REVIEW, 1813–1892 (1984). See also Gary P. Pisano and Paul Y. Mang, 'Collaborative Product Development and the Market for Know-how: Strategies and Structures in the Biotechnology Industry' in Robert A. Burgleman and Richard S. Rosenbloom (eds) *Research on Technological Innovation, Management and Policy* (JAI Press 1992), Volume 5, 109–136 at 123.

[61]   Because royalties work as a 'tax imposed on sales', royalties affect the marginal costs of the licensee. See Carl Shapiro, *Patent Licensing and R&D Rivalry*. AMERICAN ECONOMIC REVIEW, 75(2), 25–30 (1985) and Michael L. Katz and Carl Shapiro, *How to License Intangible Property*. THE QUARTERLY JOURNAL OF ECONOMICS, 567–589 (1986) at 588. See also paragraph 185 of the TTBER Guidelines, *supra* note 21 setting out circumstances where royalty obligations may amount to hardcore restrictions.

parties to conclude economically efficient agreements for the development and commercialization of new products.

Generally, TTBER does not include any specific rules on the mechanism or level of royalties in technology transfer agreements.[62] However,
in order for royalty payment clauses to be block exempted, the mechanism by which such payments are given effect must not constitute a
restriction prohibited by TTBER.[63] In other words, royalty payment
mechanisms that provide the patent holder with adequate returns on
investment need to be distinguished from mechanisms that result in
compensation that exceeds social returns. Unfortunately, for confidentiality reasons, the clauses relating to the mechanism of license payments
have been redacted from the agreements provided by the integrated drug
discovery organizations and cannot be specifically assessed. However, the
question of what constitutes adequate compensation, what mechanisms
are permitted under competition law to allow the parties to recoup costs
and receive adequate compensation, and what additional effects compensation mechanisms may have on securing other commercial objectives of
the license can still be considered in general terms within the drug
discovery and development context.

Royalty payments based on sale of end-products incorporating the
licensed technology coupled with no other restrictions such as minimum
or maximum royalties are usually seen as being pro-competitive.[64] There
appears to be support in the literature for the claim that royalties have
several beneficial effects such as resolving disputes over the future value
of the technology, providing a means of allocating risk between the
parties, and allowing the licensee to finance the license with the sales of

---

[62] Paragraph 184 of the TTBER Guidelines, *supra* note 21 states that: 'The
parties to a license agreement are normally free to determine the royalty payable
by the licensee and its mode of payment without being caught by Article 101(1)
of the Treaty. This principle applies both to agreements between competitors and
agreements between non-competitors … In cases where the licensed technology
relates to an input which is incorporated into a final product it is as a general rule
not restrictive of competition that royalties are calculated on the basis of the
price of the final product, provided that it incorporates the licensed technology'.

[63] Ibid., at paragraph 158. See also paragraphs 80 and 157 for example for
the exceptional circumstances captured by the hardcore list in Article 4 TTBER
when the underlying purpose is to accomplish price-fixing.

[64] Ibid., at paragraph 184. Applying per-unit royalties induces the licensor to
promote competition between licensees because more sales will result in higher
royalty income. See Donald F. Turner, *The Patent System and Competitive Policy*.
THE UNIVERSITY OF NEW YORK LAW REVIEW, 44, 450 (1969) at 466.

the products incorporating the licensed technology.[65] TTBER and the TTBER Guidelines take a neutral case-by-case assessment approach to royalty obligations by looking into the economic context of the agreement to determine if anticompetitive restrictions outweigh precompetitive effects.[66] It would be overly simplistic to conclude that royalty obligations have the effect of restricting competition because they have an impact on the market price of the end product. Absent the license agreement, the parties would not be able to use each other's technologies to exploit the resulting intellectual property. On the other hand, a successful license, irrespective of the royalty mechanism, would create competition by introducing a new competing product into the market. If TTBER is construed as viewing royalty obligations as restrictive compared with other payment mechanisms, parties would be forced to either forego the value of the technology by granting a royalty-free license or to negotiate a lump sum payment based on imperfect and asymmetric information on future demand. This would in turn increase transactional costs and uncertainty for the parties and licensing may therefore be discouraged, all of which would be inconsistent with the Commission's

---

[65] Royalty payments play a role in aligning the parties' incentives to the commercial objectives of the agreement by ensuring that the licensed technology is used in the exploitation of the contract product instead of competing or rival technologies. Royalty payments also reduce the uncertainty of assessing future demand for the technology by limiting payments to actual use or sales, thereby sharing risk between the parties and avoiding opportunistic behavior based on any asymmetry between the parties regarding information on the value of the technology. See for example Katz and Shapiro *supra* note 61; Charles W. Hill, *Strategies for Exploiting Technological Innovations: When and When Not to License*. ORGANIZATION SCIENCE, 3(3), 428–441 (1992) at 433; Nancy T. Gallini and Brian D. Wright, *Technology Transfer under Asymmetric Information*. THE RAND JOURNAL OF ECONOMICS, 147–160 (1990); Suzanne Scotchmer, *Innovation and Incentives* (MIT Press 2004). In other words, aside from being a reward, royalties also play a role in overcoming transactional hazards thereby giving rise to a commercial relationship that in turn secures rewards to compensate for ex-ante investments in R&D. See also European Commissioner for Competition Policy Mario Monti, *The New EU Policy on Technology Transfer Agreements* (SPEECH/04/19 2004) at http://ec.europa.eu/comm/competition/speeches/index_2004.html; Valentine Korah, *Draft Block Exemption for Technology Transfer*. EUROPEAN COMPETITION LAW REVIEW, 25(5), 247–262 (2004) at 255–256.

[66] TTBER, *supra* note 22 at recitals 3–5 and paragraphs 184–188 of the TTBER Guidelines, *supra* note 21.

own view that diffusion of technology is pro-competitive.[67] Nevertheless, language in the TTBER Guidelines seem to suggest a disapproval of royalties by stating that less restrictive alternative payment options, such as lump sum payments, are available even in cases where the licensor makes significant investments specific to tailor the licensed technology to the needs of the licensee.[68] The TTBER Guidelines recognize that in such circumstances, minimum royalty obligations may be necessary to induce licensors to make the investment, but at the same time, the TTBER Guidelines state, 'normally, the licensor will be able to charge directly for such investments by way of a lump sum payment'.[69] By suggesting that lump sum payments may be a viable alternative, the TTBER Guidelines overlook the transactional risks associated with determining such an amount and the disincentive to the licensee since lump sum payments represent a sunk cost which increases the amount of risk.[70] The preference for lump sum payments according to the TTBER Guidelines implies that transactional costs and hazards that are typical of licensing agreements may be overlooked in the TTBER framework.

Calculating royalties based on a percentage of the selling price or a fixed amount of the end-product or the input of the end-product incorporating the licensed technology is not problematic according to TTBER.[71]

Net sales shall mean the gross amount invoiced by industry to independent third parties for the sale or disposition of products incorporating the licensed intellectual property in a first commercial sale at arm's length transaction, less the following: (i) any taxes or duties imposed on the sale or import of products which are actually paid; (ii) any outbound transportation costs and costs of insurance in transit; (iii) customary trade, cash or quantity discounts or rebates, to the extent actually allowed and taken; and (iv) amounts repaid or credited by reason of rejection or return.

---

[67] As expressed in recital 4 of TTBER, *supra* note 22 and paragraphs 9, 17 and 176 of the TTBER Guidelines, *supra* note 21.

[68] Paragraph 233 of the TTBER Guidelines, *supra* note 21.

[69] Ibid.

[70] For example, if a licensee pays a lump sum fee for the use of the licensed technology for a period of three years but the licensed technology is rendered obsolete after one year when a new technology is introduced, the licensee would incur an unrecoverable substantial loss for the years the licensed technology can no longer be used. As such, a lump sum payment represents a transactional cost that may discourage licensing whereas a royalty mechanism would not create the same problem.

[71] Paragraph 184 of the TTBER Guidelines, *supra* note 21.

In the event that a product is sold in a combination form that includes, in addition to the licensed intellectual property, at least one other pharmaceutically active ingredient, which pharmaceutically active ingredient(s) are also independently marketed during the royalty period in question in the country in question, then Net Sales, for the purposes of determining royalty payments on the combination product, shall be calculated by multiplying the net sales of the combination product by [a formula]. In the event that a product is sold in combination with other pharmaceutically active ingredients, and the product or one or more pharmaceutically active ingredients are not sold separately, then Net Sales, for the purpose of determining royalty payments on the combination product, shall be calculated by [another formula].

It is when the end-product is deemed to be comprised of two independent products with separate product markets that the royalty base may infringe Article 101(1), as in *Windsurfing v Commission*,[72] where royalties were based on the sales of an unpatented separate product combined with a patented product. The ECJ found the obligation on the licensee to sell the patented product in conjunction with a product 'outside the scope of the patent' to be restrictive of competition under Article 101 because the unpatented product was not 'indispensable to the exploitation of the product'.[73] In the integrated drug discovery and development context, the associated license agreement contemplates the sale of combination products incorporating the licensed technology in addition to other pharmaceutically active compounds. No royalty payments are payable on products that do not include the licensed technology[74] and royalties that are payable on the combination products are based on a formula designed to reflect the contribution of the licensed technology to the end-product. As such, the royalty base set out in the associated license agreement should be in compliance with TTBER.

As previously discussed, royalties are essential for the purpose of recovering ex-ante R&D investments. The need to recover such ex-ante investments naturally influences the types of contractual restrictions that may be included in the licensing agreement for the purpose of ensuring an 'appropriate' stream of revenue. Although the specific clauses relating to the mechanisms to secure a particular level of remuneration have been

---

[72]   Case 193/83 *Windsurfing International Inc. v Commission* (1986) ECR 611 at paragraphs 60–67.

[73]   Ibid.

[74]   Royalties that extend to products produced solely with the licensee's own technology rights are hardcore listed under Article 4(1)(a) and (e) of TTBER, *supra* note 22. See also paragraph 185 of TTBER Guidelines, *supra* note 21.

redacted from the agreements obtained from the integrated drug discovery organizations, the TTBER Guidelines do set out general parameters of what constitutes an adequate level of compensation for a license. The TTBER Guidelines make the general statement that '[t]he parties to a licence agreement are normally free to determine the royalty payable by the licensee and its mode of payment without being caught by Article 101(1)'.[75] Viewed in combination with the statement 'the innovator should be free to seek appropriate remuneration for successful projects that is sufficient to maintain investment incentives, taking failed projects into account',[76] these statements taken together indicate that a royalty level could be set to recoup investments in initial R&D of the licensed technology using the level of fixed costs as a reference point to determine whether a level of royalty is excessive.[77] In assessing whether royalties are disproportionate, the methodology set out in the TTBER Guidelines requires an examination of the royalties paid by other licensees on the product market for the same or substitute technologies, which appears to be a rather blunt instrument that merely establishes an approximation by reference without considering product differentiation between the substitutable technologies, assuming there are substitutable technologies on the market.[78] If the relevant parties are the only ones on the market, which is a possible scenario in the present context where novel pharmaceutical products may result from the collaboration, the methodology set out in the TTBER Guidelines would have limited applicability. Furthermore, in a recent decision involving a French pharmaceutical company and five producers of generic medicine, the Commission defined the relevant market by limiting it to a single molecule, even though there were at least

---

[75] Paragraph 184 of TTBER Guidelines, *supra* note 21.

[76] Ibid., at paragraph 8.

[77] See for example, Peeperkorn, Luc Peeperkorn, *IP Licenses and Competition Rules: Striking the Right Balance.* WORLD COMPETITION, 26(4), 527 (2003) at 532–533 where it has been contended that the Commission may not view remuneration levels as a priority because it is possible that parties may still incur ex-ante R&D investments due to pressure on firms by short-term competition.

[78] Improved quality is usually associated with a higher price, which consumers may be willing to pay in favor of acquiring a higher quality product. As such, a straight comparison between royalties paid by other licensees without considering differentiating factors between rival technologies may generate erroneous conclusions as the value attributed to each of the technologies may be different. See for example Richard J. Gilbert, 'Mobility Barriers and the Value of Incumbency' in Richard Schmalensee and Robert D. Willig (eds), *Handbook of Industrial Organization* (North-Holland 1989), Volume 1, Chapter 8, 849–908.

a dozen competing products within the same therapeutic class to which the molecule belongs.[79] This definition further narrows the already controversial market definition set out in the *AstraZeneca* case as previously discussed (which is still the only fully litigated EU pharmaceutical antitrust case to date). Following the *Servier* case, if a single molecule can constitute the relevant market, then it is entirely possible that there are no substitutable technologies to assess whether royalties are disproportionate according to the proposed methodology in the TTBER Guidelines. In other words, the TTBER Guidelines fail to directly address the issue of what an adequate level of compensation is, and the proposed methodology can result in an over- and under-inclusive way to capture anticompetitive royalty arrangements, making the assessment of what constitutes disproportionate royalties quite complex in practice. From a patent reward perspective, innovators must be able to receive adequate remuneration to appropriate a reasonable portion of the benefit of the invention in order to be suitably rewarded and encouraged.[80] The maximum royalty that can be extracted is the difference between the marginal cost and the price. If the market can bear a monopoly price because the product is superior to all other technologies, the social benefit of the innovation is represented by the monopoly profit, which according to patent reward theory would not be disproportionate.

---

[79] See European Commission Press Release: Decision in Servier Case European Commission SPEECH/14/541 09/07/2014 (accessible at http://europa. eu/rapid/press-release_SPEECH-14-541_en.htm). Arguably, given that this decision relates to settlement agreements between Servier and the generic manufacturers, it can be said that this narrow market definition applies to the unique circumstances of patent settlement agreements. However, it does set a precedent for the pharmaceutical industry that the Commission prioritizes preventing 'pay for delay' over commercial concerns and transaction costs. Servier released a press release stating, among other things, '[t]he European Commission's decision against our intellectual property rights sends a very bad signal to companies of all sizes that make the choice to innovate in Europe. This kind of sanction jeopardizes the pharmaceutical companies' commitment to research and this is thus detrimental to patients'. Servier intends to file an appeal before the European Union Court of Justice. See Press Release, The European Commission limits the legitimate exercise of intellectual property rights and thus weakens the competitiveness of European industry, July 9, 2014 (accessible at http://www. servier.com/content/european-commission-limits-legitimate-exercise-intellectual-property-rights-and-thus-weakens).

[80] Joachim Inkmann, *Horizontal and Vertical R&D Cooperation*, Discussion Paper No. 2000-02, Department of Economics and Center of Finance and Economics (2000); Carl Shapiro, *Patent Reform: Aligning Reward and Contribution*. INNOVATION POLICY AND THE ECONOMY, 8, 111–156 (2008).

The TTBER Guidelines state that the parties can normally agree to extend royalty obligations beyond the patent term without falling afoul of Article 101(1) because actual and potential competition from third parties once the period of exclusivity expires should be sufficient to balance against any anticompetitive effects.[81] Curiously, the TTBER Guidelines fail to explain how extended royalty obligations could have any appreciable anticompetitive effect at all if third parties can legally exploit the technology and compete in the market, unless there is very little or no third party competition, which is highly unlikely in the present context where generic manufacturers usually enter the market immediately after a pharmaceutical patent expires.

Royalty term shall mean, on a Product-by-Product and country-by-country basis, the term during which royalties on Net Sales are due and payable for a Product, which term shall commence on the first commercial sale at arm's length of a Product in a country, and shall end on the later of (i) the expiration or abandonment of all issued patents and filed patent applications within the Licensed Patent Rights in the country in which such Product is manufactured, used or sold, in each case with a claim covering such Product, or (ii) the 10th (tenth) anniversary date of the first commercial sale of such Product in such country, or (iii) the expiration of all Data Exclusivity periods for such Product in such country. For the avoidance of doubt, in case the Licensed Know-How survives the expiration of the Royalty Term, the LICENSEE may use the Licensed Know-How after the Royalty Term on a fully paid-up basis.

Given that no extension is contemplated in the associated license agreement, there is no need for further analysis on this point. Suffice it to say that from an economic point of view, spreading royalties over a longer period by way of extending royalty obligations beyond the patent term lowers the marginal costs of the licensee, which may be an important advantage during the initial commercialization period when demand for products incorporating the new technology is unknown and

---

[81]   Paragraph 187 of the TTBER Guidelines, *supra* note 21. Interestingly, TTBER is more interested in ensuring the increased competitiveness from third parties rather than being concerned with the disadvantage to the licensee with the enduring obligation to pay royalties. This demonstrates that TTBER measures anticompetitiveness in terms of consumer welfare in contrast with old case law where the burden on the licensee was considered an anticompetitive effect. See Case 320/87, *Kai Ottung v Klee & Weilbach A/S and Thomas Schmidt A/S* [1989] ECR 1177.

uncertain.[82] It is conceivable that a licensee may elect not to enter into a license agreement without a lower royalty rate to be compensated for by an extended royalty obligation due to certain inherent transactional risks.[83] Although certain restrictions will not be caught by Article 101(1) if they are deemed objectively necessary in order to conclude a license agreement, it would be unrealistic to expect that all types of restrictions would be deemed objectively necessary to alleviate transactional problems. In the context of drug discovery and development, because of the unpredictable nature of whether the licensed technology will ultimately survive clinical trials despite proof of concept, an argument can be made that more restrictions should be considered objectively necessary to mitigate against the risks. However, if the collaborative R&D is successful, the demand for the developed technology could be roughly assessed based on statistics regarding how many people suffer from a particular disease. The problem is with hindsight. Given that the license agreement may fall under the scrutiny of Article 101 for years after the conclusion of the agreement, it will be examined with the benefit of ex-post information, whereas at the time the agreement is concluded, the risks are unforeseeable. The analysis seems to support the position that extended royalty requirements should not be caught by Article 101 in the drug discovery and development context because the parties are likely to be able to prove a genuine concern regarding uncertainty of success at the time the licensing agreement was concluded.

As previously discussed, according to the definition set out in the TTBER Guidelines, integrated drug discovery organizations and industry are not considered actual or potential competitors on the product market but they are most likely considered competitors on the technology market.[84] TTBER and the TTBER Guidelines are primarily concerned

---

[82]   Because demand is unpredictable, creditors are unable to foresee demand or the value of the licensed technology in order to determine their willingness to finance investments of the licensee. See Hill, *supra* note 65; Katz and Shapiro, *supra* note 61.

[83]   Paragraph 12(b) of the TTBER Guidelines, *supra* note 21 provides examples of where the nature of the agreement or characteristics of the market is such that certain restraints are objectively necessary for the existence of an agreement and therefore not caught by Article 101(1). In other words, gaining access to new or improved products may offset the negative effects of certain restrictions. However, not all investments into developing technology will result in improved or new products.

[84]   Ibid at paragraph 35 which states that parties are actual competitors on the technology market if the licensee is already licensing out its technology rights, which industry is most likely doing, and the licensor enters the technology

with preventing the use of royalties in sham agreements and agreements as a means for price-fixing in reciprocal licensing arrangements.[85] In the integrated drug discovery and development context, since there are no reciprocal licensing and no price-related provisions to analyze, no further assessment is possible. Royalty arrangements calculated on the basis of sales of products irrespective of whether they incorporate the licensed technology, are prohibited by hardcore restrictions as a price fixing mechanism.[86] As discussed above, since royalties in the associated license agreement are calculated based on net sales of products that incorporate the licensed technology, no further analysis is required. However, a statement that reach-through royalties are a form of price-fixing in the absence of an explicit explanation is difficult to understand. The TTBER Guidelines explain that reach-through royalties restrict competition by raising the cost of using the licensee's own competing technology rights and restrict competition that existed in the absence of the agreement, which was the situation in *Windsurfing v Commission*.[87] A reach-through royalty base has arguably been equated with a non-compete obligation where licensee R&D is discouraged.[88] Although no explicit support for this interpretation has appeared in recent case law or decisions, the economic literature appears to support the notion that reach-through royalties may be used to discourage the use of competing technology with anticompetitive effects.[89] However, under freedom to contract, a licensee may elect to put itself in a competitive disadvantage because accepting the license may improve its overall position on the market. In any event, there are no reach-through royalty arrangements in the associated license agreement.

---

market by granting a license for competing technology rights to the licensee. Integrated drug discovery organization does indeed enter the technology market by granting a license to industry, and because the proposed projects are likely, but not necessarily in the field of industry's expertise, the resulting technology developed through the collaboration will likely be a competing technology to that of industry.

[85]   Ibid. at paragraph 185 and Article 4(1)(a) of TTBER, *supra* note 22.

[86]   Paragraph 101 of the TTBER Guidelines, *supra* note 21.

[87]   *Supra* note 72.

[88]   Commission Decision 76/29/EEC *AOIP/Beyrard* [1976] OJ L 6/8, section II, recital 4(f).

[89]   Discouraging the use of competing technology may be seen as restriction. See for example OECD, *Competition Policy and Intellectual Property Rights*, Roundtable on competition policy in relation to intellectual property rights by Committee on Competition Law and Policy, DAFFE/CLP(98)18, OECD (1998) at http://www.oecd.org/dataoecd/34/57/1920398.pdf.

Although integrated drug discovery organizations and industry may be considered potential competitors on the technology market under TTBER, they are treated as non-competitors for the purpose of TTBER analysis.[90] However, Article 5(2) TTBER may be relevant because it is possible that the associated license agreement includes limits to the licensee's ability to exploit its own technology or the ability of the parties to carry out research and development.[91]

The integrated drug discovery organization may, during the term of the agreement and upon requesting industry's written consent, such consent to be at industry's sole discretion, use the resulting project's intellectual property royalty- and milestone-free for internal research purposes. Such research use must not include any commercial purposes nor may the integrated drug discovery organization involve a third party in such research use. After the resulting project's intellectual property is rightfully published (e.g. in the course of a standard patent application procedure), the integrated drug discovery organization may use the resulting project intellectual property for its internal research purposes, provided, however, that the integrated drug discovery organization shall inform industry in writing about such intended use. If commercial use is intended, the integrated drug discovery organization must obtain a license from industry to be negotiated in good faith between the parties.

Industry shall have the exclusive right, and sole responsibility and decision-making authority, to research and develop any products/compounds and to conduct all clinical trials and non-clinical studies. Industry shall have the sole right and responsibility for preparing the development plan for each product, and shall in all events have the sole decision-making authority regarding each development plan and the development of each product, including the determination of the Indications in which to pursue Development.

Both industry and the integrated drug discovery organization have the express ability to carry out its own R&D. There are no restrictions on industry's use of its own technology rights, which are considered to be restrictive of competition and does not satisfy the conditions of Article 101(3), and there are no reach-through royalty obligations.[92] Both

---

[90]   Paragraph 36 of TTBER Guidelines, *supra* note 21.
[91]   Ibid., at paragraph 142.
[92]   Ibid. Contrary to the situation in agreements between competitors, reach-through royalties may be justified in the case of agreements between non-competitors as a means to facilitate the metering of royalties. Although the arrangement may lead to foreclosure by increasing the cost of using third party inputs if royalties are paid on products produced with the licensed technology and on products produced with third party technology, the question of whether

integrated drug discovery organizations and industry are important sources of innovation, particularly because they possess the skills and assets to carry out further R&D, especially in areas where there are few technologies available in a particular field.[93] Given that both parties are free to carry out independent R&D, both integrated drug discovery organizations and industry maintain their ability to innovate, and the associated license agreement is not restrictive of competition. However, it has been contended that restricting the use of the licensee's substitutable technologies may facilitate optimal use of the licensed technology, especially in the case of an exclusive license and when the licensee has market power in the relevant product market,[94] which in effect is a non-compete obligation.[95] If the licensee's market share exceeds the TTBER threshold and has market power, foreclosing substitutable technologies will likely not satisfy the conditions of Article 101(3) because the licensor can use a minimum production quota system as a less restrictive alternative. This indicates that TTBER prioritizes competition on the product market and not on recovering R&D investments because the focus is on the competitive position of the parties rather than the transactional costs and hurdles of concluding the agreement.

Respecting contractual freedom of the parties to negotiate and mutually agree on restrictions that strategically facilitate the conclusion of a licensing agreement seems to have taken a back seat to static efficiency and an assessment of the market effects of licensing restrictions. In the context of collaborative drug discovery and development, there is a likelihood that the industry partner has market power so the market share thresholds in Article 3 of TTBER will typically disqualify the associated license agreement from block exemption and subject it to the uncertainty of assessment on an individual basis. In such a case, the analysis and assessment of the restrictions should focus on its rationale in light of the

---

the restriction has foreclosure effects must therefore be considered on a case-by-case basis. See also paragraph 188.

[93]   Ibid., at paragraph 143. A restriction preventing independent R&D by the parties when there are few alternative technologies in the market may infringe Article 101(1) and it is unlikely that the conditions under Article 101(3) TFEU would be satisfied.

[94]   John W. Schlicher, *Some Thoughts on the Law and Economics of Licensing Biotechnology Patent and Related Property Rights in the United States.* JOURNAL OF THE PATENT AND TRADEMARK OFFICE SOCIETY, 69, 263 (1987) at 270.

[95]   Paragraph 232 of the TTBER Guidelines, *supra* note 21, which supports the use of non-compete obligations to ensure that the licensee has an incentive to invest in and exploit the licensed technology effectively.

surrounding circumstances as well as the relationship between the parties, thereby explicitly considering the effects of transactional hazards. Unfortunately, TTBER in its current state prioritizes static efficiency at the expense of limiting transactional hazards in licensing agreements. TTBER's approach to the distinction made between licenses concluded between competitors and non-competitors demonstrates the conflict between transaction costs and static efficiency considerations. For example, reach-through royalties are blacklisted under Article 4 in relation to agreements between competitors but only excluded under Article 5 in relation to licenses between non-competitors. However, an agreement between competitors can benefit equally if not more from justifications based on transactional hazards as certain transactional hazards have graver consequences between competitors than non-competitors. Consequently, licensing between competitors may not be able to rely on rules that are otherwise available to non-competitors to alleviate contractual obstacles, which may negatively impact efficient licensing. The lack of awareness of transactional hazards may create disincentives for the conclusion of efficient contracts and make it harder for the licensor to appropriate its developed invention. If the parties are not able to protect their interests, the technology may simply not be licensed.

iv. Field of Use

Field of use restraints are defined as provisions limiting the exploitation of the licensed technology to a specific technical field of application or product market.[96] Field of use restrictions are seen as hardcore listed under Article 4(1)(c) of TTBER but subject to exclusions as well as individual assessment over the market share thresholds.[97]

By encouraging the licensee to apply the licensed technology to areas outside a particular field, such as in areas of focus where other third parties are active, field of use restrictions may have pro-competitive effects.[98] In other words, a field of use restriction imposed on the licensee would not restrict competition in the protected field of use

---

[96]   Ibid., paragraph 208.

[97]   Article 4(1)(c)(i)–(iv) of TTBER, *supra* note 22. TTBER's approach to field of use restrictions is directed at preventing market sharing and market power to be balanced against the pro-competitive effect of dissemination (i.e. the need to protect the licensor's main area of activity, and the need to protect the licensee's investments into the technology).

[98]   Paragraph 212 of the TTBER Guidelines, *supra* note 21.

because the restriction allows the licensee to develop the licensed technology and compete in the field without fear of infringement claims, thereby increasing competition by permitting the licensee to enter the market as a new competitor. However, in the case where the licensor and licensee are considered competitors in the specific field of use, such a restraint may restrict competition by restricting the licensor's activity within the particular field of use.

> 'Field' shall mean any uses in the diagnosis, cure, mitigation, treatment or prevention of diseases in humans or animals.

In the present case, the grant given by the integrated drug discovery organization to industry is an exclusive worldwide license to research, develop, manufacture, have manufactured, use and commercialize products or compounds in the broad field[99] of diagnosis, cure, mitigation, treatment or prevention of diseases in humans or animals. In other words, only industry has the right to carry out pharmaceutical development based on the licensed technology in regard to all types of medical applications. Because integrated drug discovery organizations do not have expertise in the development of technology for the purpose of commercialization, integrated drug discovery organizations would not be active in the 'field' as defined in the associated licensing agreement. The field of use restriction would therefore not have a restrictive impact on the activities of integrated drug discovery organizations. With regard to restricting activities of third party licensees, as the exclusive worldwide licensee of the licensed technology, the field of use restriction will not affect any third party licensee competition as no other licensees have access to the licensed technology. As previously mentioned, such a grant may be seen as hindering intra-technology competition since no third parties are permitted to practice the licensed technology.[100] In such a

---

[99]   In *Rich Products/Jus-rol* [1988] OJ L 069/21, the Commission found that a field of use restraint imposed on the licensee concerning know-how did not fall within Article 101(1). The field of use in the license was broad and encompassed all possible fields of use. Nonetheless the Commission stated that even if a field of use had been reserved the clause would not have constituted a restriction of competition. Unfortunately, the Commission did not justify this statement.

[100]   Paragraph 215 of the TTBER Guidelines, *supra* note 21. The exclusion of intra-technology competition by third parties may facilitate collusion between parties, especially when the parties have market power, but in the case of

case, third parties employing competing technologies will be the only source of competition in the particular field of use capable of disciplining the licensees' behavior on the market. From an economics perspective, licensing agreements associated with high transaction costs (as is the case with drug discovery and development) usually require strong contractual restrictions as safeguards against opportunistic behavior from third parties and to minimize risks.[101] As such, any balancing analysis under Article 101(1) of suspicious or highly restrictive licenses should be viewed with an open mind and degree of flexibility because such licenses may potentially be the most efficient way to disseminate technology, especially with respect to radical improvements. Although justifications based on objective necessity of field of use restrictions are not discussed in the TTBER Guidelines, the argument will likely be based on the general assertion that such protection of licensees may be necessary to induce them to invest and develop the licensed technology.[102] With respect to the indispensability assessment under Article 101(3), the TTBER Guidelines are equally silent on its view on transactional costs. According to the TTBER Guidelines, the exemption provided under Article 4(1)(c)(i) of TTBER to non-reciprocal agreements that grant exclusive license between competitors gives incentives to the licensee to invest in and develop the licensed technology, and may indirectly suggest an economic approach.[103] However, the legal uncertainty on how TTBER will view transactional costs under Article 101(3) makes the potential for over-inclusion under Article 101(1) a point of concern.[104]

---

non-reciprocal exclusive licensing between competitors where the licensor and the licensee only compete on the technology market (i.e. the licensor being a research-based undertaking and not engaging in production and distribution to bring products to market) such cases typically do not infringe Article 101(1). See paragraph 193 of the TTBER Guidelines. This implies that if the licensor is not a competitive force in the licensee's field of use, there are no competition concerns. However, if the licensee's position is strong, a sole or exclusive license may have negative effects, and is likely to be caught by Article 101(1) and unlikely to fulfil the conditions of Article 101(3). See also paragraph 195 of the TTBER Guidelines.

[101] Ibid., at paragraph 213.
[102] Ibid., at paragraph 212.
[103] Ibid., at paragraphs 107 and 212.
[104] There is a risk that market power alone will be used as the decisive factor. Market power or dominance will not eliminate opportunistic behavior such as free riding if investments made into developing the technology can benefit rivals. As such, field of use is still indispensable to resolve the transactional hazard.

Turning to case law, there is no real decision that specifically addresses the issue of field of use restrictions. In *Windsurfing v Commission*,[105] the court considered a clause that required the licensee to sell patented rigs in conjunction with specific non-patented boards that were subject to approval by the licensor. From the perspective of field of use restrictions, arguably, the clause restricted the use of the licensed technology in association with specific boards set out in the licensing agreements.[106] Because the board was not covered by the patent that protected the licensed technology, the court found the restraint went beyond the scope of the patent by forcing consumers to purchase both board and rig as an end-product.[107] The court rejected the argument that the clause was intended for quality control purposes and found instead that the restriction limited the licensee's freedom of action.[108]

v. Restriction on Own Use

> The integrated drug discovery organization shall not during the term of the agreement develop, manufacture, have manufactured, use, sell, offer for sale, import, or export a competing product, nor enter into any relationship with any third party with respect to the resulting project's intellectual property. In the event that the integrated drug discovery organization enters into such activities and a competing product enters clinical trials, then the integrated drug discovery organization shall thereupon be considered to be in breach of this agreement, and industry shall have the right to terminate this agreement.
>
> Notwithstanding the foregoing, the integrated drug discovery organization may, during the term, upon an individual request to industry and only after industry's prior written consent, such consent to be at industry's sole discretion, use the licensed technology royalty- and milestone-free for internal research purposes only (e.g. use as internal reference, selectivity marker and use for internal screening). Such research use must not include any commercial purposes nor may integrated drug discovery organization involve a third party in such research use. After the resulting project's intellectual property has been rightfully published, the integrated drug discovery organization may use the licensed technology for its internal research purposes, provided, however, that the integrated drug discovery organization shall inform industry in writing about such intended use. If commercial use is intended, the integrated drug discovery organization must obtain a license from industry.

---

[105] Supra note 72.
[106] Whether the restrictive clause could be construed as a field of use restriction is debatable.
[107] *Supra* note 72 at paragraphs 45 and 54–59.
[108] Ibid., at paragraph 49.

> Industry shall have the right, in its sole discretion, to grant sublicenses, in whole or in part, provided however that the granting by industry of a sublicense shall be subject to, and be consistent with, the terms and conditions of this license agreement, and shall not relieve industry of any of its obligations hereunder.

TTBER restricts prohibitions placed on the parties' ability to carry out research and development, unless the restriction is indispensable to prevent the disclosure of the licensed technology to third parties.[109] As such, the restriction on integrated drug discovery organizations from engaging in activities with third parties relating to the licensed technology is explicitly exempted from the hardcore restriction.[110] A restraint on use may promote the dissemination of new technology by assuring one party that the other does not create a competing technology or product. However, in the drug discovery and development context where it is possible that only a few technologies are available in the relevant market, a restriction on the ability to carry out independent research and development may be restrictive of competition and is unlikely to satisfy the conditions of Article 101(3) because the parties may be an important source of competition.[111] However, the right to terminate the agreement,

---

[109]   Article 4(1)(d) of TTBER, *supra* note 22.

[110]   Paragraph 115 of the TTBER Guidelines, *supra* note 21, states that in order for the exception to apply, the restrictions imposed on the licenser to prevent disclosure to third parties must be necessary and proportionate to ensure such protection. However, the Guidelines fail to provide any further guidance in regards to how such necessity and proportionality is to be accessed. For the purposes of assessing the associated license agreement, the restriction is directed towards preventing third party free-riding on the licensed technology to commercialize a competing product. From previous analysis, restrictions designed to safeguard against opportunistic behavior have been viewed favorably by TTBER as acceptable justifications to protect the licensee's investment. With respect to proportionality, other than a simple prohibition against the integrated drug discovery organization from entering into a relationship with a third party with respect to the resulting project's intellectual property, there is no other alternate less restrictive way to prevent free-riding.

[111]   Ibid., at paragraph 143. Although this section deals with non-competitors, applied to the drug discovery and development context where there is a significant likelihood that only a few technologies may be available, restriction on the ability of the parties to carry out independent research and development may be restrictive of competition, regardless of their 'competitive status' as defined by TTBER. As discussed in Chapter 3, industry and integrated drug discovery organization may be an important and potential source of innovation in the market, especially since they belong to a small group that possess the

triggered only after the integrated drug discovery organization has successfully engaged in the research and development with third parties to the point where a competing product is ready to enter clinical trials, is likely to fall outside the of Article 101(1).[112] In such a case, a termination clause coupled with a restriction on use is arguably a less restrictive alternative given that the integrated drug discovery organization's ability to conduct further research and development and innovate remains unaffected until the triggering event when a commercially viable technology has been developed.

Since there are no restrictions on the industry's ability to sublicense or to conduct research and development, and industry has the exclusive right and sole responsibility and decision-making authority on all matters relating to the exploitation of the licensed technology, no further analysis on restrictions on the licensee will be required. As competitors on the technology market, the concern is that such restrictions on the licensee will reduce existing competition on the technology and innovation market.[113] However, the clauses relating to development and manufacturing in the associated license agreement protect industry's incentives to innovate by granting full control over the exploitation of the licensed technology, including access to any background or related intellectual property belonging to both the integrated drug discovery organization and industry.

With respect to the requirement imposed on integrated drug discovery organizations to seek consent from industry in order to conduct internal research based on the licensed technology merits further investigation. Integrated drug discovery organizations are not restricted from carrying out research and development but the requirement of consent at the sole discretion of industry can have the effect of a restriction should industry refuse consent. The hardcore restriction of Article 4(1)(d) states that the parties 'must be free to carry out independent research and development',

---

necessary assets and skills to carry out further research and development. See also Paragraph 157 where the Commission takes the view that outside the area of hardcore restrictions Article 101 is unlikely to be infringed where there are four or more independently controlled technologies in addition to the technologies controlled by the parties to the agreement that may be substitutable for the licensed technology.

[112]   Ibid.

[113]   Ibid., at paragraph 116. Given that the TTBER and the TTBER Guidelines do not require an analysis of market position in relation to restriction on use clauses, it can be argued that TTBER views such restrictions as being anticompetitive by nature, suggesting the protection of the licensee's ability to conduct R&D directly protects innovation.

so arguably the requirement of consent does constitute a restriction.[114] However, the effect on competition of the consent will need to be assessed in the light of the circumstances and will likely not give rise to appreciable anticompetitive concerns unless it can be established that consent is unreasonably denied.

vi. No-Challenge

> Integrated drug discovery organization shall have the right to terminate the agreement immediately upon written notice if industry challenges or assists a third party to challenge the validity, scope or enforceability of or otherwise opposes any licensed patent right. If a sub-licensee of industry challenges the validity, scope or enforceability of or otherwise opposes any licensed patent right then industry shall, upon written notice from the integrated drug discovery organization terminate such sublicense.

A no-challenge clause is an excluded restriction that directly or indirectly prohibits a party from challenging the validity of the other party's patent.[115] According to the TTBER Guidelines, because licensees are normally in the best position to determine whether or not the intellectual property associated with the licensed technology is valid or not, for reasons of public interest, invalid intellectual property rights should be eliminated.[116] However, the exclusion is exempted in the case of an exclusive license where the licensor reserves the right to terminate the license in the event the licensee challenges the validity of the licensed technology rights.[117] It is believed that because of the licensor's dependency on the licensee to exploit the licensed technology in order to generate royalty income, the incentives for innovation and for licensing

---

[114]   Note that the agreement is silent as to the need for industry to provide reasons for not granting consent.

[115]   Article 5(1)(b) TTBER, *supra* note 22 as well as by paragraphs 133–140 of the TTBER Guidelines, *supra* note 21.

[116]   Paragraph 134 of the TTBER Guidelines, *supra* note 21. Invalid intellectual property stifles innovation so Article 101(1) is likely to apply to non-challenge clauses because they create a competitive disadvantage for undertakings. In such cases the conditions of Article 101(3) are unlikely to be fulfilled.

[117]   Article 5(1)(b) TTBER, *supra* note 22 and paragraph 139 of the TTBER Guidelines, *supra* note 21. On balance, termination clauses are usually less likely to have anticompetitive effects in the case of exclusive licensing.

out could be undermined. As such, the no-challenge clause that accompanies the exclusive license found in the associated license agreement is exempted as long as other conditions of the safe harbour such as market share threshold are fulfilled. Outside the safe harbour, a case-by-case assessment has to be carried out.

The literature has made the argument that no-challenge provisions may be a precondition for licensing as a means to protect investment in the licensed technology.[118] The TTBER Guidelines specifically recognize that benefits derived from know-how would be impossible to recover subsequent to disclosure so an obligation on the licensee not to challenge in such circumstances will be viewed more favorably.[119] In other words, because the nature of know-how is such that it cannot be taken back once it is disclosed, the indispensability requirement of Article 101(3) should be satisfied because the licensor cannot protect against use of the licensed technology after challenge.[120] The described circumstances should support an argument for the need for strong protection in favor of the licensor in the form of a no-challenge clause as a condition of granting a license. However, the TTBER Guidelines only provide exclusion to challenges against know-how and not patents, even though it is recognized in the literature that the transfer of know-how in a license agreement typically makes exploitation of the patent more efficient. The current TTBER rules (unfairly) expose the licensor to the risk of losing

---

[118] Korah (2006), supra note 31; Anderman and Kallaugher *supra* note 40. Curiously, because the TTBER Guidelines exclude no-challenge clauses set out in settlement agreements in recognition that such clauses eliminate the risk of future litigation, it is surprising that TTBER would not apply the same justification to license agreements given the desire to avoid future disputes is equally important in license agreements, especially when high transactional costs and investments are involved. See paragraph 242 of the TTBER Guidelines, suggesting that no-challenge clauses in settlement agreements are seen as objectively necessary in the settlement context.

[119] Paragraph 140 of the TTBER Guidelines, *supra* note 21. No challenge clauses in such circumstances may promote dissemination of new technology and are particularly advantageous when weaker licensors license to stronger licensees, as they can do so without fear of a challenge once the know-how has been absorbed by the licensee. However, the exclusion will only apply to non-challenge and termination clauses solely concerning know-how.

[120] Ashish Arora, *Contracting for Tacit Knowledge: The Provision of Technical Services in Technology Licensing Contracts.* JOURNAL OF DEVELOPMENT ECONOMICS, 50(2), 233–256 (1996) at 237; Christian Bessy and Eric Brosseau, *Technology Licensing Contracts Features and Diversity.* INTERNATIONAL REVIEW OF LAW AND ECONOMICS, 18(4) 451–489 (1999) at 461.

royalty payments from a successful patent challenge as well as competitive pressure that would otherwise not be available but for the unrecoverable advantage gained from disclosure of the licensor's know-how.

D. REMARKS

When analyzing the collaboration agreements and associated license agreements obtained from the integrated drug discovery organizations, the TTBER Guidelines specifically provide that TTBER should not be applied mechanically but '[e]ach case must be assessed on its own facts and the guidelines must be applied reasonably and flexibly'.[121] In other words, when applying TTBER to the analysis of the agreements obtained from the integrated drug discovery organizations, TTBER must consider the specific circumstances of the agreement and should provide legal certainty as to whether the agreements taken as a whole qualify for block exemption.

The problem is the R&D Regulation and TTBER reviews the agreements ex-post. The market share requirement assumes that there is already a market; the contract product requirement assumes that the technology is at a commercializable point. The collaboration agreements under the integrated drug discovery and development platform are exploratory at its inception and because of the nature of the drug discovery and development, something or nothing may materialize from the collaboration. As discussed in earlier chapters, some of the literature argues that patent law already assesses competition issues through the prosecution process of obtaining a patent grant, and therefore the role of competition law is simply to protect product market competition.[122] Others argue for the protection of innovation under competition law, calling for intervention when it is necessary to balance between market rivalry and innovation. From the analysis of this chapter, it appears that the Commission has adopted an approach that considers and attempts to balance the different types of efficiencies that may arise in a given agreement. However, the Commission generally intervenes when there is presence of market power, in which case, the balancing exercise tends to

---

[121]   Paragraph 3 of the TTBER Guidelines, *supra* note 21.

[122]   See for example, Nancy T. Gallini and Michael Trebilcock, 'Intellectual Property Rights and Competition Policy: A Framework for Analysis of Economic and Legal Issues' in Robert D. Anderson and Nancy T. Gallini (eds), *Competition Policy and Intellectual Property Rights in the Knowledge-Based Economy* (University of Calgary Press 2002).

favour preserving and maintaining market rivalry when there is a conflict with innovation.

As recognized in the TTBER Guidelines, licensees often commit substantial investments in production and marketing to commercialize the licensed technology and the risks are therefore substantial when the costs are sunk with no guarantee of return.[123] As such, it is understandable why industry partners need to ensure that the associated licensing agreement provides for a certain level of protection (for example, with respect to time, territory, and field of use) to ensure their interests are safeguarded. In order for competition law to fulfill its mandate to protect innovation, the context and objective of the agreement must be understood when evaluating agreement against competition law principles. TTBER recognizes that licensing in general has pro-competitive effects of granting access to new technologies, lowering transaction costs, and allowing for efficient exploitation. However, in practice, when assessing individual restraints, the Commission does not appear to consider efficiency as a determining factor.

Technology transfer through licensing in technology-intense industries such as the pharmaceutical sector, is much more dynamic than traditional product markets. The purpose of the TTBER is to facilitate the dissemination of technology by simplifying the regulatory framework and its application to license agreements. The question is whether TTBER succeeds in achieving its goal of facilitating the dissemination of technology given the peculiar and particular characteristics of the drug discovery and development process and the pharmaceutical industry.

---

[123] Paragraph 101 of the TTBER Guidelines, *supra* note 21.

PART IV

Conclusion

7. Conclusion and implications

A. ROLE OF COMPETITION LAW IN DRUG DISCOVERY AND DEVELOPMENT

Strategies for lowering risk and making collaborative R&D efforts more efficient must be acknowledged if markets and competition are to evolve dynamically, particularly in high-tech markets where dominance and high profits are not necessarily signs of ineffective competition but the result of efficient and successful enterprise. To answer the question of whether competition policy can incorporate dynamic considerations into assessing collaborative drug discovery and development, various agreements between integrated drug discovery organizations and industry were examined. In response to the broad question of whether the current legal framework supports the integrated drug discovery and development model, there is no simple answer as the existing competition law regime gives rise to both positive and negative effects on innovation in drug discovery and development when applied to collaboration agreements between integrated drug discovery organizations and industry. In theory, intellectual property and competition law complement one another, as they share the common objective of facilitating innovation, competition, and benefits to consumers. In reality, the socio-economic environment that affects drug discovery and development can be described as a delicate balance of interests between various stakeholders involved in the innovation process (i.e. academia, government, industry, and the general public). As such, social, economic, and political considerations (i.e. access to medicine, public spending and funding limits on health-related R&D, sustainability of industry, and the need for new medicines for an aging global population) give rise to competing priorities that have an impact on legal policies, including those of intellectual property and competition.

The nature of the pharmaceutical industry is such that it invites inquiries into exclusionary behavior that may be in violation of Article

101.[1] However, the Commission recognizes the positive effects of collaborative R&D and licensing on innovation, as expressly stated in the R&D Regulation and TTBER. By adopting an economics and effects-based approach to analyzing collaborative R&D and licensing agreements in integrated drug discovery and development, the overall beneficial effect should exclude or exempt such agreements from Article 101 if the particular dynamics of the pharmaceutical industry are considered. As established, the evaluation of individual clauses and restraints in case law and Commission decisions seem to indicate a general awareness or understanding of the transactional risks and hazards parties face when entering into complex collaborative relationships. However, case law and the literature also seems to firmly establish that the Commission's overall approach to Article 101 is to preserve market rivalry over welfare effects. As long as the conventional wisdom of competition law relating to market power and maintaining market rivalry continues to be applied without sufficient regard to the efficiencies created and transactional hazard resolved by restrictive conditions mutually agreed to by parties to an agreement, collaborations between integrated drug discovery organizations and industry will always be vulnerable to challenge under competition policy. Efficiency is particularly relevant and desirable in the context of drug discovery and development. It should not be ignored that collaborative drug development involving industry players, including dominant players, may bring more benefits to the market than the potential negative effects.

Collaborations between integrated drug discovery organizations and industry can maximize publically funded research by pooling resources and sharing the risk of demonstrating proof of concept so that promising discoveries can be translated into commercializable products. However, adequate incentives must be made available in order to motivate and incentivize the parties to invest the time and resources to conduct the necessary R&D and development of new pharmaceutical products. Pharmaceutical companies are businesses after all, and, by definition, they are motivated primarily by commercial interests, including profit. Without proper incentives, industry will have no reason to engage

---

[1]   See for example *WANO/Schwarzpulver*, OJ L 322/26, at 31, 2(d) (1978), [1979] 1 where the Commission was concerned that a joint venture was not only interested in R&D but provided the opportunity for the parties and induced market sharing. See also Valentine Korah, *Collaborative Joint Ventures for Research and Development where Markets are Concentrated: The Competition Rules of the Common Market and the Invalidity of Contracts.* FORDHAM INTERNATIONAL LAW JOURNAL, 15(2), 248–302 (1991).

academia in collaborative R&D in drug discovery and development. Because of the inherent uncertainties, risks, substantial time delays to enter the market, as well as the considerable financial commitment required to see the project through to commercialization, integrated drug discovery organizations and industry must be given the contractual freedom to enter into collaboration agreements that provide for a mutually agreed upon degree of control and protection. The 'quid pro quo' for the development of promising discoveries to return the benefit of publically funded research back to the public is some form of exclusivity or competitive advantage to industry, such as securing some rights to revenue that may arise from successful development. However, under the present legal framework, such collaboration agreements invite the scrutiny of the Commission.

The underlying question is to what extent is innovation promoted by existing competition rules when applied to collaboration agreements between integrated drug discovery organizations and industry for the purposes of drug discovery and development. The innovation process encompasses not only the scientific research that gives rise to the resulting technology or pharmaceutical product, but also the economic benefits of collaborative R&D and licensing agreements aimed at translating and commercializing science into products that can benefit the public. In other words, the coordination of innovation efforts, merging of complementary resources, and the subsequent licensing of successful results to bring life-saving therapies to market efficiently and in a cost-effective manner must also be protected under competition law in order to promote the innovation process. This is supported by both the R&D Regulation and TTBER, which recognizes the role of collaborative R&D and licensing in promoting technical and economic progress. In this sense, competition law views these objectives as legitimate interests that may justify competitive restraints under certain circumstances. Recognizing that both collaborative R&D and subsequent licensing of successful results are both important parts of the innovation process, both elements of the collaboration agreement between integrated drug discovery organizations and industry should be exempted under competition rules if innovation is to be promoted. As concluded in Chapter 4, the R&D component of the collaboration agreements generally do not fall under Article 101 and/or qualifies for exemption under the R&D Regulation because the subject matter of the agreement typically involves early stage discoveries far removed from the potential of exploiting the results. Furthermore, because integrated drug discovery organizations and industry are considered non-competitors under the R&D Regulation, such

agreements generally do not give rise to restrictive effects on competition. However, with respect to competition on the innovation market,
depending on the subject matter of the collaboration agreement, integrated drug discovery organizations and/or industry may be considered
credible R&D poles. And in the interest of preserving market rivalry,
there is still a risk that the collaborative R&D component of the
collaboration agreement may be deemed to create foreclosure effects.

Because the collaboration agreement incorporates and contemplates a
licensing component of the results if the collaborative R&D is successful,
it is not entirely clear whether the subsequent licensing falls under the
R&D Regulation (in which case the exemption should extend to the
licensing component) or if TTBER applies. As concluded in Chapter 5
and 6, should TTBER apply to the associated license agreement, an
argument can be made for individual restrictions typically found in such
agreements to qualify for exemption under TTBER. Advantageously,
TTBER recognizes dissemination of new technology, reduction of R&D
costs, and the possibility for both licensor and licensee to gain access to
new assets as positive effects of licensing.[2] However, it is equally
foreseeable that some contractual restrictions in the licensing agreements
may be seen as legitimately restricting competition even if they are
necessary to induce licensing. Because existing competition policy
focuses on market power and protecting markets as a decisive factor in
considering the permissibility of individual clauses,[3] there is still a risk
that the overall benefits of the associated licensing agreement may not
qualify for exemption under TTBER. Understandably, determining the
balance between maintaining a competitive market and efficient innovation would require the Commission to somehow quantify the different
types of efficiencies in order to calculate the net welfare effect, which
can be difficult. However, considering what is at stake is the danger of
discouraging innovation in an area as important as drug discovery and
development, where inefficiencies and transactional hazards are known to

---

[2]   Recital 4 of TTBER, Commission Regulation No 316/2014 on the
application of Article 101(3) of the Treaty on the Functioning of the European
Union to categories of technology transfer agreements, OJ 2014 L93/17
('TTBER') and Communication from the Commission, *Guidelines on the application of Article 101 of the Treaty on the Functioning of the European Union to
technology transfer agreements*, Official Journal C89, 28.03.2014, 3–50 (hereinafter referred to as 'TTBER Guidelines') at paragraph 176.

[3]   See for example TTBER Guidelines, *supra* note 2 at paragraphs 130 and
199.

have a negative impact on the rate of innovation, perhaps the Commission should make the extra effort to assess the delicate balance. Because the onus is on the parties to self-assess the agreements to determine compliance with the R&D Regulation and/or TTBER, integrated drug discovery organizations and industry need to invest further resources in obtaining legal advice. But even with legal counsel, significant legal uncertainty still remains with the law and how the Commission will apply the law to assess collaboration agreements between integrated drug discovery organizations and industry for compliance with competition policy.

Understanding the context of an agreement is important if the assessment under competition law is to protect innovation. The objective of the agreement should have an impact on the evaluation of its competitive effects. If the contractual restraints included in the collaboration agreements and associated license agreements are construed with regard to their function in light of the difficulties associated with drug discovery and development, competition law may better serve its mandate of promoting market competition by exempting or excluding the collaboration agreements and associated licensing agreements so as to facilitate the innovation process in drug discovery and development. Generally, the Commission does consider or integrate the evaluation of the aim and function of agreements in both the R&D Regulation and TTBER by considering economic benefits and indispensability under Article 101(3). However, the overriding concern with market power and market protection generally leads to the striking out of agreements, even if they are welfare enhancing on balance. In the context of the integrated drug discovery and development model, certain restrictive clauses may be included to increase licensing efficiency or to address transactional hazards. Blindly using market power to assess clauses in the context of competitive harm without considering the true intentions and function of the clauses may lead to erroneous conclusions of prohibiting agreements that do not give rise to competitive harm when considered in context.

As discussed repeatedly in preceding chapters, the dynamics and nature of the pharmaceutical industry is quite different compared to most other traditional industry sectors. Compared to other established industries where development time and cost are generally much lower and where products can enter the market shortly after development to recoup costs and generate revenue for the development and commercialization of new products, it is difficult to see how conventional wisdom relating to the analysis and application of competition law, which has been shaped and developed over the years and applied to issues that arise in established or mature industries, can apply in a meaningful way to highly innovative markets such as the particular dynamics of the pharmaceutical industry. It is unlikely that competition policy can achieve its purpose across all industries when the pharmaceutical industry is so different from traditional industries. If one of the mandates of the competition law framework is to promote innovation and facilitate the dissemination of new technologies, then the framework must also provide for the protection of the interests of parties contributing to the innovation process, such as through collaborative R&D. Arguably, competition law should incorporate a broad perspective and approach to assessing collaborative innovation to promote innovation and competition by facilitating parties to enter the market, which can result in more competition.[4] If the objective of competition policy is to enhance economic and public welfare, the traditional approach of discouraging conduct that limits competitors and their ability to compete in the market fails to achieve this objective in the context of the pharmaceutical industry. A more nuanced framework that takes into the account the nature of the pharmaceutical industry would help facilitate drug discovery and development while traditional competition law assessment can provide guidance on a case-by-case basis.

The significant R&D costs associated with drug discovery and development constitute a high entry barrier making industry players hard to replace if they cannot survive in the market. If industry players cannot survive, then there will be fewer players to develop and bring new products to market. As stated by Judge Jacob at a presentation relating to the Pharma-sector inquiry:

> Before the invention of a new drug, we would willingly pay for it. After the risking and investment have produced a new medicine there is a great temptation to say the price is too high. ... The Commission repeatedly says that it does not want to damage the pharmaceutical industry and that it recognises how important patents are to it – it sounds to me a bit like Mark Anthony emphasising that Brutus was an honourable man. The big truth is that if you damage the income stream of research companies, you are going to

---

[4]   An efficient framework for collaboration between public research organizations and industry must include mechanisms for encouraging cooperative behavior, in a manner that is optimal for all parties, rather than adopting a traditional competitive approach. See Constance E. Bagley and Christina D. Tvarnø, *Pharmaceutical Public-Private Partnerships: Moving from the Bench to the Bedside*. HARVARD BUSINESS LAW REVIEW, 4, 373 (2014) at pp. 383–384.

imperil future research at the expense of European – indeed World – citizens. Yes, you will save money now, but at the cost of fewer future medicines.[5]

As such, an argument can be made that competition authorities should adopt a more flexible approach to collaborations between industry and integrated drug discovery organizations in order to facilitate drug discovery and development.

B. ECONOMIC THEORY AND THE PHARMACEUTICAL INDUSTRY

The question of whether competition or monopoly best promotes innovation has been long disputed.[6] While legal professionals tend to accept the premise that intellectual property law acts as a balance between public access or dissemination and incentivizing innovation, economists generally find this trade-off between dynamic and static efficiency difficult to achieve in reality.[7] Although the cost-benefit principles and perfect competition models of economics is well established and deeply rooted in conventional mainstream economics analysis, competition and innovation in the pharmaceutical context is not a phenomenon that can be fully understood by traditional economic analysis. For example, the perfect competition model attempts to achieve allocative efficiency,

---

[5]   Rt Hon Sir Robin Jacob, *Patents and Pharmaceuticals* – a Paper given on 29th November at the Presentation of the Directorate-General of Competition's Preliminary Report of the Pharma Sector Inquiry (accessible at http://ec.europa.eu/competition/sectors/pharmaceuticals/inquiry/jacob.pdf) at 2 and 11.

[6]   See for example Jonathan B. Baker, *Beyond Schumpeter vs. Arrow: How Antitrust Fosters Innovation.* ANTITRUST LAW JOURNAL, 74(3), 575–602 (2007), who stated that 'one view often associated with Joseph Schumpeter argues that monopolies favor innovation. An opposite view, often associated with Kenneth Arrow, argues that competition favors innovation. Taking the cue from this debate, some commentators qualify their support for antitrust policy, reserving judgment as to whether antitrust enforcement is good for innovation'. See also Carl Shapiro, 'Competition and Innovation: Did Arrow Hit the Bull's Eye?' in Josh Lerner and Scott Stern (eds), *The Rate and Direction of Inventive Activity Revisited* (University of Chicago Press 2011) 361–404 at 362 where it was stated that Arrow's view that competition incentivizes innovation makes sense: a company that is earning substantial profits has an interest in protecting the status quo and is thus less likely to be the instigator of innovating and producing new technologies.

[7]   Suzanne Scotchmer, *Innovation and Incentives* (MIT Press 2004).

productive efficiency, and maximum total welfare,[8] which is inconsistent with the typical industry practice of acquiring and strengthening market power through various means, including strategic collaborations and monopolization. According to the perfect competition model, among other undesirable effects, companies with substantial market power produce deadweight loss and reduce total welfare by decreasing market output and raising market price; reducing consumer choice by discouraging competitors; and reducing innovation. Since real markets do not simulate the perfect competition model, using policies to force market conditions to produce perfect competition would be intrusive and may not create the desired end result.[9]

By recognizing that the real market is an imperfect market and that companies will employ various commercial strategies, whether co-operative or not, to acquire and strengthen market power, a more realistic approach and rationale to competition law and market functioning can be devised to better understand the pharmaceutical industry and its market structure. Economic theories that represent competition as a dynamic and on-going process of development may provide a more realistic understanding of competition and the market in the pharmaceutical context. For example, the cycle of innovation in the pharmaceutical industry typically begins with a new innovation whereby a leader rises above its competitors with its new technological advance and is rewarded with a competitive edge, market share, and profits. This stimulates other competitors to innovate to participate in the success enjoyed by the market leader. When a competitor succeeds in innovating, the state of the art advances incrementally to the benefit of the public and the market levels out with the new innovation taking a share of the

---

[8]   See Victor J. Tremblay and Carol H. Tremblay, 'Perfect Competition and Market Imperfections' in *New Perspectives on Industrial Organization* (Springer New York 2012) 123–143 at 123, which states that no real-world market is perfectly competitive but the model provides a benchmark of market efficiency from which real markets can be judged. See also Roger J. van den Bergh and Peter D. Camesasca, *European Competition Law and Economics: A Comparative Perspective* (Intersentia 2001). See also John Weeks, 'The Fallacy of Competition: Markets and the Movement of Capital' in Jamee K. Moudud, Cyrus Bina, and Patrick L. Mason (eds), *Alternative Theories of Competition: Challenges to the Orthodoxy* (Routledge 2012) at 15.

[9]   Several empirical studies show that perfect markets and firms without market power do not necessarily facilitate innovation. See Wesley M. Cohen and Richard C. Levin, *Empirical Studies of Innovation and Market Structure* in Richard Schmalensee and Robert D. Willig (eds), *Handbook of Industrial Organization* (North-Holland 1989), Volume 2, 1059–1107.

competitive advantage and profits previously enjoyed solely by the market leader. The cycle then repeats itself, stimulating another round of innovation to broaden the competitive gap between the market players. As such, an argument can be made that in the pharmaceutical industry, what may appear inefficient in the short term, by way of market power and barriers to entry, may actually be a necessary step towards achieving greater efficiency in the long-term by stimulating future innovations that improve the state of the art.[10] Furthermore, the fact that companies achieve market power and can affect market entry of competitors is evidence that the companies have made a significant contribution to innovation by developing new products that satisfy consumers to the point where they become dominant players. Although markets that allow for companies to maintain a dominant position can cause harm to consumers and competitors by reducing both consumer surplus and total welfare, in the pharmaceutical industry, if efficient actions are deterred because of the fear of achieving market power, it would undermine incentives to innovate and take risks, thereby diminishing the driving force for innovation and productivity in the pharmaceutical industry. The competition law framework calls for an economics-based approach to analyzing commercial arrangements and, in the pharmaceutical context, it can be argued that total welfare may be achieved by allowing dominant firms to engage in aggressive yet efficient conduct. Without certain contractual restrictions, pro-competitive collaboration agreements may not be reached at all.

---

[10] For example, Cimetidine, the prototype of H2 blockers used in the treatment of dyspepsia was first marketed in 1976 and became recognized as a blockbuster drug by 1979. By 1981, Ranitidine was introduced into the market as an improvement of the H2 blocker with fewer adverse drug reactions and longer lasting action. Ranitidine went on to be the world's biggest-selling prescription drug by 1988. Despite the commercial success of H2 blockers, AstraZeneca invested in the R&D of proton pump inhibitors (PPI) for the treatment of dyspepsia and Losec was launched in 1989. By 1992, H2 blockers were surpassed by the more effective PPI. This example demonstrates that in the pharmaceutical industry, achieving blockbuster success did not discourage or prevent competitors from improving on the existing technology (i.e. Ranitidine was an improvement of H2 blockers in direct competition with the blockbuster drug Cimetidine) or investing in the development of new technology (i.e. PPIs) for the treatment of the same condition, which turned out to be more effective than the original technology.

C. POLICY RECOMMENDATIONS – A NUANCED APPROACH TO DRUG DISCOVERY AND DEVELOPMENT

With respect to the integrated drug discovery platform, the current competition law regime places too much consideration on traditional factors and general considerations, such as market power and maintaining market rivalry. A greater understanding of the specific industry dynamics, such as the transactional hazards and resulting efficiencies that may be created through collaborations between integrated drug discovery organizations and industry may result in a more accurate and nuanced evaluation of such agreements. Such an approach still views the preservation of market rivalry as a priority, but allows for flexibility to argue in favor of efficiency, given the particular industry dynamics as justification. This would therefore increase the weight of innovation in balance with market rivalry. Should concerns relating to market power and market rivalry arise as a result of applying such flexibility, such anti-competitive concerns could be dealt under Article 102 as a case of abuse of dominance, particularly since Article 102 takes precedence over any block exemption regulation.

An argument that the results of publically funded research should be dedicated and made available to the public is logically and morally grounded on the premise that the public paid for the research through tax dollars and should therefore benefit from the results without further payment. However, because the availability of public funding for R&D has decreased over the years, other funding methods must be explored and considered in order to push forward with developing life-saving technologies. When public and private resources are pooled together in order to pursue efficient drug discovery and development, the argument against seeking profit from the resulting research becomes harder to make. The reality is that the pharmaceutical industry is comprised of commercial enterprises that can only survive by making a profit. Similarly, the reality of academic research is that funds are required in order to pay for research, lab equipment, salaries, and materials needed to conduct research. The money to 'get it done' needs to come from somewhere. If the public system alone can no longer sustain R&D for drug discovery and development, then the public needs to support other methods of ensuring public health and understand that other stakeholder interests need to be considered.

What the drug discovery and process development needs is a more nuanced competition law framework to assess the collaboration agreements between integrated drug discovery organizations and industry. Advocating for a sector specific approach may not be the solution[11] but the relevant authorities should adopt a specific awareness or recognition of the particular dynamics that plague the drug discovery and development process to allow for some flexibilities and concessions to the traditional competition law framework in order for integrated drug discovery organizations and industry to facilitate the development and commercialization of much needed therapies to benefit the public. As one scholar concluded:

> [The pharmaceutical industry] is an environment typified by imperfect competition, where the legislative and judicial organs of the Community must maintain a balance between realising the Single Market while respecting the function and integrity of IP rights, as well as ensuring the social element of the pharmaceutical industry is not sacrificed on the altar of the Single Market. Unlike other sectors, the barriers to entry are such as to naturally exclude new entrants – for the pharmaceutical industry requires huge sums to be invested with no guarantee of any return and high risk of failure. There is no scope for pursuing the wrong economic policy in a market in which the chances of success are between 0.02 and 0.03% of a successful new discovery.[12]

Although there is no direct case on point that would suggest the Commission will adopt a traditional analysis approach to non-traditional industries such as the pharmaceutical sector, existing cases, policy statements, reports, and guideline examples involving the pharmaceutical industry provide a reasonable indication of how the Commission will likely construe competition policy in the context of drug discovery and development. For example, in merger cases involving pharmaceutical companies, when assessing the future effects of the merger, the Commission evaluated the ability of the parties to anticompetitively reduce R&D efforts when assessing future effects on the market.[13] The Commission

---

[11] See for example, Nina Boeger and Joseph Corkin, 'The Resilience of Sector Specific Competition Law in the Liberalized Sectors' in Caroline Heide-Jørgensen, Christian Bergqvist, Ulla Neergaard, and Sune T. Poulsen (eds), *Aims and Values in Competition Law* (Djøf Publishing 2013).

[12] Russell G. Hunter, *The Pharmaceutical Sector in the European Union: Intellectual Property Rights, Parallel Trade and Community Competition Law*, Institute for European Law at Stockholm University (2001) at 5.

[13] See for example Case No COMP/M.1846, *Glaxo Wellcome/SmithKline Beecham* (2000); Case COMP/M.5479, *Lonza/Teva/JV* (2005); Case COMP/M.5530, *Glaxo Smith Kline/Stiefel Laboratories* (2009).

considered existing competing compounds in development, 'resourceful-ness' of competitors, and market position of the parties in question and found that elimination of one party as competitor could strengthen the other's position, which could discourage third party research attempts. Applied to integrated drug discovery and development, this case may suggest that tying up of R&D could be anticompetitive and therefore barred. However, the Commission's analysis of merger cases typically involves competitive situations with regard to products that have reached such a level of development that their competitive impact can be assessed. In the case of integrated drug discovery and development where the potential for future product development is not yet clear at the outset, the transactions are not transparent so the competition structure relating to innovation at this stage might not be as conducive to traditional analysis. Because anticompetitive challenges are initiated ex-post after the collaboration has led to successful translation and commercialization and when the competitive impact can be assessed by traditional analysis, the precedents set by merger cases may still be applicable to integrated drug discovery and development without being helpful in providing guidance to avoid anticompetitive pitfalls ex ante.

When decision-making is based on analysis of current structures and future developments in dynamic markets, there is inherent uncertainty and speculation involved. If the intention of law is to be reflective of societal interests, in principle, the commitment of competition policy to economic rationality should give the law the flexibility to cope with evolving issues as they arise in a particular context. In the Sector Report,[14] the Commission recognized that unique competition law issues arise in the pharmaceutical context. This is an indication that there is room for some sector-specific considerations.

---

[14]   European Commission Pharmaceutical Sector Inquiry, Final Report, July 8, 2009, at 23.

Bibliography

Aarnio, A. (1997) *Reason and Authority – A Treaty on the Dynamic Paradigm of Legal Dogmatics.* Cambridge University Press

Adams, J.D. (1990) *Fundamental Stocks of Knowledge and Productivity Growth.* JOURNAL OF POLITICAL ECONOMY, 98(4), 673–702

Anderman, S. (2002) *EC Competition Law and Intellectual Property Rights in the New Economy.* ANTITRUST BULLETIN, 47, 285

Anderman, S.D. and Kallaugher, J. (2006) *Technology Transfer and the New EU Competition Rules: Intellectual Property Licensing after Modernisation,* Oxford University Press

Andrews, L.B. (2002) *Genes and Patent Policy: Rethinking Intellectual Property Rights.* NATURE REVIEWS GENETICS, 3(10), 803–808

Andries, P. and Debackere, K. (2007) *Adaptation and Performance in New Businesses.* SMALL BUSINESS ECONOMICS, 29(1–2), 81–99

Angell, M. and Relman, A.S. (2002) *Patents, Profits & American Medicine: Conflicts of Interest in the Testing & Marketing of New Drugs.* DAEDALUS, 102–111

Arena, A., Bergmann, B., and Himes, J.L. (2013) *Two Bodies of Law Separated by a Common Mission: Unilateral Conduct by Dominant Firms at the IP/Antitrust Intersection in the EU and the US.* EUROPEAN COMPETITION JOURNAL, 9(3), 623–675

Arkin, M.R. and Wells, J.A. (2004) *Small-Molecule Inhibitors of Protein-Protein Interactions: Progressing Towards the Dream.* NATURE REVIEWS DRUG DISCOVERY, 3(4), 301–317

Arora, A., Fosfuri, A., and Gambardella, A. (2001) *Markets for Technology and their Implications for Corporate Strategy.* INDUSTRIAL AND CORPORATE CHANGE, 10(2), 419–451

Arrow, K. (1962) 'Economic Welfare and the Allocation of Resources for Invention' in *The Rate and Direction of Inventive Activity: Economic and Social Factors.* Princeton University Press, 609–626

Ayres, I. and Parchomovsky, G. (2007) *Tradable Patent Rights.* STANFORD LAW REVIEW, 863–894

Bagley, C. and Tvarnø, C.D. (2014) *Pharmaceutical Public-Private Partnerships: Moving from the Bench to the Bedside.* HARVARD BUSINESS LAW REVIEW, 4(2), 373–401

Baker, J.B. (1995) *Fringe Firms and Incentives to Innovate.* ANTITRUST LAW JOURNAL, 63(2), 621–641

Baker, J.B. (2007) *Beyond Schumpeter vs. Arrow: How Antitrust Fosters Innovation*. ANTITRUST LAW JOURNAL, 74, 575

Balkin, J.M. (1996) *Interdisciplinarity as Colonization*. WASHINGTON & LEE LAW REVIEW, 53, 949–970

Banakar, R. (2000) *Reflections on the Methodological Issues of the Sociology of Law*. JOURNAL OF LAW AND SOCIETY, 27, 273–295

Banakar, R. and Travers, M. (2005) 'Introduction' in R. Banakar and M. Travers (eds), *Theory and Method in Socio-legal Research*. Bloomsbury Publishing

Bellamy, C. and Child, G.D. (2013) *Bellamy & Child European Union Law of Competition*, Roth, P.M. and Rose, V. (eds). Oxford University Press

Ben-Asher, D. (2000) *In Need of Treatment? Merger Control, Pharmaceutical Innovation, and Consumer Welfare*. JOURNAL OF LEGAL MEDICINE, 21(3), 271–349

Benavente, J.M. and Lauterbach, R. (2008) *Technological Innovation and Employment: Complements or Substitutes?* EUROPEAN JOURNAL OF DEVELOPMENT RESEARCH, 20(2), 318–329

Bergek, A. and Bruzelius, M. (2010) *Are Patents with Multiple Inventors from Different Countries a Good Indicator of International R&D Collaboration? The Case of ABB*. RESEARCH POLICY, 39(10), 1321–1334

Bergman, M.A. (2001) *The Role of the Essential Facilities Doctrine*. ANTITRUST BULLETIN, 46, 403

Berneman, L. (2003) *University-Industry Collaborations: Partners in Research Promoting Productivity and Economic Growth*. RESEARCH MANAGEMENT REVIEW, 13(2), 28–37

Bishop, S. and Walker, M. *The Economics of EC Competition Law: Concepts, Application, and Measurement*. Sweet & Maxwell

Boeger, N. and Corkin, J. (2013) 'The Resilience of Sector Specific Competition Law in the Liberalized Sectors' in C. Heide-Jørgensen, C. Bergqvist, U. Neergaard, and S.T. Poulsen (eds), *Aims and Values in Competition Law*. Djøf Publishing

Boldrin, M. and Levine, D.K. (2008). *Against Intellectual Monopoly*. Cambridge University Press

Boolell, M., Allen, M.J., Ballard S.A., Gepi-Attee, S., Muirhead, G.J., Naylor, A.M., Osterloh, I.H, and Gingell, C. (1996) *Sildenafil: An Orally Active Type 5 Cyclic GMP-specific Phosphodiesterase Inhibitor for the Treatment of Penile Erectile Dysfunction*. INTERNATIONAL JOURNAL OF IMPOTENCE RESEARCH, 8(2), 47–52

Booth, B. (2005) *From the Analyst's Couch: Valuation with Cash Multiples*. NATURE REVIEWS DRUG DISCOVERY 4, 533–534

Bottazzi, G., Dosi, G., Lippi, M., Pammolli, F., and Riccaboni, M. (2001) *Innovation and Corporate Growth in the Evolution of the Drug Industry*. INTERNATIONAL JOURNAL OF INDUSTRIAL ORGANIZATION, 19(7), 1161–1187

Bowman, W.S. (1973) *Patent and Antitrust Law: A Legal and Economic Appraisal*. The University of Chicago Press

Braunerhjelm, P. and Svensson, R. (2010) *The Inventor's Role: Was Schumpeter Right?* JOURNAL OF EVOLUTIONARY ECONOMICS, 20(3), 413–444

Brodley, J.F. (1987) *The Economic Goals of Antitrust: Efficiency, Consumer Welfare, Technological Progress*. NEW YORK UNIVERSITY LAW REVIEW, 62, 1020

Bruneel, J., D'Este, P., and Salter, A. (2010) *Investigating the Factors that Diminish the Barriers to University-industry Collaboration*. RESEARCH POLICY, 39(7), 858–868

Burci, G.L. (2009) *Public/Private Partnerships in the Public Health Sector*. INTERNATIONAL ORGANIZATIONS LAW REVIEW, 6(2), 359–382

Butler, D. (2008) *Translational Research: Crossing the Valley of Death*. NATURE NEWS, 453(7197), 840–842

Caballero, R.J. and Jaffe, A.B. (1993) 'How High are the Giants' Shoulders: An Empirical Assessment of Knowledge Spillovers and Creative Destruction in a Model of Economic Growth' in O.J. Blanchard and S. Fischer, (eds), *NBER Macroeconomics Annual, Volume 8*. The University of Chicago Press

Caballero-Sanz, F., Moner-Colonques, R., and Sempere-Monerris, J.J. (2005) *Licensing Policies for a New Product*. ECONOMICS OF INNOVATION AND NEW TECHNOLOGY, 14(8), 697–713

Cabral, L.M.B. (2000) *R&D Cooperation and Product Market Competition*. INTERNATIONAL JOURNAL OF INDUSTRIAL ORGANIZATION, 18(7), 1033–1047

Campbell, C.M. and Wiles, P. (1976) *The Study of Law in Society in Britain*. LAW AND SOCIETY REVIEW, 10, 547–578

Carlson, S.C. (1999) *Patent Pools and the Antitrust Dilemma*. YALE JOURNAL ON REGULATION, 16, 359

Carlton, D. and Gertner, R. (2003) 'Intellectual Property, Antitrust and Strategic Behavior' in A.B. Jaffe, J. Lerner, and S. Stern (eds), *Innovation Policy and the Economy, Volume 3*. MIT Press

Carone, G., Schwierz, C., and Xavier, A. (2012) *Cost-containment Policies in Public Pharmaceutical Spending in the EU*, available at SSRN http://papers.ssrn.com/sol3/papers.cfm?abstract_id=2161803

Carrier, M.A. (2002) *Unraveling the Patent-Antitrust Paradox*. UNIVERSITY OF PENNSYLVANIA LAW REVIEW, 150(3), 761–854

Carrier, M. (2003) *Resolving the Patent-Antitrust Paradox through Tripartite Innovation.* VANDERBILT LAW REVIEW, 56, 101

Caves, R.E., Crookell, H., and Killing, J.P. (1983) *The Imperfect Market for Technology Licenses.* OXFORD BULLETIN OF ECONOMICS AND STATISTICS, 45(3), 249–257

Chalmers, D., Davies, G., and Monti, G. (2010). *European Union Law: Cases and Materials.* Cambridge University Press

Chesbrough, H. (2003) *Open Innovation.* Harvard Business School Press

Cockburn, I.M. (2004) *The Changing Structure of the Pharmaceutical Industry.* HEALTH AFFAIRS, 23(1), 10–22

Cohen, F.J. (2005) *Macro Trends in Pharmaceutical Innovation.* NATURE REVIEWS DRUG DISCOVERY, 4(1), 78–84

Cohen, W.M., Nelson, R.R., and Walsh, J.P. (2000) *Protecting their Intellectual Assets: Appropriability Conditions and Why US Manufacturing Firms Patent (or Not).* No. w7552. National Bureau of Economic Research

Coller, B.S. and Califf, R.M. (2009) *Traversing the Valley of Death: A Guide to Assessing Prospects for Translational Success.* SCIENCE TRANSLATIONAL MEDICINE, 1(10), 109

Conti, A. and Gaule, P. (2011) *Is the US Outperforming Europe in University Technology Licensing: A New Perspective on the European Paradox.* RESEARCH POLICY, 40, 123–135

Cornish, W., Llewelyn, D., and Aplin, T. (2013) *Intellectual Property, Patents, Copyrights, Trademarks and Allied Rights.* Chapter 7: 'Property Rights and Exploitation'. Sweet & Maxwell

Correa, C.M. (2004) *Ownership of Knowledge: The Role of Patents in Pharmaceutical R&D.* BULLETIN OF THE WORLD HEALTH ORGANIZATION, 82(10), 784–787

Cressey, D. (2011) *Traditional Drug Discovery Model Ripe for Reform.* NATURE NEWS, 47(7336), 17–18

Criscuolo, C., Haskel, J.E., and Slaughter, M.J. (2010) *Global Engagement and the Innovation Activities of Firms.* INTERNATIONAL JOURNAL OF INDUSTRIAL ORGANIZATION, 28(2), 191–202

Dahdouh, T.N. (1996) *The Shape of Things to Come: Innovation Market Analysis in Merger Cases.* ANTITRUST LAW JOURNAL, 64(2), 405–441

Danzon, P.M. (2006) *Economics of the Pharmaceutical Industry*, BER Reporter Online, 14–17

Danzon, P.M. and Epstein, A.J. (2012) *Effects of Regulation on Drug Launch and Pricing in Interdependent Markets.* ADVANCES IN HEALTH ECONOMICS AND HEALTH SERVICES RESEARCH, 23, 35–71

Danzon, P.M. and Nicholson, S. (eds) (2012) *The Oxford Handbook of the Economics of the Biopharmaceutical Industry.* Oxford University Press

Danzon, P.M. and Towse, A. (2003). *Differential Pricing for Pharmaceuticals: Reconciling Access, R&D and Patents.* INTERNATIONAL JOURNAL OF HEALTH CARE FINANCE AND ECONOMICS, 3(3), 183–205

David, P.A. and Hall, B.H. (2006) *Property and the Pursuit of Knowledge: IPR Issues Affecting Scientific Research.* RESEARCH POLICY, 35(6), 767–771

Davis, L., Larsen, M.T., and Lotz P. (2011) *Scientists' perspectives concerning the effects of university patenting on the conduct of academic research in the life sciences.* THE JOURNAL OF TECHNOLOGY TRANSFER, 36(1), 14–37

Davis, R.W. (2003) *Innovation Markets and Merger Enforcement: Current Practice in Perspective.* ANTITRUST LAW JOURNAL, 71(2), 677–703

Debackere, K. (2012) *The TTO, A University Engine Transforming Science Into Innovation*, Advice Paper No. 10, League of European Research Universities

Debackere, K. and Reinhilde, V. (2005) *The Role of Academic Technology Transfer Organizations in Improving Industry-science Links.* RESEARCH POLICY, 34(3), 321–342

DeRuiter J. and Holston, P.L. (2012) *Drug Patent Expirations and the 'Patent Cliff'.* US PHARMACIST 37(6) (Generic Suppl), 12–20

DeSanti, S. and Cohen, W. (2001) 'Competition to Innovate: Strategies for Proper Antitrust Assessments' in R.C. Dreyfuss, D.L. Zimmerman and H. First (eds), *Expanding the Boundaries of Intellectual Property: Innovation Policy for the Knowledge Society.* Oxford University Press

Diathesopoulos, M.D. (2012) *Competition Law and Sector Regulation in the European Energy Market after the Third Energy Package: Hierarchy and Efficiency.* University of Cambridge Faculty of Law Research Paper

Dickson, M. and Gagnon, J.P. (2004) *Key Factors in the Rising Cost of New Drug Discovery and Development.* NATURE REVIEWS DRUG DISCOVERY, 3(5), 417–429

DiMasi, J.A. and Grabowski, H.G. (2007) *The Cost of Biopharmaceutical R&D: Is Biotech Different?* MANAGERIAL AND DECISION ECONOMICS, 28(4–5), 469–479

DiMasi, J.A. and Grabowski, H.G. (2012) *R&D Costs and Returns to New Drug Development: A Review of the Evidence.* Tufts Center for the Study of Drug Development. March/April CSDD Impact Report

DiMasi, J.A., Feldman, L., Seckler, A. and Wilson, A. (2010) *Trends in Risks Associated with New Drug Development: Success Rates for Investigational Drugs.* CLINICAL PHARMACOLOGY AND THERAPEUTICS, 87(3), 272–277

DiMasi, J.A., Hansen, R.W. and Grabowski, H.G. (2003) *The Price of Innovation: New Estimates of Drug Development Costs.* JOURNAL OF HEALTH ECONOMICS, 22(2), 151–185

Dolmans, M. and Piilola, A. (2004) *The New Technology Transfer Block Exemption.* WORLD COMPETITION, 27(3), 351–363

Dubois, P., Lam, W.M.W., de Mouzon, O., Scott-Morton, F. and Seabright, P. (2012) *Innovation in the Pharmaceutical Industry and Market Size.* Science, Innovation, Firms and Markets in Europe, Centre for Economic Policy Research 49

Easterbrook, F.H. (1985) *Workable Antitrust Policy.* MICHIGAN LAW REVIEW, 84, 1696–1713

Easterbrook, F.H. (1984) *Limits of Antitrust.* TEXAS LAW REVIEW, 63(1), 1–40

Edler, J., Fier, H., and Grimpe, C. (2011) *International Scientist Mobility and the Locus of Knowledge and Technology Transfer.* RESEARCH POLICY, 40(6), 791–805

Eisenberg, R. (1989) *Patents and the Progress of Science: Exclusive Rights and Experimental Use.* THE UNIVERSITY OF CHICAGO LAW REVIEW, 56, 1017–1086

Eisenberg, R.S. (2003) *Patents, Product Exclusivity, and Information Dissemination: How Law Directs Biopharmaceutical Research and Development.* FORDHAM LAW REVIEW, 72, 477

Eisenberg, R.S. and Nelson, R.R. (2002) *Public vs Proprietary Science: A Fruitful Tension?* DAEDALUS, 131, 89–91

Ess, S.M., Schneeweiss, S., and Szucs, T.D. (2003) *European Healthcare Policies for Controlling Drug Expenditure.* PHARMACOECONOMICS, 21(2), 89–103

Etzkowitz, H. and Leydesdorff, L. (2000) *The Dynamics of Innovation: From National Systems and 'Mode 2' to a Triple Helix of University–Industry–Government Relations.* RESEARCH POLICY, 29(2), 109–123

Evangelista, R. and Vezzani, A. (2010) *The Economic Impact of Technological and Organizational Innovations: A Firm-level Analysis.* RESEARCH POLICY, 39(10), 1253–1263

Fagerberg, J., Scrholec, M., and Verspagen, B. (2010) 'Innovation and Economic Development' in B.H. Hall and N. Rosenberg (eds), *Handbook of the Economics of Innovation*, Volume 2. North-Holland, 833–872

Faull, J. and Nikpay, A. (1999) *The EC Law of Competition.* Oxford University Press

Fazackerley, A., Smith, M., and Massey, A. (2009) *Innovation and Industry: The Role of Universities.* Policy Exchange

Feldstein, P. (2011). *Health Care Economics.* Chapter 2: 'The Role of Government in Health and Medical Care'. Cengage Learning

Fine, F. (2004) *The EU's New Antitrust Rules for Technology Licensing: A Turbulent Harbour for Licensors.* EUROPEAN LAW REVIEW, 29(6), 766–787

Fisher, K. (2007) *Building a New Economy with Biotechnology.* THE CHRONICLE OF HIGHER EDUCATION, 54(2), A1

Foray, D. (2009) *The New Economics of Technology Policy.* Edward Elgar Publishing.

Foray, D. and Lissoni, F. (2010) 'University Research and Public-Private Interaction' in B.H. Hall and N. Rosenberg (eds), *Handbook of the Economics of Innovation, Volume 1.* North-Holland

Friedl, K.E. (2006) *Overcoming the 'Valley of Death': Mouse Models to Accelerate Translational Research.* DIABETES TECHNOLOGY & THERAPEUTICS, 8(3), 413–414

Friedman, J. and Silberman, J. (2003) *University Technology Transfer: Do Incentives, Management, and Location Matter?* THE JOURNAL OF TECHNOLOGY TRANSFER, 28(1), 17–30

Gallini, N. and Scotchmer, S. (2002) 'Intellectual Property: When is it the Best Incentive System?' in A.B. Jaffe, J. Lerner, and S. Stern (eds), *Innovation Policy and the Economy, Volume 2.* MIT Press, 51–78

Gallini, N.T. and Trebilcock, M. (1998) *Intellectual Property Rights and Competition Policy: A Framework for Analysis of Economic and Legal Issues.* Competition Policy and Intellectual Property Rights in the Knowledge-Based Economy, 17 (DAFFE/CLP(98)) at 18

Gallini, N. and Wright, B.D. (1990) *Technology Transfer under Asymmetric Information.* THE RAND JOURNAL OF ECONOMICS, 21(1), 147–160

Gambardella, A., Orsenigo, L., and Pammolli, F. (2001) *Global Competitiveness in Pharmaceuticals: A European Perspective.* Office for Official Publications of the European Communities

Ganslandt, M. and Maskus, K.E. (2004) *Parallel Imports and the Pricing of Pharmaceutical Products: Evidence from the European Union.* JOURNAL OF HEALTH ECONOMICS, 23(5), 1035–1057

Gaulé, P. (2006) *Towards Patent Pools in Biotechnology?* CDM Working Paper, CEMI Report 2006-010, École Polytechnique Fédérale de Lausanne

Gertner, D., Roberts, J., and Charles, D. (2011) *University-Industry Collaboration: A CoPs Approach to KTPs.* JOURNAL OF KNOWLEDGE MANAGEMENT, 15(4), 625–647

Getz, K. and Kaitin, K.I. (2012) *Open Innovation: The New Face of Pharmaceutical Research and Development.* EXPERT REVIEW OF CLINICAL PHARMACOLOGY, 5(5), 481–483

Gilbert, R.J. (1989) 'Mobility Barriers and the Value of Incumbency' in R. Schmalensee and R.D. Willig (eds), *Handbook of Industrial Organization.* Elsevier Science

Gilbert, R.J. (2004) *Converging Doctrines? U.S. and EU Antitrust Policy for the Licensing of Intellectual Property.* ANTITRUST, 19, 51

Gilbert, R.J. and Sunshine, S.C. (1995) *Incorporating Dynamic Efficiency in Merger Analysis: The Use of Innovation Markets.* ANTITRUST LAW JOURNAL, 569–601

Ginsburg, D.H. and Wright, J.D. (2012) *Dynamic Analysis and the Limits of Antitrust Institutions.* ANTITRUST LAW JOURNAL, 78(1), 12–48

Glader, M. (2000) *Research and Development Cooperation in European Competition Law: A Legal and Economic Analysis.* CFE Working Paper Series, 6

Glader M. (2004) *Innovation Markets and Competition Analysis: EU Competition Law and US Antitrust Law.* Faculty of Law, Lund University

Glader, M. (2006) *Innovation Markets and Competition Analysis*: *EU Competition Law and US Antitrust Law.* New Horizons in Competition Law and Economics. Edward Elgar Publishing

Glasgow, L.J. (2001) *Stretching the Limits of Intellectual Property Rights: Has the Pharmaceutical Industry Gone too Far?* IDEA, 41(2), 227

Gotts, I.K. and Rapp, R.T. (2004) *Antitrust Treatment of Mergers Involving Future Goods.* ANTITRUST, 10

Grabowski, H.G., Vernon, J.M., and DiMasi J.A. (2002) *Returns on Research and Development for 1990s New Drug Introductions.* PHARMACOECONOMICS, 20(3), 11–29

Greaves, R. (2013) 'EU Competition Law, and Research and Development Agreements' in M. Pittard, A.L. Monotti, and J. Duns (eds), *Business Innovation and the Law: Perspectives from Intellectual Property, Labour, Competition and Corporate Law.* Edward Elgar Publishing, 299–311

Griffiths, A. (2005) 'Using Ethnography as a Tool in Legal Research: An Anthropological Perspective' in R. Banakar and M. Travers (eds), *Theory and Method in Socio-Legal Research.* Hart Publishing, 133–132

Griliches, Z. (1980) *R&D and the Productivity Slowdown.* THE AMERICAN ECONOMIC REVIEW, 70(2), 343–348

Grossman, G.M. and Shapiro, C. (1986) *Research Joint Ventures: An Antitrust Analysis.* JOURNAL OF LAW, ECONOMICS AND ORGANIZATION, 2(2), 315–337

Grover, A., Citro, B., Mankad, M., and Lander, F. (2012) *Pharmaceutical Companies and Global Lack of Access to Medicines: Strengthening Accountability under the Right to Health.* THE JOURNAL OF LAW, MEDICINE & ETHICS, 40(2), 234–250

Guellec, D. and van Pottelsberghe de la Potterie, B. (2007) *The Economics of the European Patent System: IP Policy for Innovation and Competition.* Oxford University Press

Gutterman, A.S. (1997) *Innovation and Competition Policy: A Comparative Study of the Regulation of Patent Licensing and Collaborative Research & Development in the United States and the European Community.* Kluwer Law International

Hagedoorn, J. and Roijakkers, N. (2006) *Inter-firm R&D Partnering in Pharmaceutical Biotechnology since 1975: Trends, Patterns, and Networks.* RESEARCH POLICY, 35(3), 431–446

Heller, M.A. and Eisenberg, R.S. (1998) *Can Patents Deter Innovation? The Anticommons in Biomedical Research.* SCIENCE, 280(5364), 698–701

Henderson, R. and Cockburn, I. (1996) *Scale, Scope and Spillovers: The Determinants of Research Productivity in Drug Discovery.* THE RAND JOURNAL OF ECONOMICS, 27(1), 32–59

Herranz, N. and Ruiz-Castillo, J. (2013) *The End of the 'European Paradox'.* SCIENTOMETRICS, 95, 453–464

Hovenkamp, H. (1985) *Antitrust Policy after Chicago.* MICHIGAN LAW REVIEW, 84, 214–284

Hudson, J. and Khazragui, H.F. (2013) *Into the Valley of Death: Research to Innovation.* DRUG DISCOVERY TODAY, 18(13), 610–613

Hughes, B. (2009) *FDA Drug Approvals: A Year of Flux.* NATURE REVIEWS DRUG DISCOVERY, 7(2), 107–109

Hull, D.W. (2011) *The Application of EU Competition Law in the Pharmaceutical Sector.* JOURNAL OF EUROPEAN COMPETITION LAW & PRACTICE, 2(5), 480–488

Hunter, J. (2010) *Is the Pharmaceutical Industry Open for Innovation?* DRUG DISCOVERY WORLD, 9

Hunter, R.G. (2001) *The Pharmaceutical Sector in the European Union: Intellectual Property Rights, Parallel Trade and Community Competition Law.* Juristforlaget

Hutchison, T. and Duncan, N. (2012) *Defining and Describing What We Do: Doctrinal Legal Research.* DEAKEN LAW REVIEW, 17(1), 83–119

Ivinson, A.J. (2005) *University Investment in Drug Discovery.* SCIENCE, 310(5749), 777

Jacobs, M.S. (1995) *Essay on the Normative Foundations of Antitrust Economics.* NORTH CAROLINA LAW REVIEW, 74, 219

Jaquemin, A. (1994) *Goals and Means of European Antitrust Policy After 1992*. In H. Demsets and A. Jaquemin, *Anti-trust Economics*. Lund University Press, 34

Jones, A. and Clifford, L. (2005) *Drug Discovery Alliances*. NATURE REVIEWS DRUG DISCOVERY, 4(10), 807–808

Jones, B.F. (2009) *The Burden of Knowledge and the 'Death of the Renaissance Man': Is Innovation Getting Harder?* REVIEW OF ECONOMIC STUDIES, 76(1), 283–317

Joskow, P.L. (2002) *Transaction Cost Economics, Antitrust Rules and Remedies*. JOURNAL OF LAW, ECONOMICS AND ORGAN-IZATION, 18(1), 95–116

Just, R.E. and Huffman, W.E. (2009) T*he Economics of Universities in a New Age of Funding Options*. RESEARCH POLICY, 38(7), 1102–1116

Kaczorowska, A. (2011) *European Union Law*, 2nd edn. Routledge

Kaitin, K.I. (2010) *Deconstructing the Drug Development Process: The New Face of Innovation*. CLINICAL PHARMACOLOGY AND THERAPEUTICS, 87(3), 356–361

Kaitin K.I. (2011) *21st Century Bioinnovation: Academic-Industry Part-nerships are Increasingly Important in Biopharmaceutical Innov-ation*. PHARMACEUTICAL TECHNOLOGY, 35(6), 32

Kaitin, K.I. (2012) *Translational Research and the Evolving Landscape for Biomedical Innovation*. JOURNAL OF INVESTIGATIVE MEDI-CINE, 60(7), 995–998

Kallay, D. (2004) *The Law and Economics of Antitrust and Intellectual Property*. Edward Elgar Publishing

Kaplow, L. (1984) *The Patent-Antitrust Intersection: A Reappraisal*. HARVARD LAW REVIEW 1813–1892

Kaplow, L. and Shavell, S. (2006) *Fairness Versus Welfare*. Harvard University Press

Kattan, J. (1993) *Antitrust Analysis of Technology Joint Ventures: Alloca-tive Efficiency and the Rewards of Innovation*. ANTITRUST LAW JOURNAL, 97, 937–973

Katz, M.L. (1996) *An Analysis of Cooperative Research and Develop-ment*. THE RAND JOURNAL OF ECONOMICS, 17(4), 527–543

Kern, B.R. (2014) *Innovation Markets, Future Markets, or Potential Competition: How Should Competition Authorities Account for Innov-ation Competition in Merger Reviews?* WORLD COMPETITION: LAW AND ECONOMICS REVIEW, 37(2), 173–206

Kern, S. and van Reekum, R. (2012) *The Use of Patents in Dutch Biopharmaceutical SME: A Typology for Assessing Strategic Patent Management Maturity*. NEW TECHNOLOGY-BASED FIRMS IN THE NEW MILLENNIUM, 9, 131–149

Klausner, A. (2005) *Mind the (Biomedical Funding) Gap.* NATURE BIOTECHNOLOGY, 23(10), 1217–1218

Koch, V.G. (2012) *Incentivizing the Utilization of Pharmacogenetics in Drug Development.* JOURNAL OF HEALTH LAW & POLICY, 15, 263

Korah, V. (1981) *The Rise and Fall of Provisional Validity*: *The Need for a Rule of Reason in EEC Antitrust.* NORTH WESTERN JOURNAL OF INTERNATIONAL LAW AND BUSINESS, 3, 320

Korah, V. (1985) *Patent Licensing and EEC Competition Rules Regulation 2349/84.* ESC Publishing

Korah, V. (1986) *EEC Competition Policy – Legal Form or Economic Efficiency.* CURRENT LEGAL PROBLEMS, 39(1), 85–109

Korah, V. (1991) *Collaborative Joint Ventures for Research and Development where Markets are Concentrated: The Competition Rules of the Common Market and the Invalidity of Contracts.* FORDHAM INTERNATIONAL LAW JOURNAL, 15(2), 248–302

Korah, V. (1996) *Technology Transfer Agreements and the EC Competition Rule*s. Clarendon Press

Korah, V. (2002) *The Interface Between Intellectual Property and Antitrust: The European Experience.* ANTITRUST LAW JOURNAL, 69(3), 801–839

Korah, V. (2004) *Draft Block Exemption for Technology Transfer.* EUROPEAN COMPETITION LAW REVIEW, 25(5), 247–262

Korah, V. (2007) *An introductory Guide to EC Competition Law and Practice*, 9th edn. Hart Publishing

Kortum, S. and Lerner, J. (1999) *What is Behind the Recent Surge in Patenting?* RESEARCH POLICY, 28(1), 1–22

Kroeze I.J. (2013) *Legal Research Methodology and the Dream of Interdisciplinarity.* POTCHEFSTROOM ELECTRONIC LAW JOURNAL, 16(3), 35–65

Lande, R.H. (1988) *The Rise and (Coming) Fall of Efficiency as the Ruler of Antitrust.* THE ANTITRUST BULLETIN, 33, 429

Landes, W.M. and Posner, R.A. (2009) *The Economic Structure of Intellectual Property Law.* Harvard University Press

Landman, L.B. (1997) *The Economics of Future Goods Markets.* WORLD COMPETITION, LAW AND ECONOMICS REVIEW, 21(3), 63–90

Landman, L.B. (1998) *Innovation Markets in Europe.* EUROPEAN COMPETITION LAW REVIEW, 19, 21–31

Lang, T. (1996) *European Community Antitrust Law: Innovation Markets and High Technology Industries.* FORDHAM INTERNATIONAL LAW JOURNAL, 20, 717

Langenfeld, J. (2001) *Intellectual Property and Antitrust: Steps Toward Striking a Balance.* CASE WESTERN RESERVE LAW REVIEW, 52, 91

Larenz, K. (1991) *Methodenlehre der Rechtswissenschaft.* Springer

Lavi, S. (2010) *Turning the Tables on 'Law and …': A Jurisprudential Inquiry into Contemporary Legal Theory.* CORNELL LAW REVIEW, 96, 811

Ledford, H. (2011) *Drug Buddies.* NATURE, 474(7352), 433–434

Lee, P. (2012) *Transcending the Tacit Dimension: Patents, Relationships, and Organizational Integration in Technology Transfer.* CALIFORNIA LAW REVIEW, 100, 1503

le Frapper, I. (2012) *Striking the Right Balance Between Co-operation and Competition: Several Antitrust Pitfalls in R&D Alliances and Other Strategic Partnerships.* INTERNATIONAL IN-HOUSE COUNSEL JOURNAL, 5(18), 1–18

Lehmann, M. (1985) *The Theory of Property Rights and the Protection of Intellectual and Industrial Property.* INTERNATIONAL REVIEW OF INDUSTRIAL PROPERTY AND COPYRIGHT LAW, 16(5), 525–540

Leibenstein, H. (1966) *Allocative Efficiency vs. 'X-Efficiency'.* AMERICAN ECONOMIC REVIEW, 56(3), 392–415

Lemley, M.A. (2007) *A New Balance between IP and Antitrust.* SOUTHWESTERN JOURNAL OF LAW & TRADE IN THE AMERICAS, 13, 237

Lerner, J. and Tirole, J. (2004) Efficient Patent Pools. THE AMERICAN ECONOMIC REVIEW, 94(3), 691–711

Levin, R.C. (1986) *A New Look at the Patent System.* AMERICAN ECONOMIC REVIEW, 76(2), 199–202

Levy, R. (1999) *FTC Bureau of Economics Staff Report – The Pharmaceutical Industry: A Discussion of Competitive and Antitrust Issues in an Environment of Change.* Diane Publishing

Lianos, I. (2005) *Competition Law and Intellectual Property Rights: Is the Property Rights Approach Right?* CAMBRIDGE YEARBOOK OF EUROPEAN LEGAL STUDIES, 8, 153

Light, D.W. (2009) *Advanced Market Commitments: Current Realities and Alternate Approaches.* HAI Europe/Medico International Publication

Light, D.W. and Warburton, R. (2011) *Demythologizing the High Costs of Pharmaceutical Research.* BIOSOCIETIES, 6(1), 34–50

Lind, R.C. and Muysert, P. (2004) *The European Commission's Draft Technology Transfer Block Exemption Regulation: A Significant Departure from Accepted Competition Policy Principles.* EUROPEAN COMPETITION LAW REVIEW, 25(4), 181–189

Lipinski, C.A. (2006) *The Anti-Intellectual Effects of Intellectual Property.* CURRENT OPINION IN CHEMICAL BIOLOGY, 10(4), 380–383

Litan, R.E. and Mitchell, L. (2010) *Breakthrough Ideas for 2010. A Faster Path from Lab to Market.* HARVARD BUSINESS REVIEW, 88(1–2), 52

Loury, G.C. (1979) *Market Structure and Innovation.* THE QUARTERLY JOURNAL OF ECONOMICS, 93(3), 395–410

Luintel, K.B. and Khan, M. (2011) *Basic, Applied and Experimental Knowledge and Productivity: Further Evidence.* ECONOMICS LETTERS, 111(1), 71–74

Maggiolino, M. (2011) 'The Economics of Antitrust and Intellectual Property Rights' in S.D. Anderman and A. Ezrachi (eds), *Intellectual Property Rights and Competition Law: New Frontiers.* Oxford University Press

Mansfield, E. (1986) *Patents and Innovation: An Empirical Study.* MANAGEMENT SCIENCE, 32(2), 173–181

Marquis, M. (2007) *O2 (Germany) v Commission and the Exotic Mysteries of Article 81(1) EC.* EUROPEAN LAW REVIEW, 32(1), 29–47

Maurer, S. and Scotchmer, S. (2006) *Profit Neutrality in Licensing: The Boundary between Antitrust Law and Patent Law.* AMERICAN LAW AND ECONOMICS REVIEW, 8(3), 476–522

McCrudden, C. (2006) *Legal Research and the Social Sciences.* LAW QUARTERLY REVIEW, 122, 632

McDermott, E. (2012) *How to Survive the Patent Cliff.* MANAGING INTELLECTUAL PROPERTY, 216, 22

Merges, R.P. (1996) *Contracting Into Liability Rules: Intellectual Property Rights and Collective Rights Organizations.* CALIFORNIA LAW REVIEW, 1293–1393

Merges, R.P. (2001) 'Institutions for Intellectual Property Transactions: The Case of Patent Pools' in R.C. Dreyfuss, D.L. Zimmerman, and H. First (eds), *Expanding the Boundaries of Intellectual Property: Innovation Policy for the Knowledge Society.* Oxford University Press

Mestre-Ferrandiz, J., Sussex, J., and Towse, A. (2012) *The R&D Cost of a New Medicine.* Office of Health Economics

Meyer-Krahmer, F. and Reger, G. (1999) *New Perspectives on the Innovation Strategies of Multinational Enterprises: Lessons for Technology Policy in Europe.* RESEARCH POLICY, 28, 751–776

Milne, C.P. and Kaitin, K.I. (2009) *Translational Medicine: An Engine of Change for Bringing New Technology to Community Health.* SCIENCE TRANSLATIONAL MEDICINE, 1(5), 1–4

Monti, G. (2011) *EC Competition Policy.* Cambridge University Press

Morales, T.L. and Rivas, J. (2008) *Merger Control in the Pharmaceutical Sector and the Innovation Market Assessment: European Analysis in Practice and Differences with the American Approach*. CEU Ediciones

Moran, N. (2007) *Public Sector Seeks to Bridge 'Valley of Death'*. NATURE BIOTECHNOLOGY, 25, 266

Moreno-Torres, I., Puig-Junoy, J., and Raya, J.M. (2011) *The Impact of Repeated Cost Containment Policies on Pharmaceutical Expenditure: Experience in Spain*. THE EUROPEAN JOURNAL OF HEALTH ECONOMICS, 12(6), 563–573

Moudud, J.K., Bina, C., and Mason, P.L. (eds). (2012) *Alternative Theories of Competition: Challenges to the Orthodoxy*. Routledge

Murphy K.M. and Topel R.H (2006) *The Value of Health and Longevity*. JOURNAL OF POLITICAL ECONOMY, 114(5), 871–904

Nazzini, R. (2006) *Article 81 EC between Time Present and Time Past: A Normative Critique of 'Restriction of Competition' in EU Law*. COMMON MARKET LAW REVIEW, 43(2), 497

Nazzini, R. (2012) *The Foundations of European Union Competition Law: The Objective and Principles of Article 102*. Oxford University Press

Nelson, R.R. (1982) *The Role of Knowledge in R&D Efficiency*. QUARTERLY JOURNAL OF ECONOMICS, 97, 467–468

Nelson, R.R. (2004) *The Market Economy, and the Scientific Commons*. RESEARCH POLICY, 33(3), 455–471

Nicolaides, P. (2005) *The Balancing Myth: The Economics of Article 81(1) & (3)*. LEGAL ISSUES OF ECONOMIC INTEGRATION, 32(2), 123–145

Odrobina, A. (2014). *Patent Pools in Light of European Union Competition Law*. EKONOMIA I PRAWO. ECONOMICS AND LAW, 13(4), 523–532

Odudu, O. (2001) *Interpreting Article 81(1): Demonstrating Restrictive Effect*. EUROPEAN LAW REVIEW, 26(4), 379–390

Ordover, J.A. (1984) *Economic Foundations and Considerations in Protecting Industrial and Intellectual Property*. ANTITRUST LAW JOURNAL, 53(3), 503–511

Pammolli, F., Magazzini, L., and Riccaboni, M. (2011) *The Productivity Crisis in Pharmaceutical R&D*. NATURE REVIEWS DRUG DISCOVERY, 10(6), 428–438

Pattaro, E. (2007) *A Treatise of Legal Philosophy and General Jurisprudence, Volume 4: Scienta Juris, Legal Doctrine as Knowledge of Law and as a Source of Law*, Chapter 1: 'Legal Doctrine and Legal Theory'. Springer Science & Business Media

Paul, S.M., Mytelka, D.S., Dunwiddie, C.T., Persinger, C.C., Munos, B.H., Lindborg, S.R., and Schacht, A.L. (2010) *How to Improve R&D*

Productivity: The Pharmaceutical Industry's Grand Challenge. NATURE REVIEWS DRUG DISCOVERY, 9(3), 203–214

Peeperkorn, L. (2003) *IP Licenses and Competition Rules: Striking the Right Balance.* WORLD COMPETITION, 26(4), 527

Peeters, J. (1989) *The Rule of Reason Revisited: Prohibition on Restraints of Competition in the Sherman Act and the EEC Treaty.* THE AMERICAN JOURNAL OF COMPARATIVE LAW, 37(3), 521–570

Perkmann, M., Tartari, V., McKelvey, M., Autio, E., Brostrom, A., D'Este, P., Fini, R., Geuna, A., Grimaldi, R., Hughes, A., Krabel, S., Kitson, M., Llerena, P., Lissoni, F., Salter, A., and Sobrero, M. (2013) *Academic Engagement and Commercialization: A Review of the Literature on University-Industry Relations.* RESEARCH POLICY, 42(2), 423–442

Pisano G.P. (2006) *Can Science be a Business? Lessons from Biotech.* HARVARD BUSINESS REVIEW, 84(10), 114–125

Posner, R. (1975) *The Economic Approach to Law.* TEXAS LAW REVIEW, 53, 757

Posner, R. (1979) *The Chicago School of Antitrust Analysis.* UNIVERSITY OF PENNSYLVANIA LAW REVIEW, 127, 925–948

Posner, R.A. (1987) *The Decline of Law as an Autonomous Discipline: 1962–1987.* HARVARD LAW REVIEW, 100, 761

Posner, R. (1988) *Conventionalism: The Key to Law as an Autonomous Discipline.* UNIVERSITY OF TORONTO LAW JOURNAL, 38, 333–354

Posner, R.A. (1995) *Overcoming Law.* Harvard University Press

Pottage, A. (2007) *The Socio-legal Implications of the New Biotechnologies.* ANNUAL REVIEW OF LAW AND SOCIAL SCIENCE, 3, 321–344

Powell, W.W. (2001) 'Networks of Learning in Biotechnology: Opportunities and Constraints Associated with Relational Contracting in a Knowledge-Intensive Field' in R. Dreyfuss, D.L. Zimmerman, and H. First (eds), *Expanding the Boundaries of Intellectual Property.* Oxford University Press

Powers J.B. (2006) *Between Lab Bench and Marketplace: The Pitfalls of Technology Transfer.* THE CHRONICLE OF HIGHER EDUCATION, 53, 5, B18

Priddis, S. and Constantine, S. (2011) 'The Pharmaceutical Sector, Intellectual Property Rights, and Competition Law in Europe' in S. Anderman and A. Ezrachi (eds), *Intellectual Property and Competition Law.* Oxford University Press

Prodan, I. (2005) *Influence of Research and Development Expenditures on Number of Patent Applications: Selected Case Studies in OECD*

Countries and Central Europe 1981–2000. APPLIED ECONO-
METRICS AND INTERNATIONAL DEVELOPMENT, 5(4), 5–22

Rahnasto, I. (2003) *Intellectual Property Rights, External Effects and Antitrust Law: Leveraging IPRs in the Communications Industry.* Oxford University Press

Rai, A.K., Reichman, J.H., Uhlir, P.F., and Crossman, C.R. (2008) *Pathways Across the Valley of Death: Novel Intellectual Property Strategies for Accelerated Drug Discovery.* YALE JOURNAL OF HEALTH POLICY, LAW, AND ETHICS, 8(1), 20–30

Rapp, R.T. (1995) *The Misapplication of the Innovation Market Approach to Merger Analysis.* ANTITRUST LAW JOURNAL, 64(1), 19–47

Reed, J.C. (2011) *NCATS Could Mitigate Pharma Valley of Death.* GENETIC ENGINEERING & BIOTECHNOLOGY, 31(10), 6–8

Rehman, H.A. ur (2010) *Equitable Licensing and Publicly Funded Research: A Working Model for India?* SOUTHWESTERN JOURNAL OF INTERNATIONAL LAW, 16, 75–78

Reichman, J.H. and Uhlir, P. (2003) *A Contractually Reconstructed Research Commons for Scientific Data in a Highly Protectionist Intellectual Property Environment.* LAW & CONTEMPORARY PROBLEMS, 66, 315–462

Rey, P. and Stiglitz, J. (1995) *The Role of Exclusive Territories in Producers' Competition.* THE RAND JOURNAL OF ECONOMICS, 26(3), 431–451

Roessner, D., Bond, J., Okubo, S., and Planting, M. (2013). *The Economic Impact of Licensed Commercialized Inventions Originating in University Research.* RESEARCH POLICY, 42(1), 23–34

Rottleuthner, H., Shiner, R.A., Peczenik, A., Sartor, G., Postema, G.J., and Stein, P. (2007) *A Treaties of Legal Philosophy and General Jurisprudence, Volume 4: Scienta Juris, Legal Doctrine as Knowledge of Law and as a Source of Law.* Springer Science & Business Media

Russ, A.P. and Lampel, S. (2005) *The Druggable Genome: An Update.* DRUG DISCOVERY TODAY, 10(23), 1607–1610

Sampat, B.N. and Lichtenberg, F.R. (2011) *What Are the Respective Roles of the Public and Private Sectors in Pharmaceutical Innovation?* HEALTH AFFAIRS, 30(2), 332–339

Scherer, F.M. (1987) *Antitrust, Efficiency, and Progress.* NEW YORK UNIVERSITY LAW REVIEW, 62, 998

Scherer, F.M. (2010) 'Pharmaceutical Innovation' in B.H. Hall and N. Rosenberg (eds), *Handbook of the Economics of Technological Innovation, Vol. 1.* Elsevier, 539–574

Schmidt, H. and Anderman, S.D. (2011) *EU Competition Law and Intellectual Property Rights: The Regulation of Innovation.* Oxford University Press

Schumpeter, J.A. (2008) *Capitalism, Socialism and Democracy*. Harper Perennial, New York, reprint of 1950 edition

Schwartz, R. (1992) *Internal and External Method in the Study of Law*. LAW AND PHILOSOPHY, 11(3) 179–199

Scotchmer, S. (2004) *Innovation and Incentives*. MIT Press

Senderovitz, T. (2009) *How Open Innovation Could Reinvigorate the Pharmaceutical Industry with Fresh R&D Opportunities*. EXPERT REVIEW OF CLINICAL PHARMACOLOGY, 2(6), 585–587

Service, R.F. (2004) *Surviving the Blockbuster Syndrome*. SCIENCE, 303(5665), 1796

Shapiro, C. (1985) *Patent Licensing and R&D Rivalry*. AMERICAN ECONOMIC REVIEW, 75(2), 25–30

Shapiro, C. (2001) 'Navigating the Patent Thicket: Cross Licenses, Patent Pools, and Standard Setting' in *Innovation Policy and the Economy, Volume 1*. MIT Press

Shapiro, C. (2008) *Patent Reform: Aligning Reward and Contribution*. INNOVATION POLICY AND THE ECONOMY, 8, 111–156

Shapiro, C. (2011) 'Competition and Innovation: Did Arrow Hit the Bull's Eye?' in *The Rate and Direction of Inventive Activity Revisited*. University of Chicago Press

Sidak, J.G. and Teece, D.J. (2009) *Dynamic Competition in Antitrust Law*. JOURNAL OF COMPETITION LAW AND ECONOMICS, 5(4), 581–631

Simoens, S. (2011) *Pricing and Reimbursement of Orphan Drugs: The Need for More Transparency*. ORPHANET JOURNAL OF RARE DISEASES, 6(42), 1–8

Singer, J.W. (2009) *Normative Methods for Lawyers*. UCLA LAW REVIEW, 56, 899–904

Smits, J.A. (2011) *The Mind and Method of the Legal Academic*. Edward Elgar Publishing

Smits, J. (2012) *The Mind and Method of the Legal Academic*. Edward Elgar Publishing

Smits J.M. (2014) *Law and Interdisciplinarity: On the Inevitable Normativity of Legal Studies*. CRITICAL ANALYSIS OF LAW, 1(1), 75–86

Stephan, P.E. (2010) 'The Economics of Science' in B.H. Hall and N. Rosenberg (eds) *Handbook of the Economics of Innovation, Volume 1*. North-Holland, 217–273

Stossel, T.P. (2005) *Regulating Academic-Industrial Research Relationships – Solving Problems or Stifling Progress?* NEW ENGLAND JOURNAL OF MEDICINE, 353(10), 1060

Swamidass, P.M. and Vulasa, V. (2009) *Why University Inventions Rarely Produce Income? Bottlenecks in University Technology Transfer*. THE JOURNAL OF TECHNOLOGY TRANSFER, 34(4), 343–363

Szydlo, M. (2009) *Sector-Specific Regulation and Competition Law: Between Convergence and Divergence.* EUROPEAN PUBLIC LAW, 15(2), 257–275

Tamanaha, B. (2006) *Law as a Means to an End: Threat to the Rule of Law.* Cambridge University Press

Teece, D.J. (1986) *Profiting from Technological Innovation: Implications for Integration, Collaboration, Licensing and Public Policy.* RESEARCH POLICY, 15(6), 285–305

Tether, B.S. (2002) *Who Co-operates for Innovation, and Why: An Empirical Analysis.* RESEARCH POLICY, 31(6), 947–967

Tether, B.S. and Tajar, A. (2008) *The Organisational-Cooperation Mode of Innovation and Its Prominence Amongst European Service Firms.* RESEARCH POLICY, 37(4), 720–739

Thomas, P.A. (1997) 'Socio-Legal Studies: The Case of Disappearing Fleas and Bustards' in P.A. Thomas (ed.), *Socio-Legal Studies.* Dartmouth Publishing Company

Tiller, E.H. and Corss, F.B. (2006) *What is Legal Doctrine?* NORTH-WESTERN UNIVERSITY LAW REVIEW, 100(1), 517–534

Timmermann, C. and van den Belt, H. (2013) *Intellectual Property and Global Health: From Corporate Social Responsibility to the Access to Knowledge Movement.* LIVERPOOL LAW REVIEW, 34(1), 47–73

Tom, W.K. and Newberg, J.A. (1997) *Antitrust and Intellectual Property: From Separate Sphere to Unified Field.* ANTITRUST LAW JOURNAL, 66, 167–229

Tralau-Stewart, C.J., Wyatt, C.A., Kleyn, D.E., and Ayad, A. (2009) *Drug Discovery: New Models for Industry–Academic Partnerships.* DRUG DISCOVERY TODAY, 14(1), 95–101

Treacy, P. and Heide, T. (2004) *The New EC Technology Transfer Block Exemption.* EUROPEAN INTELLECTUAL PROPERTY REVIEW, 26, 414–420

Tremblay, V.J. and Tremblay, C.H. (2012) 'Perfect Competition and Market Imperfections' in *New Perspectives on Industrial Organization.* Springer New York

Tuominen, N. (2012). *Patenting Strategies of the EU Pharmaceutical Industry: Regular Business Practice or Abuse of Dominance.* WORLD COMPETITION, 35(1), 27–54

Turner, D.F. (1984) *Basic Principles in Formulating Antitrust and Misuse Constraints on the Exploitation of Intellectual Property Rights.* ANTITRUST LAW JOURNAL, 53(3), 485–502

van Looy, B., Callaert, J., and Debackere, K. (2006) *Publication and Patent Behavior of Academic Researchers: Conflicting, Reinforcing or Merely Co-existing?* RESEARCH POLICY, 35(4), 596–608 van Looy, B., Landoni, P., Callaert, J., van Pottelsberghe, B., Sapsalis, E., and Debackere, K. (2011) *Entrepreneurial Effectiveness of European Universities: An Empirical Assessment of Antecedents and Trade-offs.* RESEARCH POLICY, 40(4), 553–564

van Looy, B., Ranga, M., Callaert, J., Debackere, K., and Zimmermann, E. (2004) *Combining Entrepreneurial and Scientific Performance in Academia: Towards a Compounded and Bi-directional Matthew-effect.* RESEARCH POLICY, 33(3), 425–441

van Zimmeren, E., Vanneste, S., Matthijs, G., Vanhaverbeke, W., and van Overwalle, G. (2011) *Patent Pools and Clearinghouses in the Life Sciences.* TRENDS IN BIOTECHNOLOGY, 29(11), 569–576

Verbeure, B. (2009) 'Patent Pooling for Gene-based Diagnostic Testing: Conceptual Framework' in G. van Overwalle (ed.), *Gene Patents and Collaborative Licensing Models: Patent Pools, Clearinghouse, Open Source Models and Liability Regimes.* Cambridge University Press

Verbeure, B., van Zimmeren, E., Matthijs, G. and Van Overwalle, G. (2006) *Patent Pools and Diagnostic Testing.* TRENDS IN BIO-TECHNOLOGY, 24(3), 115–120

Vincent-Lancrin, S. (2006) *What is Changing in Academic Research? Trends and Future Scenarios.* EUROPEAN JOURNAL OF EDU-CATION, 41(2), 169–202

Vollebregt, E. (2004) *The Changes in the New Technology Transfer Block Exemption Compared to the Draft.* EUROPEAN COMPETITION LAW REVIEW, 25(10), 660

Wald, D.L. and Feinstein, D.L. (2004) *Merger Enforcement in Innovation Markets: The Latest Chapter – Genzyme/Novazyme.* THE ANTITRUST SOURCE, 1–11

Walsh, J.P., Cohen, W.M., and Cho, C. (2007) *Where Excludability Matters: Material Versus Intellectual Property in Academic Biomedical Research.* RESEARCH POLICY, 36(8), 1184–1203

Wheeler, S. and Thomas, P.A. (2002) 'Socio-Legal Studies' in D.J. Hayton (ed.), *Law's Future(s).* Hart Publishing

Whish, R. and Bailey, D. (2012) *Competition Law.* Oxford University Press

Whitty, A. and Kumaravel, G. (2006) *Between a Rock and a Hard Place?* NATURE CHEMICAL BIOLOGY, 2(3), 112–118

Williamson, O.E. (1985) *The Economic Institutions of Capitalism.* The Free Press

Woolman, S., Fishman, E., and Fisher, M. (2013) *Evidence of Patent Thickets in Complex Biopharmaceutical Technologies.* IDEA, 53, 1

Wright, M., Clarysse, B., Mustar, P. and Lockett, A. (eds) (2007) *Academic Entrepreneurship in Europe.* Edward Elgar Publishing

Yeh, R.M. (2012) *The Public Paid for the Invention: Who Owns It?* BERKELEY TECHNOLOGY LAW JOURNAL, 27, 453

Zambrowicz, B.P. and Sands, A.T. (2003) *Knockouts Model the 100 Best-Selling Drugs – Will They Model the Next 100?* NATURE REVIEWS DRUG DISCOVERY, 2(1), 38–51

SECONDARY RESOURCES

Ahn, S. (2002) *Competition, Innovation and Productivity Growth: A Review of Theory and Evidence.* OECD, Economic Department Working Paper no. 317

Almunia, Joaquín (2012) Vice President of the European Commission Responsible for Competition Policy, *Industrial and Competition Policy: Quo vadis Europa?*, Address at the New Frontiers of Antitrust 3rd International Concurrences Conference (Feb. 10)

American Bar Association's Section of Antitrust Law, Section of International Law and Section of Intellectual Property Law on Commission Regulation on the Application of Article 81(3) of the EC Treaty to Categories of Technology Transfer Agreements and Commission Notice on Guidelines on the Application of Article 81 to Technology Transfer Agreements (February 2012)

AUTM US Licensing Activity Survey Highlights (FY2011)

Blumenstyk, G. (2012) *Universities Report $1.8 Billion in Earnings on Inventions in 2011.* THE CHRONICLE OF HIGHER EDUCATION

Cameron, D.M. and Borenstein, R. (2003) *Key Aspects of IP License Agreements.* Ogilvy Renault LLP

Clark, J. (2000) *Patent Pools: A Solution to the Problem of Access in Biotechnology Patents?* US Patent and Trademark Office

Contrasting European and U.S. Patent Laws: Issues for the Pharmaceutical Industry. Wiley Handbook of Current and Emerging Drug Therapies

Council for American Medical Innovation (CAMI) (2010) *Gone Tomorrow: A Call to Promote Medical Innovation, Create Jobs, and Find Cures in America*, prepared by the Battelle Technology Partnership Practice, June 10

Danish Agency for Science, Technology and Innovation (2009) *Proof of Concept Financing of Public Research Institutions, Midterm Report*, prepared by IRIS Group for Research and Innovation

DeBacker, K., Lopez-Bassols, V., and Martinez, C. (2008) *Open Innovation in a Global Perspective – What Do Existing Data Tell Us?* OECD STI Working Paper, 2008/4

Directorate General for Internal Policies, Policy Department A: Economic and Scientific Policy (2011) *Differences in Costs of and Access to Pharmaceutical Products in the EU*

EC Expert Group Report: *Management of Intellectual Property in Publicly-funded Research Organisations: Towards European Guidelines*, 2004

EFPIA, *The Pharmaceutical Industry in Figures*, 2010

EFPIA, *Competition Occurs through Successful R&D*

ERC-2015-PoC Call for Proposal for ERC Proof of Concept Grant

EUA 2012 Annual Conference on 'The Sustainability of European Universities'

Europa Press Release 'Commission Fines AstraZeneca €60 Million for Misusing Patent System to Delay Market Entry of Competing Generic Drugs', IP/05/737, 15 June 2005

European Federation of Pharmaceutical Industries and Associations (2012) *The Pharmaceutical Industry in Figures*

European Federation of Pharmaceutical Industries and Associations *Submission to the European Commission in Relation to the Pharmaceutical Sector Inquiry*

Executive Summary of EvaluatePharma World Preview 2013, Outlook to 2018, Returning to Growth

The Financing of Biopharmaceutical Product Development in Europe: The Framework Contract of Sector Competitiveness Studies – ENTR/06/054 Final Report 2009

Food and Drug Administration's Approved Drug Products with Therapeutic Equivalence Evaluations

Freund, N. and Ruhle, E.O. (2011) *The Evolution from Sector-specific Regulation Towards Competition Law in EU Telecom Markets from 1997 to 2011: Different Effects in Practical Implementation*. In 22nd European Regional Conference of the International Telecommunications Society (IT2011), Budapest, 18–21 September

FT Global Pharmaceutical and Biotechnology Conference on 6 December 2011

Hall, S.S. (2001) *Prescription for Profit*. NEW YORK TIMES MAGAZINE (March)

Hall, B., Helmers, C., von Graevenitz, G., and Rosazza-Bondibene, C. (2014) *Technology Entry in the Presence of Patent Thickets*. Working Paper

Harris, G. (2011) 'Federal Research Centre Will Help Develop Medicines'. *The New York Times*

House of Commons Science and Technology Committee (March 2013) *Bridging the Valley of Death: Improving the Commercialization of Research, Eighth Report of Session 2012–13*

IMS Health World Review Analyst 2013

IMS Institute for Healthcare Informatics (2012) *The Global Use of Medicines: Outlook Through 2016*, July

Inkmann, J. (2000) *Horizontal and Vertical R&D Cooperation*, Discussion Paper No. 2000–02, Department of Economics and Center of Finance and Economics, University of Konstanz

International Federation of Pharmaceutical Manufacturers & Associations, *The Pharmaceutical Industry and Global Health Facts and Figures 2012*

Italianer, Alexander (2013) Director General of the European Commission Directorate-General for Competition, Prepared Remarks on: Level-Playing Field and Innovation in Technology Markets, Address at the Conference on Antitrust in Technology (Jan. 28)

Jack, Andrew (2012) 'Pharma Tries to Avoid Falling Off "Patent Cliff"'. *Financial Times* (London, 6 May) (accessible at http://www.ft.com/cms/s/0/572ea510-9452-11e1-bb47-00144feab49a.html#axzz4EmCT0 HIL

Khan, M. and Luintel, K.B. (2006) *Sources of Knowledge and Productivity: How Robust is the Relationship?* OECD STI Working Papers, 2006/06

King, S. (2014) *Firstword Lists – Pharma's 50 biggest selling drugs*, March

'KU Leuven – Prestigious University Fosters Innovation-Driven Economy'. *The European Times*, 28 January 2014

Licensing Surveys of the Association of University Technology Managers

Medical Research Council (2012) Press Release, 'Academia-Pharma Collaboration Attracts £14.4 million Funding in the UK to Accelerate Drug Discovery', 16 May

Monti, M. (2004) *The New EU Policy on Technology Transfer Agreements*. Speech at École de Mines, Paris, 16th January

National Institute of Health (2012) *Impacts on U.S. Economy*, March

National Science Board (2012) *Science and Engineering Indicators 2012*. Arlington VA, National Science Foundation

OECD Directorate for Financial, Fiscal and Enterprise Affairs, Competition Committee *Merger Review in Emerging High Innovation Markets 2003*

OECD Health Statistics 2013

OECD Policy Brief, *What is Competition on the Merits?* June 2006

OECD Policy Roundtable: Competition and Regulation Issues in the Pharmaceutical Industry, 6 February, 2001 DAFFE/CLP(2000)29

OECD Research and Development Database, May 2011

OECD Roundtable on Market Definition DAF/COMP/WD(2012)28, 31 May 2012

OECD Working Papers, Application of Competition Policy to High Technology Markets, 1997

OECD (1997) *Application of Competition Policy to High Tech Markets*, OECD Working Papers, Series Roundtables on Competition Policy No. 9, Paris

OECD (2003) *Turning Science into Business: Patenting and Licensing at Public Research Organisations.* http://www.keepeek.com/oecd/media/science-and-technology/turning-science-into-business_9789264100244-en#.V5dwWT_6tes

OECD (2009) *Open Innovation in Global Networks.* Organisation for Economic Co-operation and Development

OECD (2009) Working Party of National Experts in Science and Technology (NESTI) Innovation Microdata Project Based on CIS-2006, June

OECD (2010) *Measuring Innovation – A New Perspective.* Organisation for Economic Co-operation and Development

OECD (2010) *Innovation in Firms.* Organisation for Economic Co-operation and Development

OECD (2010) *The OECD Innovation Strategy: Getting a Head Start on Tomorrow.* Paris: Organisation for Economic Co-operation and Development

Overview of Submissions Received from Stakeholders in the Public Consultation on the Draft Proposal for a Revised Block Exemption Regulation for Technology Transfer Agreements and for Revised Guidelines

PAREXEL International (2010) *PAREXEL Biopharmaceutical R&D Statistical Sourcebook 2010/2011* Waltham, MA, PAREXEL International

Patents and Pharmaceuticals – a Paper given on 29th November at the Presentation of the Directorate-General of Competition's Preliminary Report of the Pharma-Sector Inquiry

Pfizer 2011 Financial Report

Pharmaceutical Research and Manufacturers of America (2013), *2013 Biopharmaceutical Research Industry Profile.* Washington, DC: PhRMA, July

Pigott, R., Barker, R., Kaan, T., and Roberts, M. (2014) *Shaping the Future of Open Innovation: A Practical Guide for Life Sciences Organizations.* The Wellcome Trust

PricewaterhouseCoopers, and National Venture Capital Association (2007) *MoneyTree! Survey Report.* 2007

Responsible Partnering Guidelines (2009) *Joining Forces in a World of Open Innovation: Guidelines for Collaborative Research and Knowledge Transfer Between Science and Industry*

Riemenschneider, K. (2006) *New Economy: Antitrust Review of Merger Analysis Using Innovation Markets*. Antitrust Modernization Commission Public Comment

The Role of Static and Dynamic Analysis in Pharmaceutical Antitrust, at the Fifth Annual In-House Counsel Forum on Pharmaceutical Antitrust (18 February 2010)

Royal Society (March 2011) *Knowledge, Networks and Nations: Global Scientific Collaboration in the 21st Century*

Rt. Hon. Sir Robin Jacob, *Patents and Pharmaceuticals* – a Paper given on 29th November at the Presentation of the Directorate-General of Competition's Preliminary Report of the Pharma Sector Inquiry

Saftlas, H. (2009) 'Healthcare: Pharmaceuticals'. *Standard & Poor's Industry Surveys*, 4 June

Schlicher, J.W. (1987) *Some Thought on the Law and Economics of Licensing Biotechnology Patent and Related Property Rights in the United States*. JOURNAL OF THE PATENT AND TRADEMARK OFFICE SOCIETY, 69, 264, 270

Science Business Innovation Board (2012) *Making Industry-University Partnerships. Work Lessons from Successful Collaborations*

Standard and Poor's Rating Services (2012) *European Pharma Roadshow 2012 Corporate Ratings*, September

Standard and Poor's Rating Services (2012) *Global Pharmaceutical Companies, Strongest to Weakest*, Ratings Direct, 18 December

Subseries I: Impact on Manufacturing, Vol. 2: Pharmaceutical Products, 'The Pharmaceutical Sector in the EU' (1997), The Single Market Review

UNESCO (2010) *UNESCO Science Report 2010*. Paris: United Nations Educational, Scientific and Cultural Organization

University of Kansas Cancer Center, Friends of Cancer Research, Kansas Bioscience Authority, Council for American Medical Innovation, and Ewing Marion Kauffman Foundation, *The New Role of Academia in Drug Discovery and Development: New Thinking, New Competencies, New Results* (December 1, 2010). Ewing Marion Kauffman Foundation Research Paper

U.S. Food and Drug Administration (2004) *Innovation or Stagnation: Challenge and Opportunity on the Critical Path to New Medical Products*

U.S. Food and Drug Administration Center for Drug Evaluation and Research (2011) *New Molecular Entity Approvals for 2010 Report*, 1 March

Veltri, G., Grablowitz, A., and Mulatero, F. (2009) *Trends in R&D Policies for a European Knowledge-based Economy*, JRC Scientific and Technical Reports Series

VentureOne (2006), 'Venture Capital Industry Report'. Dow Jones

WIPO Economics & Statistics Series, *2011 World Intellectual Property Report: The Changing Face of Innovation*, Chapter 4: 'Harnessing Public Research for Innovation – The Role of Intellectual Property'

WIPO Press Release (5 March 2012) *International Patent Filings Set New Record in 2011*, Geneva, PR/2012/703

Zycher, B. (2006) *The Human Cost of Federal Price Negotiations: The Medicare Prescription Drug Benefit and Pharmaceutical Innovation.* Manhattan Medical Institute Medical Progress Report, No. 3

Index